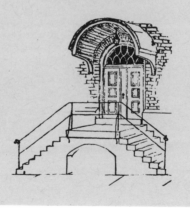

THE POETICS OF DISAPPOINTMENT

THE POETICS OF DISAPPOINTMENT

WORDSWORTH TO ASHBERY

Laura Quinney

UNIVERSITY PRESS OF VIRGINIA

CHARLOTTESVILLE AND LONDON

The University Press of Virginia
© 1999 by the Rector and Visitors of the University of Virginia
All rights reserved
Printed in the United States of America
First published 1999

⊗ The paper used in this publication meets the minimum requirements
of the American National Standard for Information Sciences—Permanence
of Paper for Printed Library Materials, ANSI Z39.48-1984.

Library of Congress Cataloging-in-Publication Data
Quinney, Laura.
    The poetics of disappointment : Wordsworth to Ashbery / Laura
Quinney.
        p.   cm.
    Includes bibliographical references and index.
    ISBN 0-8139-1858-8 (alk. paper)
    1. English poetry—19th century—History and criticism.
2. Disappointment in literature. 3. American poetry—20th century—
History and criticism. 4. Poetry—Psychological aspects.
5. Frustration in literature. 6. Self in literature. I. Title.
PZ7.B43485wh 1999   98-55128
                                                          CIP

FOR BILLY AND DANIEL

CONTENTS

THIS BOOK MAKES an argument for a thematic continuity from Words-worth to Ashbery. Neither this argument per se nor this lineage of authors is new. Whatever novelty the book has to offer lies in its description of what the poets share. I advance an account of romanticism without con-solations. In the conventional version of romanticism and its legacy, the loss of vitality and self-esteem bewailed in major first-person poems is surreptitiously compensated by a gain in intellectual or artistic entitle-ment; in the account given here, the losses are subtly compounded, mov-ing up the levels into reaches of ontological catastrophe where restitution is no longer possible. The pleasures of the self are obliterated rather than solemnized, and the self disappointed with its portion is simultaneously stripped of the comfort of art. This rereading of romanticism turns in par-ticular on a rereading of Wordsworth, because Wordsworth is credited with inaugurating the romantic celebration of the self. As I understand it, however, the reverse is true: rather than embracing the riches of the inner life, he is often bewildered and oppressed by self-disenchantment.

Disappointment is the name I give to the state of the self estranged from the hopes of selfhood. The meaning of disappointment may seem obvious enough, if it is taken to be simply the frustration of wishes or ex-pectations. Yet what I am isolating under this name—failure, defeat, and mortification—signifies a more complex and traumatic experience. For it is disappointment as a distinct, fearsome psychological state—a twilight of paralysis—that the preromantic, romantic, and postromantic lyric portrays. Poems about *this* form of disappointment are not poems about the failure of literary ambition or romantic love; they are about a more generalized—and deeper—frustration of eros, in which the self is frozen and isolated, has lost all purchase for its continuing resources, and is in fact humiliated both in itself and in its idea of what it means to be a subject.

I became interested in the topic of disappointment when I was work-ing on the Shelley chapters of my book *Literary Power and the Criteria of*

Truth. That book studies the prestige of tragic sense and its enhancement by the authority of severe style. Shelley was drawn to perfect this style—concise, bitter, hieratic—out of his literary ambition, and in spite of his opposing respect for the lyrical and optimistic. "The Triumph of Life" represents the culmination of his severity in its fierce pessimism and its antithetical poetics. But at the same time that he was working on this poem, Shelley was also writing his last lyrics, which adopt a rhetoric quite distinct from the lofty, impersonal style of "The Triumph of Life," with its tendency toward apothegm and its interest in philosophical generalization. Shelley's late lyrics are instead quiet and sad. They explore a psychological state in which the speaker is so thoroughly demoralized as to have lost even his capacity for disillusionment. For disillusionment still harbors some degree of pride and a respect for the intellect, whereas disappointment inflicts what Freud called a "narcissistic wound" on the self and its conception of its powers. (As Wallace Stevens incisively remarked, disillusion is the last illusion.) Shelley sought to represent this curious condition of self-entrapment and self-defeat, but obviously he could not do so by means of the same elevated rhetoric he was using so dazzlingly in "The Triumph of Life." To represent this state in the first person he had to abandon high style and grim rhetoric—the very rhetoric and style that make a swift route to literary power. It is striking that the subject remained so compelling for him when its exploration required the sacrifice of authority.

In studying how Shelley had arrived at portraying this state of mind, I turned to Wordsworth as a possible influence, only to discover that Wordsworth had been there before Shelley, and more, that a major strain of romantic and postromantic lyric devotes itself to capturing the sadness of disappointment. This disoriented sense of sadness is to be found in poetry of the tradition from Wordsworth's

> Turn whereso'er I may,
>   By night or day,
> The things which I have seen I now can see no more.

to John Ashbery's "I tried each thing, only some were immortal and free." These poems concern not specific disappointments but rather the psychic state of being disappointed, which results in a complex condition of psychological deadlock. An experience of loss fractures and paralyzes the formerly hopeful self, because it makes that self seem in retrospect to have been arrogant and naive. The self now regards itself as having grossly overestimated its power and significance, and it loses ontological status in its own eyes: it seems to itself a mediocre thing and is at a loss to know how to employ its remaining energies of thought and desire. As Ashbery puts it, the dream sustaining all other dreams dies; one is left "To awake and try to begin living in what / Has now become a slum."

The paradigm of such discomfiture is to be found in Wordsworth's crisis lyrics. By examining his major autobiographical poems, including "Tintern Abbey" and the Intimations Ode, I suggest that his interest is not, as it has always been taken to be, in portraying a loss and the discovery of a more or less successful "recompense" for it, but on the contrary that he works to describe the psychological impasse of disappointment, in which the self is compromised to the extent that it has lost its resources of pride and defiance and is reduced to seeking comfort in pieties it does not really accept (including the claim that it has received "abundant recompense" for its losses). This compounded influence of disappointment —its self-consciousness, its haunting self-doubt, and its oppression— constitute what we might call its second-order effects.

The exploration of such effects was crucial to the development of the romantic and postromantic lyric. It governs the poetry of many Wordsworth successors, particularly Shelley and Wallace Stevens—Shelley with his emphasis on the results of "desolation," Stevens with his study of the "malady" continually recurring in alternation with "inescapable romance." All of these poets represent the self struggling not only to recover an interest in the experience of the world but also in the experience of being an experiencing subject. Stevens and Ashbery then go on explicitly to detail a disappointment with the ontological status of the self, a disappointment that is expressed abstractly but felt individually as an emotional deprivation. There is no clearer example of this ontological disappointment than Ashbery's startling declaration of sorrow over the paltriness of the "soul":

> The pity of it smarts,
> Makes hot tears spurt: that the soul is not a soul,
> Has no secret, is small, and it fits
> Its hollow perfectly.

This version of romanticism and its legacy diverges from received notions in that it uncovers an emphasis on a desolation unredeemed; the sadness of disappointment does not enter into the dialectic of loss and gain, despair and triumph, with which romanticism is usually identified. On the contrary, in disappointment it is precisely the self's confidence in the fascination and the power of its subjectivity that is suspended. Disappointment is a condition of *"désoeuvrement"*—to use Maurice Blanchot's suggestive concept—being put out of place or put out of work, in this case as an experiencing subject. In such an abyss, bewilderment and sadness have no grandeur.

The poets I study here are the poets of Harold Bloom's "high romantic" canon. I adopt his canon but depart from his account of what the poets have in common. For in his rendering of the romantic tradition, each poet wages a battle to triumph in his originality, and the successful poems are the records of successful struggles. Bloom has grouped these central poems together under the name of the "crisis lyric," a work in which, by dint of the author's "strength," poetic self-doubt wins its way through to its own cure. It is precisely this description of the crisis lyric, with its emphasis on fortunate conclusion (or the appearance of it), that I wish to challenge. My difference with Bloom turns on a redescription of the rhythm of the crisis lyric. As I see it, the crisis is psychic rather than vocational—it is a crisis for the poet as person not the poet as poet —and it most pointedly meets with no resolution. The history of romantic and postromantic poetry is not a history of ambitious self-assertion but a collective testimony of chagrin over the broken promises of the self.

This book concentrates on four poets of the romantic and postromantic tradition. In order to discuss the poets whose portrayal of disappointment I have found most profound, I have omitted some others (such as Coleridge) who might have figured more largely in this history, and I skip straight from the romantic poets Wordsworth and Shelley to two twentieth-century American writers, Stevens and Ashbery. This work passes over romanticism's endowment to the second half of the nineteenth and the early twentieth centuries, when a number of major poets—including Tennyson, Browning, Hardy, and Yeats—pursued the representation of impasse and self-disenchantment. The theme of the self stripped of its pretensions and floundering remains vivid from Tennyson's *In Memoriam* through Yeats's "The Circus Animals Desertion." It is not incidental that the poets in this list are all male: though some women write about the self-disenchanted self (Charlotte Smith, Mary Shelley, and Elizabeth Bishop), it has been an especially prominent topic in poetry by men. Perhaps the upset of self-confidence comes as a particular affront to men or remains a particularly absorbing experience.

What romanticism bequeathed to Victorian poetry, and then, oddly enough, to modernism and postmodernism, is the psychology of unresolved disappointment. Romantic, Victorian, modernist, and postmodernist literature have all been characterized as literatures of disillusionment in which past traditions—cultural, poetic, and religious—are rejected with either impatience or angst. But in individual poets and individual poems, the brisk freedom of disillusionment is superseded by the stumbling and undignified confusions of disappointment. Muted and self-effacing, disappointment naturally does not advertise itself, and so it has been overlooked. Yet psychological representation in modern poetry would not be nearly as subtle as it is if it did not so often concern disappointment.

It may seem paradoxical to claim that a series of first-person poems can share in the representation of "self-effacement" or that aesthetically successful poems can speak for an abyss of failure. I believe that both paradoxes are superficial. The first springs from confusing self-representation with self-regard, while the second depends on slighting the distinction between the poet as poet, who may enjoy or profit from his or her success, and the poet as person, whose plight is unrelieved by poetic achievement. In his essays on Kafka, Maurice Blanchot demonstrates how Kafka gradually abandoned the shy pride he took in his writing and experienced it more and more as a form of grim exile or unrewarding "*désoeuvrement*." This transition was occurring at the same time that his writing was becoming increasingly powerful, but that makes no difference: the triumph of this alien expenditure could not exalt him in his own eyes. He had been surprisingly disappointed in his hopes for writing —surprisingly, not because he failed in his ambitions (since he actually succeeded), but rather, because his success itself failed to be rewarding.

This is the ultimate disappointment for the writer per se, and any work that evinces the pleasure of its composition cannot represent disappointment persuasively. A compelling poem will make it manifest that disappointment obsessively seeks its place in writing because it is as irresolvable as writing is purposeless.

However, I do not expect to dispel the force of paradox with abstract argument. This book will demonstrate through examples that a work in the first person can deny the ascendancy of the self and that poems of considerable aesthetic merit can show there is no compensation in art.

I present this work as a study in the discrimination of literary affects. For all the varieties of disheartenment—all its different sources and levels —are too often subsumed under the general rubric of disillusionment, just as literature's diverse evocations of sadness are lumped together under the bare and uninformative name of "pathos." Words like "disillusionment," "pathos," and "tragedy" do not sufficiently differentiate the emotions traced in many romantic poems, where the apprehension of irredeemable loss can find no means by which to dignify and approve itself. In the paradigm of disappointment, there is no reassertion of pleasure in the motions of the self, not even one veiled under the mantle of tragic recognition. In isolating such a paradigm, I wish to recover the subtleties of literary affect and to liberate so-called pathos from its association with indulgence, mystification, and banality.

A number of people furthered the thought or writing in this book, and I thank them here: Harold Bloom, Marshall Brown, John Burt, Stanley Cavell, Jerome Christensen, Burton Dreben, Juliet Floyd, Frances Ferguson, William Flesch, Deborah Gordon, Moshe Halbertal, Neil Hertz, Richard Moran, Jeff Nunokawa, Adela Pinch, Christopher Pye, Marc Redfield, Thomas Reinert, Shirley Samuels, Steven Shaviro, and Karen Swann.

I remember Walter Hughes, 1960–95, with gratitude for his friendship.

I am indebted to the Society for the Humanities at Cornell, where I had a fellowship the year I finished this book.

A portion of my chapter on Wordsworth appeared previously, under the title "'Tintern Abbey,' Sensibility and the Self-Disenchanted Self," in *ELH*, 64 (1997), 131-56; I thank the journal for permission to reprint that writing. I am also grateful for permission to quote:

Excerpts from "The Book of Ephraim" from *The Changing Light at Sandover* by James Merrill, copyright © 1980, 1982 by James Merrill. Reprinted by permission of Alfred A. Knopf Inc.

Excerpts from *Collected Poems* by Wallace Stevens, copyright 1954 by Wallace Stevens. Reprinted by permission of Alfred A. Knopf Inc. and Faber & Faber Ltd.

Excerpts from *Self-Portrait in a Convex Mirror* by John Ashbery. Copyright © 1972, 1973, 1974, 1975 by John Ashbery. Used by permission of Viking Penguin, a division of Penguin Putnam Inc.

Excerpts from "Crazy Weather" and "The Gazing Grain" by Ashbery from *Houseboat Days* (New York: Viking, 1977). Copyright © 1975, 1976, 1977 by John Ashbery. Excerpts from "Soonest Mended" and "Variations, Calypso and Fugue on a Theme of Ella Wheeler Wilcox" by John Ashbery from *The Double Dream of Spring* (New York: Dutton, 1970). Copyright © 1970, 1969, 1968, 1967, 1966 by John Ashbery. Reprinted by permission of Georges Borchardt Inc. for John Ashbery.

A NOTE ON CITATION

Citations from primary sources are included in the body of the text, in parentheses after the quotation. Line numbers are given for poems by Wordsworth and Shelley, and other poets for whose work there are lineated editions; page numbers are given for Stevens, Ashbery, and Merrill. References to secondary sources appear in the endnotes.

Wordsworth's shorter poems are quoted from *Poetical Works*, ed. Hutchinson and Selincourt. The *Prelude* used here is the 1805 version. Shelley is cited from the Reiman and Powers *Selected Poetry and Prose*, except where otherwise indicated. Stevens is quoted from *The Collected Poems*; Ashbery, from *The Double Dream of Spring* (abbreviated as *DDS*), *Houseboat Days* (abbreviated as *HD*), and *Self-Portrait in a Convex Mirror* (abbreviated as *SP*).

THE POETICS OF DISAPPOINTMENT

IN ITS FIRST USE, disappointment meant "to undo the appointment of; to deprive of an appointment, office, or possession" (*O.E.D.*, 1483). Disappointment in this sense entailed losing one's hold on public identity and public space, losing a goal for one's energies and an occupation for one's time. Most primitively, disappointment meant ceasing to be "*à point,*" in the right place at the right moment, and thus implied a breakdown in one's relation to time, a falling out and away from a recognizable order. In the seventeenth and eighteenth centuries, disappointment came to have its more familiar meaning, "the frustration or non-fulfillment of expectation, intention or desire," and "the state or condition of being disappointed, with the resultant feeling of dejection." This book uses disappointment to mean less the frustration of specific intentions than the frustration of general expectations of experience, general hopes for the self and its destiny, through the loss of which one is exposed to disorientation and existential vagrancy.

The customary name for the loss of hopes and ideals is disillusionment, and disappointment clearly entails disillusionment insofar as it exposes what are perceived to have been naive illusions about the self: belief in its grandeur, its intellectual capacity, its continuity, its uniqueness, and its possession of a special destiny. Yet a distinction can be drawn between disillusionment, which brings with it the compensation of intellectual progress, and disappointment, in which esteem for the self is so seriously compromised as to cripple the pride of intellectual accomplishment. Etymologically, disillusionment means the loss of illusion, rather than loss of position or place. Thus, disillusionment carries a sense of potential advantage in a newfound acquaintance with the truth, whereas there is no obvious advantage in being cast away. Popular usage discounts disappointment as insignificant and ephemeral whereas disillusionment is valued as a portentous experience. In this book, the terms are used with the opposite valence: disappointment is the more involved condition because it goes deeper in rooting out the hopes of the self. We may be able to recognize such a distinction in our own affects—between, for example, the feeling of disgust that accompanies de-idealization and the devastation of irredeemable loss. But it is primarily in rhetorical form—in the linguistic representation of psychological states—that this distinction becomes vivid.

The abysmal quality of disappointment makes it intimate with writing and drawn to unfurl there. To judge by the evidence, poetry in particular offers the best forum for this exploration. A disproportionate number of lyric and meditative poems concern disappointment—not just those that address individual disappointments, as for example, disappointments in love, but those that plumb the generalized, chronic condition. The condensed and complex moment of the poem gives a proper home to the dilation of disappointment.

Coleridge's "Dejection: An Ode" draws out the subtlety of disappointment in a paradigmatic way: by contrasting the naive and disappointed (as opposed to disillusioned) states. Coleridge compares his present debilitation with his stamina in an earlier time. But he does not say that he was simply younger then, nor that he was carefree:

> There was a time when, though my path was rough,
>   This joy within me dallied with distress,
> And all misfortunes were but as the stuff
>   Whence Fancy made me dreams of happiness.   (76–79)

He had tribulations then, too—perhaps the same kind of difficulties he has now—but his attitude toward them was different. With a bold and surprising choice of verb, Coleridge avers that in the old days the persisting joy within him "dallied" with distress. He was evidently able to toy with his griefs, as if he had reserves of self-confidence, or self-exhilaration,

that protected him from the worst disheartenment. His troubles, however painful, lay more or less lightly on his spirit. They even gave rise to
"dreams of happiness"; they seemed perhaps to be the necessary trials for
one on his way to greater things. But now affliction has become a sorrow
in itself, an incessant reminder to Coleridge, the sufferer, that he is such
as to be made to suffer. It is humiliating to him to be unhappy, because
he must therefore see himself as enregistered among the unfortunate
and unthriving.

Between then and now he has lost what Freud would have termed his
"narcissistic supplies." Disappointment has inflicted a narcissistic wound,
a wound not to spoiled self-love, but to constitutive self-regard. As
Coleridge's "joy" constituted an overflowing of narcissistic excitement
("We in ourselves rejoice! / And thence flows all that charms or ear or
sight"), so his present demoralization follows from the decay of the pleasure he took in being himself. He is divided against himself, beleaguered
by anachronistic emotion, and yet discouraged by the benumbing effect
of self-discipline:

> But now afflictions bow me down to earth:
> Nor care I that they rob me of my mirth;
>   But oh! each visitation
> Suspends what nature gave me at my birth,
>   My shaping spirit of Imagination.
> For not to think of what I needs must feel,
>   But to be still and patient, all I can;
> And haply by abstruse research to steal
>   From my own nature all the natural man—
>   This was my sole resource, my only plan.   (82–91)

Now that his wishes for the future have been cut off, he has entered a
curious limbo, wherein he must find employment for his unhappily surviving appetites. His new purpose is to suppress feeling and self-
consciousness, and ultimately to distract himself from his own existence.
He does not look beyond the goal of anesthetization, but even becoming
numb is only a temporary good. Its consequences in the long run are destructive. Without larger aims, his "plan" is deprived of a significant
teleology; Coleridge's course is halted and suspended without hope of

rescue. Such a fraught condition of paralysis hardly conduces to ease self-consciousness—quite the reverse—and so he is doubly afflicted: not only humbled but also confined to the occupation of beholding his degraded state.

This is a life of disappointment: to have to labor at an existence deprived of self-delight and the related pleasure of teleology. Coleridge does not alter or modify this self-description in the rest of the poem; nor does he "work through" to any resolution. All he does, rather sadly, is to leave off here, and offer his good wishes to another:

> Tis midnight, but small thoughts have I of sleep:
> Full seldom may my friend such vigils keep!
> Visit her, gentle Sleep! with wings of healing.   (126–28)

The poem remains true to itself as a delving in the state of disappointment, which appears to be chronic and insurmountable. Though it may be common to cease to feel disappointed, as one may cease to despair, too, it is constitutive of both states that they seem to be irreversible.

In the cul-de-sac of disappointment, the subject loses the inner assurance of purpose at the same time when external frustrations have made his need for that assurance more acute. He finds himself stripped of existential support, cast adrift in what suddenly seems to him an unsponsored life. Coleridge is stunned by his precipitate banishment from a normal relation to his own life. Cowper's "The Castaway" focuses on this condition of existential exile even more explicitly. "The Castaway" is so saturated with pathos that it might seem to be an aesthetic disaster. Yet it is not a poem of mere self-pity and self-lamentation; it is hard-pressed to delineate the state it laments, and that delineation is its real labor. Cowper frames his brief, elliptical description of his own state with ten stanzas describing someone else's situation, which is only roughly analogous to his own. There was no ship, sea, storm, cask, coop, and "stifling wave" in Cowper's case, no narrative and no physical facts. And yet the state is much more particular than the broad comparison ("I was like the sailor drowning in sight of his friends") would suggest.

The sailor went over; he did not drown immediately, but swam with "strength" and "courage"; he "waged" a fierce battle for life, and could have been saved, if not for a storm that compelled his friends to sail be-fore the wind for their own sake; he knew this and forgave them; they threw him casks and coops to hold him up, but these could only prolong his vigil, and he perished within hearing distance. In what respect is this drowning like Cowper's experience?

The castaway sailor's psychological ordeal springs from his having instinctively had to struggle to survive in spite of his knowing he could not survive. He is compelled to see himself as a lost thing. The peculiar-ity of this state is suggested by Cowper's grammatically tortured, am-biguous description: he "waged with death a lasting strife, / Supported by despair of life." Either the strife or the sailor paradoxically derives en-ergy from "despair of life"; such is the introversion of his struggle and the dissemination of the layers of self-consciousness that "despair of life" provides a desperate sustenance. "Supported" is in any case a macabre choice, because it calls attention to the plight of the man supporting him-self through his desperate exertions in the water. In fact, he has to sup-port himself in every way. The universe has worked against him, and thereby shown its indifference to him (which is not the same as its indif-ference in general). For he has been doomed by a combination of acci-dents. Now, like Shakespeare's Antony, he must see himself as suffering the abandonment of fortune and must knowingly endure the space of pointlessly prolonged survival. Cowper focuses on that stretch of anti-grace: "He long survives, who lives an hour / In ocean, self-upheld." It is this self-conscious loneliness that Cowper identifies with his own condi-tion; like the sailor, he has fallen into a life that has to regard itself as posthumous—omitted from history, confined to itself:

> No voice divine the storm allayed,
> > No light propitious shone,
> When, snatched from all effectual aid,
> > We perished, each alone.
> But I beneath a rougher sea,
> And whelmed in deeper gulphs than he.   (61–66)

Cowper emphasizes the image of death in solitude, the harsh end of a life that knows itself to be cut off from ordinary teleology, discarded, and preterite. Though this fate may be a common one, the acknowledgment of commonality is deflating and paradoxically isolating because the life of routine disappointment still has to be lived out, and apprehended, alone.

A sense of humiliation characterizes the state of disappointment as Coleridge and Cowper portray it. To demarcate this state, their poems can be contrasted with another poem that portrays a similar psychological impasse but without the element of humiliation. Byron's "January 22nd 1874, Messalonghi," subtitled "On this day I complete my thirty-sixth year," also describes a crisis of exhaustion, nostalgia, and dismay. The speaker does not, in essence, emerge from this state; and yet despite his self-contempt, from somewhere he summons up continuing resources of vigor and defiance. In the second half of the poem, the speaker repudiates his erotic claustrophobia (he loves but abhors the prospect of reentering the futile round of love), though not by means of curing it; he turns to simple repression ("Tread those reviving passions down"!(29)) or better, sublimation, demanding of himself that he should convert his ennui into valor because taking a courageous stand is bound to bring about the most effective conclusion:

> If thou regret'st thy youth, *why live?*
>   The land of honourable death
> Is here:—up to the field, and give
>   Away thy breath!
>
> Seek out—less often sought than found—
>   A soldier's grave, for thee the best;
> Then look around, and choose thy ground,
>   And take thy rest.   (33–40)

This last command is easy and efficient, albeit suicidal. The speaker finds the way out of his weariness by finding the end to life. Seeing that maturation is tantamount to decline, he rejects his inevitable fate and revenges himself upon life by dismissing it. Byron's poem leaves room for such pride in the speaker and such disdain for the condition to which he has been reduced, as to permit a lofty though destructive refusal of terms. The sense of entitlement remains strong; the speaker has not, in F. Scott Fitzgerald's words, "developed a sad attitude toward sadness" or "become identified with the objects of [his] horror or compassion."[1] Byron stages his weltschmerz as something notable and rare. By contrast, Coleridge and Cowper discover their ordinariness, but discover it exactly insofar as they feel their findings to be of merely personal interest; they have found out nothing of general importance by whose announcement they might command regard. The aggrieved indignation in Byron's dis- illusionment sets it apart from the harried perplexity of Coleridge and Cowper's disappointment.

Disillusionment maintains an assurance of authority and an enraged attitude about the future because it trusts that the self is being contoured to a purpose (it is learning) and so moving forward in a teleologically or- dered existence. What does it mean to conclude instead that experience is not teleologically ordered, that one has no destiny to pursue? In the context of constitutive narcissism, destiny and self-determination are not opposing concepts; both exert a mastery over sublunary experience. But without teleology, experience loses all shape, initiative loses its point of application, and time becomes a strange vacuum. Therefore, the idea of having a destiny is tenacious; it will not be readily abandoned, but will continue to conceal itself in the guise of various doubts. Frustrations of all kinds can be interpreted as episodes in a narrative of emotional matura- tion, or increasing insight, or vocational intensity. Jean-François Lyotard makes this point in a moment of intellectual memoir:

> The delusion that we are able to program our life is a part of an ancient fidelity to something like a destiny or destination, as if we were called by somebody or something, let us say, by an author—and this includes ourself as a hidden author—called, finally, by authorization, to perform the role he (or it) has written on our behalf. Even the early doubts I experienced could easily be inscribed in a process of destiny under the title "The years of for- mation." Wasn't the care with which I tried to direct my life the sign that I was spending my "Lehrjahre" in search of a vocation which could appear as properly mine, and wasn't the eagerness itself a part of the sought-after vocation?[2]

Deprecating the artificiality of his early anxieties, Lyotard perceives that his uncertainties never profoundly discouraged him because he tacitly understood them to be scheduled moments of struggle, hygienic and temporary. His passionate doubt of his vocation he accepted, deep down, as proof of his fledgling purpose. And the confidence of possessing this hidden purpose preserved, in turn, the still more necessary assurance that experience has a telos, that it is gathering to an end. It must have an end—with or without a heaven to follow, as Wallace Stevens might say. For the teleological paradigms provided by religion—faith in a deity who has ordered experience or hope of an afterlife to redeem it—are lavishly built upon a more primitive need to believe in the arrangement of experience, and in the self as its proud harvester. If all else fails, trust that the self is its own balanced center—the eye of its life—bestows significance on experience, while other hopes and expectations will retreat before this elemental dream.

To cease to believe in the destiny of the self empties time of its teleological promise. One loses one's orientation toward the future, and time comes to a halt, giving rise to drift and silence, the temporal equivalent of being weightless in space. However, rather than being liberated from time, the disappointed subject thrust into a temporal void feels himself to be surrounded by nothing but time, in effect, to be drowning in time. Without the promise of evolution, time is pared down to an iterative stutter, proceeding rather than progressing, creating in one moment what it dissolves in the next. All the teleological verbs by which its action is usually described are now perceived as inaccurate; it does not reveal, unfold, and bring forth, but rather idles or divagates (depending on whether it is conceived of as standing still or moving at random; these are two facets of the same intuition). The disappointed subject is panicked by the barren prospect of time, but also feels subject to time because the self stripped of ontological grandeur—and therefore of the assumption that it is a permanent essence—no longer expects to transcend time, but sees itself as agglutinated, dissolved, and rearranged in time. It loses its pride with respect to time, having been forced to concede the unlikelihood of rising above temporal chaos, either constitutively or intellectually. For when, in the manner scrupulously detailed by Proust, it beholds the discontinuity between past, present, and future selves, it recognizes itself as conatal with time, or composed of time's element; it is in flux as time is in flux and therefore, cannot hope to attain a masterly, general and permanent perspective.

It is humiliating to find that the self is steeped in time, as Kierkegaard would put it. Kierkegaard forcefully analyzes this humiliation (and what he characteristically regards as its desirability) in *Concluding Unscientific Postscript*, in which he contrasts the delusive vainglory of "objective knowledge" with the monotony of being a subject bound to time, "a poor, wretched, existing individual who stumbles again and again and progresses very slowly from year to year."[3] One would like to escape from this degrading condition through a compensatory claim to intellectual authority, but to Kierkegaard's mind, such claims simply evade the truth. The human being is not constituted to become the master of its experience and so to transcend its confinement by time: "the absolute difference between God and a human being is simply this, that a human being is an individual existing being (and this holds for the best brain just as fully as for the most obtuse), whose essential task therefore cannot be to think *sub specie aeternitatis*."[4] The subject must instead resign the consolation of knowledge and devote himself to "the task of deepening in inwardness" or "becoming subjective." This task is necessarily unrewarding because it does not grant the subject's wish for progress and tangible achievement. It is instead a thankless and belittling toil.

Kierkegaard likes to blame Hegel and the "assistant professors" for advancing the prestige of objectivity, but the logic of his general argument makes it clear that the abasement of inwardness is a structural necessity. That is, any "deepening" of inwardness will involve an experience of tedium, bewilderment, and indignity:

> It is generally thought that to be subjective is no art. Well, of course, every human being is something of a subject. But now to become what one is as a matter of course—who would waste his time on that? That would indeed be the most dispensable of all tasks in life. Quite so. But that is why it is already so very difficult, indeed, the most difficult of all, because every human being has a strong natural desire and drive to become something else and more. That is how it is with all apparently insignificant tasks: just this apparent insignificance makes them infinitely difficult, because the task does not clearly beckon and thus lend support to the aspirer, but works against him so that it

takes an infinite effort just to discover the task, that is, that this is the task, a drudgery from which one is otherwise exempted.[5]

A vertiginous labor of faltering and failing, the task of "becoming subjective" will seem repulsively empty to an "aspiring" spirit. In pursuing "inwardness," the subject discovers only its own poverty and degradation. Kierkegaard declares in no uncertain terms that the development of inwardness brings "suffering" and that this plunge into internal confusion constitutes the "martyrdom of faith." But, in an important paradox, this state, though ultimately desirable, is not to be alleviated by conviction of its inherent worth, or by any hope of reward, or even by the comfort of community and recognition. For any such reassurance would negate its constitutive features—floundering, self-doubt, humiliation, and solitude.

For Kierkegaard, the "truth of inwardness" is the experience of self-loss, but a self-loss that cannot comfort itself with the satisfaction of having attained the truth. Kierkegaard's paradigm of inwardness is thus similar to our paradigm of disappointment, in which an increasing acquaintance with what is felt to be the true nature of the self both deflates the status of the self and removes the compensation of learning. It may be difficult to sustain the credibility of this paradox; but to join these apparently competing claims—that the self has come to know its poverty and at the same time ceased to take pride in the acquisition of knowledge—is exactly what Kierkegaard and, in a different way, the romantic crisis lyric seek to do.

It is through the agency of time that the self is humbled in its regard for its own being. In James Merrill's "The Book of Ephraim," Proust is called "A GREAT PROPHET." Merrill defers to Proust because in "Ephraim" he aspires to do what Proust does—to make manifest time's erosion of personality. He sees time as having worn him down in an invisible accumulation of memory, repetition, and routine, while depriving him, step by step, of the dreams and consolations that initially rendered its burden light—fascination with oneself, erotic novelty, the pleasures of untested gifts, the delight of aesthetics, the incredulity of death, and the capacity for idealization. For the decay of the willingness to idealize both attacks the propensity for self-aggrandizement and disheartens or empties something out of the self. Thus the self is led to retire or to resign its claims, and it subsists in a state of what Merrill calls "self-effacement."

At the deepest level, this is the sense in which "Ephraim" portrays "the incarnation and withdrawal of / A god" (3). The first of the poem's gods to take form and then withdraw is Ephraim himself, though, ironically, he does not withdraw of his own accord, like the Greek gods disgusted with the world, but dies of his inventors' boredom, as they outgrow the exuberant wit that brought him into being, as well as their first love. And thus the second, greater god to vanish is the god of Eros, subject not only to the wearing effects of familiar union, but also to the general loss of the power of "sexual idealization," to use Freud's term. It is not merely that the character of erotic life changes, but that as it does so it subdues and erodes the self. Love decays, and Merrill finds that he is essentially alone, but by the influence of his long dependency on his lover DJ, he has been stripped of the fantasy that he has a permanent and autonomous self:

> And here was I, or what was left of me.
> Feared and rejoiced in, chafed against, help cheap,
> A strangeness that was us, and was not, had
> All the same allowed for its description,
> And so brought at least me these spells of odd,
> Self-effacing balance. Better to stop
> While we still can. Already I take up
> Less emotional space than a snowdrop.
> My father in his last illness complained
> Of the effect of medication on
> His real self—today Bluebeard, tomorrow
> Babbitt. Young chameleon, I used to
> Ask how on earth one got sufficiently
> Imbued with otherness. And now I see.   (76–89)

The bond of sustained love performs a reduction on the self. The fascinations of life spring from investing it with unwarranted grandeur; it turns out that the concept of the true self is one of these fascinations, and thus, one of what Proust calls *les erreurs charmantes de la jeunesse*.[6]

We might therefore distinguish disappointment, as a loss of the capacity for self-idealization, from disillusionment, which could be said to entail only the loss of external ideals. The ideals impaired by disappointment include certain primitive ontological assumptions about the constitution and destiny of the self. In his essay on the sublime, Schiller observes that it is humiliating to be checked in one's will, and that everyone's life is therefore humiliating simply by virtue of mortality. Disappointment, in this light, represents an acknowledgment of the perpetual thwarting of the will in its most basic requirements of experience.

Psychoanalysis contains a rich vein of thinking about the pains of deidealization, but naturally, it concerns clinical affects, and we are therefore hard put to know how to invoke it because disappointment is not quite a clinical affect. It shares some but not all the characteristics of melancholia. It separates its sufferer from the ordinary course of life, and thereby subjects her or him to the secondary afflictions of loneliness and shame, like Kristeva's melancholia, in which "A betrayal, a fatal illness, some accident or handicap . . . abruptly wrests me away from what seemed to me the normal category of normal people."[7] Again, like "despair" in Kristeva's description of it, disappointment is a form of sorrow specifically experienced as debasing rather than ennobling: "Such despair is not a revulsion that would imply my being capable of desire and creativity, negative indeed but present. Within depression, if my existence is on the verge of collapse, its lack of meaning is not tragic—it appears obvious to me, glaring and inescapable."[8] On the other hand, the disappointment explored in the works of the sensibility poets, Coleridge, Wordsworth, Shelley, Stevens, and Ashbery can hardly be said to share in the aphasia (the loss of "all interest in words") that characterizes melancholia. Disappointment reminds us of depression but is not identical to it. As the figurative rendition of a psychological state, disappointment conforms to psychological experience in part (otherwise it would be recognizable), but it also takes its place within a literary paradigm. It is clarified and stylized. It captures a sadness that has something in common with depression but is not pathological, for the erosion of self-regard that disappointment entails is largely conceptual. We might call it a philosophical problem. Even though the disappointed self feels itself to have shrunk down to mere particularity, it is not simply the failing of its own life that it mourns. Disappointment attacks the aggrandized onto-logical status of the self in general.

Although disappointment cannot be analyzed in a strictly psychoana-lytic vocabulary, the insights of psychoanalysis can be suggestively applied. The psychoanalytic literature on the affects of privation—on mourning, melancholia, and de-idealizing—helps to illuminate the kinds of losses or the nature of loss in the literature of disappointment. Freud and Klein show why disenchantment with idealized objects in the world leads to a diminished sense of self, or, how external disappointment is transformed into internal poverty.

In "Mourning and Melancholia," Freud began to work out an expla-nation of why loss in the outer world causes inner pain and darkness. (Giving an explanation for this turns out to be much more difficult than one would suppose.) Freud introduced the concepts of introjection and identification, and arrived at the somewhat surprising notion that identification with a lost loved object, which might seem to enrich the self, actually causes "a shadow" to "fall upon the ego."[9] The ego discovers that such introjection is not enough to sustain it—that its own resources of solipsism and self-sufficiency falter when it is thrown back upon its internalizations.

The first and most important introjections are those of one's parents, just as the parents are one's primary lost love objects, often lost through de-idealization before they are lost through death. Freud does not pursue the topic of de-idealization of one's parents in "Mourning and Melancho-lia," but in his short, sharp essay "Family Romances," he describes the cunning tenacity of the will to idealize and hints at why it is so tenacious.

Freud suggests that adults, including those who are not especially neurotic, may continue to nourish the archaic fantasies by which they expressed their love for their parents in childhood. He begins by declar-ing that "The freeing of an individual, as he grows up, from the author-ity of his parents, is one of the most necessary though one of the most painful results brought about by the course of his development."[10] Yet at the essay's close, he leaves us in some doubt as to how completely this lib-eration is achieved. Freud discovers the concealed, lingering idealism of childhood in what would appear to be rapacious disillusionment, "faith-lessness and ingratitude."

The essay describes children's necessary disenchantment with their parents, who had once seemed perfect. In the normal course of development, children's initial idealization of their parents gives way to the effects of reality testing, and the disappointments of sexual rivalry feed anger and dissatisfaction, as well as contributing a vengeful motive to critical assessments of the parents. Children replace inadequate parents with other, grander ones through the fantasy of adoption, or, after they have learned about the means of sexual reproduction, they dispose of sibling rivals by imagining them to be the product of adulterous liaisons. But, Freud cautions us with some amusement,

> If anyone is inclined to turn away in horror from this depravity of the child-ish heart or feels tempted, indeed, to dispute the possibility of such things, he should observe that these works of fiction, which seem so full of hostility, are none of them really so badly intended, and that they still preserve, under a slight disguise, the child's original affection for his parents. The faithlessness and ingratitude are only apparent. If we examine in detail the commonest of these imaginative romances, the replacement of both parents or of the father alone by grander people, we find that these new and aristocratic parents are equipped with attributes that are derived entirely from real recollections of the actual and humble ones; so that in fact the child is not getting rid of his father but exalting him.[11]

The child is disillusioned with his or her parents because they have not succeeded as avatars of the ideals for which they were themselves the originals. In seeking a new object, thwarted idealism falls back on the old object for the choice of standards. The new love rephrases the old, doing it perpetual, unthinking homage. Therefore, children's disillusionment, however painful, is hardly complete: behind their disenchantment, the old enchanting hopes persevere. A touching naiveté is at the heart of this rejection, which expresses nostalgia and regret—the strong wish not to avoid bewitchment, but to fall under the spell again. Thus an apparently linear progression toward enlightenment, growth, and autonomy conceals a recidivist movement, a circling back to reembrace the un-shakable convictions of an ignorant self.

Indeed the whole effort at replacing the real father by a superior one is only an expression of the child's longing for the happy, vanished days when his father seemed to him the noblest and strongest of men and his mother the dearest and loveliest of women. He is turning away from the father he knows to-day to the father in whom he believed in the earlier years of his childhood; and his phantasy is no more than the expression of a regret that those happy days have gone. Thus in these phantasies the over-valuation that characterizes a child's earliest years comes into its own again.[12]

The naive estimation of the parents survives, transferred to surrogates. The desire for admirable authority is maintained as an anachronistic longing that will never be fully satisfied, and this will to idealize persists under cover of local disillusionments. Freud does not describe an end to idealization here, but perhaps an end of a kind might come with perpetual frustration, which would lead one to recognize one's own psychic atavism. Such a recognition would belong to the psychology of disappointment, in which the subject helplessly beholds her or his participation in a wish she or he cannot transcend. Perceiving the witchcraft of the family romance cannot bring about its exorcism; on the contrary, in this case to be disabused of illusion only means helplessly acknowledging one's continued desire for it. The situation is as Hegel describes it in his analysis of the "unhappy consciousness": one does not believe in what one believes in. In "Mourning and Melancholia" and "Family Romances," Freud exposes the lingering idealism of disillusionment, but the state beyond it, disappointment, entails compromise of the capacity for idealization.

It was with an intuition similar to Freud's that Blake designed the frontispiece to his *Songs of Experience*, which shows two young women grieving over the bodies of a beautiful old man and woman, clearly a glamorized rendition of their parents. The girls dwell in their loss; it is a present and vivid experience, in some sense not yet relinquished. The embitterment of "Experience" evidently involves still clinging to the internalized ideal of what the parent represents. Whereas the loving and cheerful speakers of the *Songs of Innocence* trust in the benevolence of authority figures (parent, nurse, beadle, teacher, God), the paranoid speakers of Experience not only are discontented with specific incarnations of authority but also have become angry with what they regard as the pretended benignity of life. They have become resentful, like the Nurse, who sees herself as losing her adulthood to "waste" and "disguise." These speakers are defiant precisely to the extent that they have forsworn without actually abandoning the will to find a benevolent authority. They contemn the actual authorities they have encountered because they secretly hold out the hope of finding their idol incarnate.

The idealization of authority persists because it is fed by narcissistic hopes and satisfactions. Though Freud does not put it this way, the family romance—or the aggrandizement of the parent-imagoes—serves the purpose of glorifying the child in his own eyes (hence the adoption fantasy, "I am really the child of a King"). Mother, father, and child are a holy triad, larger than life, and the child's whole existence is magnified by this dream: he is one of the elect, his way is guided by a destiny. Conversely, the collapse of the family romance would inflict sore damage on what the self has taken to be its portion, and it is for this reason that investment in the family romance is so stubborn.

Klein makes this understanding of the dominion of the family romance explicit. Why does the loss of idealized authority lead to pandemic disappointment? A Kleinian analysis would say that loss of idealized authority equals, or threatens to equal, the loss of inner good objects, and the loss of inner goodness spells loss of the "belief and trust in [one's] capacity to love."[13] The greatest danger is always the danger of damage to inner good objects, the first and most elemental of which are the internalized mother and father. Any reverse imperils them, for they ensure one's confidence that there is something charitable in the world and that the self is creative. That is why external frustrations ultimately impoverish the self and diminish it in its own eyes.

Drawing upon Freud and Abraham in her essay, "Mourning and Its Relation to Manic-Depressive States," Klein argues that every loss returns us to the miseries of the infantile "depressive position," characterized by "sorrow and concern about the feared loss" of "'good' objects."[14] These are both external "good" objects—the idealized aspects of the parents, the parents insofar as they are figures of love and trust—and their introjected avatars within the self, the internal "good" objects. In the end, it is the survival of the internal good objects—the aspects of ourselves that we can love and trust, and that reassure and comfort us—

that we need most and fear for most. A loss in the external world threatens the survival of these internal good objects, and so threatens us with the prospect of "inner chaos." To recognize and confront the loss, however dreadful, of the real, external object, is preferable to surviving in a self from which the good objects have fled, abandoning it to the terrors of hatred, guilt, and persecution.

The "work of mourning" is therefore not, as Freud described it, to disinvest from the lost object, but to revive and "reinstate" inner "good" objects. Klein describes a "Mrs. A," whose son died suddenly, away from home. After a period of shock and "manic defenses," Mrs. A was finally able to know and experience her grief, by recovering her good objects, in this case her parents in memory, who encouraged her to feel that she was innocent of her son's death and entitled to mourn him: "Mrs. A, who at an earlier stage of her mourning had to some extent felt that her loss was inflicted on her by revengeful parents, could now in phantasy experience the sympathy of these parents (dead long since), their desire to support and to help her. She felt that they also suffered a severe loss and shared her grief, as they would have done had they lived. In her internal world harshness and suspicion had diminished, and sorrow had increased. The tears which she shed were also to some extent the tears which her internal parents shed, and she also wanted to comfort them as they—in her phantasy—comforted her."[15] Mrs. A. only really began to mourn—to rejoin the current of life, we might say—when she had reconstituted inner good objects who treated her with love and assured her that love has a place in the world, when, that is, she had restored an internal dream of parental benevolence.

The oppression of mourning, with its struggle to re-create phantasied idealizations, echoes the first experience of the threat of "inner chaos." This is "the depressive position," the stage of the infant's relation to its mother in which it is acutely ambivalent and fearful (fearful both of her and for her). According to Klein, every loss and disappointment brings about regression to the depressive position; in a sense, adulthood consists of a perpetual effort to avoid falling back into an early and original depression. It is not only grief that activates this struggle; "any pain caused by unhappy experiences, whatever their nature, has something in common with mourning. It reactivates the depressive position; the encountering and overcoming of adversity of any kind entails mental work similar to mourning."[16] Thus, the loss of an external "good" object— even in the form of an ideal, or a hope or expectation—can be seen, in Kleinian terms, as a danger to the self's persuasion that it has "goodness" in it. And here "good" means: forgiving, trusting, generous, creative, and adaptive. These qualities not only render the self deserving of affection, but also give it a future because "goodness" of this kind will be capable of flexibility, engagement, and interest, whereas a self embattled by guilt, hatred, and "persecutory anxieties" will be caught in a repetitive round of defenses. A de-idealized self will be paralyzed in time, unable to invest in the future by means of love or hope.

In "On the Sense of Loneliness," Klein explains directly how the loss of an ideal can cause de-idealization of the self (and thus how an instance of disillusionment can turn into an episode of disappointment): "The realization that the good object can never approximate to the perfection expected from the ideal one brings about de-idealization: and even more painful is the realization that no really ideal part of the self exists."[17] De-idealization can spell not merely the extinction of an external good object, an illusion or a dream, but also the extinction of that in the self for which this ideal stood, the lofty, confident part of the self from which it was projected. In its place will be left a lacuna or emptiness, and a corresponding feeling of defeat and disorientation.

This is the lacuna Wordsworth identifies when he says that the failure of the Revolution left him with "a sense of treachery and desertion in the place / The holiest that I knew of—my own soul" (*The Prelude*, 10.378–80).[18] Similarly, the psychological dilemma of his crisis lyrics is that he feels the loss of glamour in Nature as a loss within himself. He therefore makes a desperate effort to reconstruct the benevolence of Nature, who is clearly figured as the good mother. His future hangs in the balance, for the internalized parent is the promise of the world. Stevens makes this correlation even more lucidly. When, in "The Auroras of Autumn," he laments that the mother "is dissolved" and "is destroyed," he gives utterance to his conviction that he has lost what the idealized mother means, which is his own capacity for idealization and its hopefulness. She guarantees the pride of what is most necessary to be idealized— the self. And so she takes something fundamental with her when she grows "exhausted and a little old" ("Things of August"). As Klein puts it, "the idealized mother is the safeguard against a retaliating or a dead mother and against all bad objects, and therefore represents security and life itself."[19]

In his essay "On Idealization, Illusion and Catastrophic Disillusion," Charles Rycroft argues that "an element of illusion enters into the realistic libidinal cathexis of external reality."[20] He attributes this idea to Winnicott and Milner, but Winnicott at least probably found it in Klein, where it is latent. As Klein intimates, the inner "good" object is the product of an idealization of the mother (the "bad" is artificially distinguished from the "good" through splitting), but because the capacity to love and trust is founded on this idealization, idealization itself—"error" in a de Manian sense—is strictly necessary for mental health.[21] And after a loss or reverse, restoration of mental health depends on reviving this condition of error. Poetic disappointment—the disappointment portrayed in the romantic and postromantic tradition—involves an erosion within the self such that it cannot recover the empowering inaccuracy of self-idealization. It cannot reinstate what was created by a delusive imagination: the inner good object, or the self's happiness in itself.

1 | WORDSWORTH

The Guise of Hope

THE PARADIGM OF disappointment had a life of sorts before the eighteenth century. Moments in the Bible, Dante, and Chaucer, among other works, touch on the psychology of disappointment; during the Renaissance, the topoi of frustrated eros and spiritual confusion led poets like Wyatt and Herbert to more detailed explorations of disappointment in the lyric mode.[1] But, for whatever reason, perhaps because of developing interest in the interior life or the evolution of a language for describing it, or because of a reordering of literary values in which pathos came to be privileged, mid- and late eighteenth-century poetry began to enlarge upon the representation of the abject self and its turmoil. The poetry of sensibility offers a kind of prototradition in the representation of disappointment, but not until Coleridge and especially Wordsworth, who investigated the phenomenon with greater concentration than anyone ever had before, were its possibilities fully exploited. Because the lyric of disappointment began to thrive with Wordsworth and his immediate predecessors, it is with them that this study begins.

Disappointment, Wordsworth's favorite subject, provides the source of subtlety in many of his poems, particularly his major autobiographical works. There will seem to be nothing new in this remark. It is well known that Wordsworth owed a debt to the poets of the later eighteenth century, particularly Gray, Cowper, Bowles, and Smith (the so-called sensibility poets) for their experiments in the representation of psychological interiority and their emphasis on the themes of nostalgia, anxiety, and regret. In her book on the background and sources of *Lyrical Ballads*, Mary Jacobus gives a sympathetic account of the continuity between "Tintern Abbey" and later eighteenth-century poems of meditative "revisiting." Those poems bequeathed to "Tintern Abbey" their "saddened searching for renewal" and for "a source of restoration in the face of loneliness and distress"; therefore, even the atmosphere of exhaustion and elegy in Wordsworth's poem is conventional. Nevertheless, Jacobus continues, Wordsworth did improve on his models, wresting a credible language of loss out of the "indiscriminate melancholy" of sensibility.[2] Although one might agree with this view in general, the elegiac motifs on which Wordsworth drew were not really "indiscriminate," for he was following a theme or a specific psychological paradigm that deserves to be distinguished from the truly indiscriminate mass of eighteenth-century experiments in melancholy: "graveyard" poetry, imitations of *Il Penseroso*, meditations among ruins, didactic retirement poems, and so forth—all the varieties of melancholy "moods and themes"—cataloged in Eleanor M. Sickels's delightful *The Gloomy Egoist*.

The most popular eighteenth-century poem of melancholy was Gray's "Elegy." Critics have long recognized that despite his criticism of Gray, Wordsworth was in some way his inheritor. The nature of the debt has seemed somewhat obscure, but it can be rendered more precise. Gray's "Elegy" is a study in self-conception—more specifically, in diminished self-regard, or a diminished sense of status and possibility for the self. The speaker regards himself as "mute" and "inglorious," doomed to an invisible life and an anonymous grave. He must live out his life, side by side with this humiliated self: and what does an existence in this self have to offer? The prospect of the future, its secret, is emptied out. The remainder of his life appears to him as foreshortened, promising only meaningless repetition. He dwells in a posthumous twilight which matches the poem's mise-en-scène, for the foreshortening of life has brought his obscure death near; and now it is easy for him to imagine and anticipate. Gray's poem resolves into a representation of the speaker's disappointment and his gloomy prognosis for himself. Rather than struggle against his diminished self-regard, he embraces it, revealing his very discouragement in the exaggerated humility of his religious pieties. Thus, the poem depicts a distinct psychological predicament: the uneasy watch of a damaged self-conception. Gray is innovative in his portrayal of this crippling self-relation, wherein the self is called upon to see itself as a reduced and enfeebled thing. And yet the poem strangely characterizes this predicament as a settled, almost tranquil condition.

The self that feels overwhelmed by a consciousness of its abasement: that is also the subject of Cowper's stark, powerful poem "The Castaway," as analyzed in my introduction. It is striking how often the poetry of sensibility focuses on an inner erosion and failing—the complaint of a self that has come to be disheartened with itself and its lot. Such complaint not only is common to Gray and Cowper, but reappears as well, often more subtly, in the "elegiac" sonnets of Charlotte Smith and William Lisle Bowles. Although it led to a poetry that can seem morose, this fascination of the sensibility poets also occasioned their peculiar, and paradoxical, strength. They perceived the discursive possibilities of a particular subject: the self-disenchanted self.

The complexity of the psychological situation makes the subject fruitful. Among other difficulties, the chastened self is reduced to shifting uneasily among its mental processes, its own thoughts and desires, from which it is estranged by its want of hope and lack of a future. Nostalgic reflection is prominent and often paired with lament for the loss of a buoyant, unsuspecting youth replaced by a harrowing maturity. (Hence the standard pessimism about adulthood codified in Gray's "Ode on a Distant Prospect of Eton College.") The theme of "the burden of the past" also provides a rationale and setting for the emergence of this thwarted self, a dwindler, an inhabitant of shadows. The speaker of Collins's "Ode on the Poetical Character," finds himself stranded in such a cul-de-sac when he concludes that his "trembling feet" have pursued Milton's tracks "In vain," forever in vain, since

> Heav'n, and Fancy, kindred Pow'rs
> Have now o'erturn'd th' inspiring Bow'rs,
> Or curtain'd close such Scene from ev'ry future View.

Northrop Frye first characterized the poetry of sensibility as a poetry of "process," self-reflexively concerned with its own unfolding and taking its search for a theme as a theme. That is fair enough, but the sensibility theme of poetic failure also entails yet another and more intricate subject, the quandary of the self at a loss—and specifically, at a loss to know how to employ those capacities it no longer trusts. The peculiar humility of the sensibility poets has been taken for charmingly realistic self-assessment; but it may be rather that such humility (or rather, humiliation) was actually their topic and the object of their acute aesthetic, as well as intellectual, attention.

In his 1800 "Preface to the Second Edition of *Lyrical Ballads*," Wordsworth established his differences with the poetry of the previous age by critiquing Gray's sonnet on the death of West, distinguishing its worthy lines from the dross of its eighteenth-century artifice. He does not give a clear reason for preferring the verses he does, saying merely that the italicized lines were the only ones in the sonnet "of any value." Actually, they are the lines that sound like Wordsworth; he finds kinship in their comparative simplicity and frank emotional appeal. But it is not just any emotion whose portrayal has caught his fancy. Within the elegiac tradition, Gray works out a situation of some psychological intricacy, depicting a state of mental and emotional claustrophobia—a form of self-enclosure combined with a species of self-alienation:

> In vain to me the smiling mornings shine.
> And reddening Phoebus lifts his golden fire:
> The birds in vain their amorous descant join:
> Or cheerful fields resume their green attire:
> These ears, alas! for other notes repine,
> *A different object do these eyes require.*
> *My lonely anguish melts no heart but mine;*
> *And in my breast the imperfect joys expire;*
> Yet morning smiles the busy race to cheer,
> And new-born pleasure brings to happier men:
> The fields to all their wonted tribute bear:
> To warm their little loves the birds complain.
> *I fruitless mourn to him, that cannot hear,*
> *And weep the more, because I weep in vain.*[3]

Wordsworth dismisses Gray's mawkish lines about the untimely "cheerfulness" of the natural world. Instead, he seizes on the verses that approach the more involved psychology of self-reflection—the verses in which the mourner describes his grief and its internal relations. The self of Gray's poem undergoes a kind of inner redoubling, and it is not merely the redoubling of self-consciousness. This self has become hapless with relation to its own affects: it watches, as if from a distance, as "imperfect joys" wither and die within it (it can harbor an emotion in which, oddly, it doesn't seem to share). It sees that its mourning is "fruitless" but cannot stop mourning, so that its knowledge only exacerbates the acuteness of the emotion. It recognizes its isolation, and this recognition becomes a considerable burden. The last line underscores one "death spiral" of feeling: "[I] weep the more, because I weep in vain."

The speaker suffers from awareness of his entrapment as much as from his loss itself. Stalled by means of and within his feelings, he is oppressed by his very self-conception, the recognition of his paralysis. Through grief and its self-entanglement, he is detached from external objects of interest, and, in the words of Peter J. Manning, thus becomes "imprisoned" in an "empty now." Manning eloquently describes the peculiar "massiveness" and "stasis" of Gray's sonnet: "Death in Gray's poem institutes an absolute break in time: even as the world of natural process moves onward, the speaker's grief resists the progress of life."[4] Manning goes on to differentiate the self-hypnotized "melancholia" of Gray's speaker from the psychological and moral development of the speaker in Wordsworth's Lucy poems, who "works through" his "mourning" to emerge with a stronger appreciation of humanity and nature.

Although this is a cogent argument, Wordsworth need not be seen as departing entirely from Gray. Often he remained faithful to the psychological predicament the earlier poet explores. There is a continuity between Gray's sonnet and Wordsworth's poems of psychological crisis, particularly "Tintern Abbey" and the Intimations Ode, which also portray a self halted in time and estranged from "the progress of life." The initial situation in these poems reprises that in Gray: Wordsworth too depicts a self that has become inhibited by its self-perception and by a "fruitless" inner colloquy with emotions it does not fully trust; a self that has lost the point of application for its energies and so entered a repetitive, "empty now," with the prospect of an empty future; a self that has stumbled upon "the thorns of life" and so discovered its own abjectness. These were the refined elements of psychological representation that

Wordsworth found to inspire him in the degraded literature of the late eighteenth century.

Wordsworth owed a particular debt to William Lisle Bowles, a more immediate precursor than Gray. Coleridge wrote lovingly of his adolescent infatuation with Bowles, describing Bowles as a major influence on the development of his own poetics. And through Coleridge, Bowles affected Wordsworth as well. He was less popular with other romantic writers. When Coleridge proposed to dedicate a volume of poems to Bowles, Lamb mocked them both: "Genius of the sacred fountain of tears, it was he who led you gently by the hand through all this valley of weeping, showed you the dark green yew trees and the willow shades where, by the fall of waters, you might indulge an uncomplaining melancholy, a delicious regret for the past." Similarly, Byron later dismissed Bowles as "the maudlin Prince of mournful sonneteers."[5] These detractors are somewhat unfair; at any rate, they characterize Bowles inaccurately when they imply that he indulged only a vague and opportunistic sorrow. Coleridge's favorite poem by Bowles, the sonnet "To the River Itchin," makes it clear that within the realm of elegiac feeling, Bowles had opened up a supple and fascinating subject: the movement and variation in the contaminated affects of one who feels himself to be permanently disheartened.

> Itchin, when I behold thy banks again,
> Thy crumbling margin, and thy silver breast,
> On which the self-same tints still seem to rest,
> Why feels my heart the shiv'ring sense of pain?
> Is it, that many a summer's day has past
> Since, in life's morn, I carol'd at thy side?
> Is it, that oft, since then, my heart has sigh'd,
> As Youth, and Hope's delusive gleams, flew fast?
> Is it that those, who circled on thy shore,
> Companions of my youth, now meet no more?
> Whate'er the cause, upon thy banks I bend
> Sorrowing, yet feel such solace at my heart,
> As at the meeting of some long-lost friend,
> From whom, in happier hours, we wept to part.

This is not a poem of renewal, but rather of a "saddened searching for

[a] renewal" that does not arrive. Yet unlike Gray's sonnet on the death of West, the poem does not remain static. The speaker's grasping after consolation, and his acceptance of trivial consolation, are themselves as melancholy as any of his hypothetical sources of sadness. The speaker is in a quandary: he cannot determine why he is sad, but he insists that he feels in some way scarred and diminished; his thoughts are shadowed; his capacity for unburdened pleasure and hope is compromised. Worst, he regards this damage as the fruit of age and therefore as irreversible. That is the problem: but the poem neither rests with a statement of the problem, nor works through to a resolution. The last quatrain shows a kind of affective modulation, in which the "shiv'ring sense of pain" and "sorrow" are joined by a qualifying "solace." Yet because both emotions —pain and consolation—come from the same source in recollection, the solace does not provide an antidote to sorrow. Craving consolation, the speaker only finds the endearing familiarity of the place by the river and of his own memories. That can hardly be much consolation. The poem takes cold comfort in finding only "such solace at my heart / As at the meeting of some long-lost friend, / From whom, in happier hours, we wept to part." Neither the dissipation of happiness, nor the awareness of its dissipation, has been reversed. The consolation of tenderness represents a small movement within the trend of sorrow. This broken solace is the best that the broken self can bring forth: a timid consolation, stained by the pessimism that created the need for it.

"To the River Itchin" is widely anthologized and critically popular; yet another, less well-known Bowles sonnet still more intently portrays the enfeeblement of the disappointed self.[6] Here enfeeblement takes a classic form in the shrinking or reduction of the capacity to hope.

> O Time! who know'st a lenient hand to lay
> Softest on sorrow's wound, and slowly thence,
> (Lulling to sad repose the weary sense)
> Stealest the long-forgotten pang away;
> On Thee I rest my only hope at last,
> And think, when thou hast dried the bitter tear
> That flows in vain o'er all my soul held dear,
> I may look back on many a sorrow past,

> And meet life's peaceful evening with a smile—
> As some poor bird, at day's departing hour,
> Sings in the sunbeam, of the transient shower
> Forgetful, tho' its wings are wet the while:—
> Yet ah! how much must that poor heart endure,
> Which hopes from thee, and thee alone, a cure!

The true subject of this poem comes out in its last lines, which focus on the speaker's assessment of his own condition as the major cause of his distress. Like Gray, Bowles cultivates a self-reflexive sadness: the disappointed self is doubly discouraged because in addition to its actual sorrows, it feels chastised and undergoes the mortification of perceiving its own (apparently endemic) debilitation. Its "only hope" is small, being merely that its "pang" should "steal away," or subside, over time. But worse, the passage of time that will bring this benumbing forgetfulness has itself to be borne: "Yet ah! how much must that poor heart endure, / Which hopes from thee, and thee alone, a cure!" How is this disheartened speaker to occupy himself while waiting for time to anesthetize him? He is resigned, but his resignation provides no help because the self reduced to awaiting the dullness of time has lost its aims and purposes; it is out of work, *désoeuvré*. Though in one sense empty, it still has resources of anticipation—residual hopes and drives—that want to find objects, but are debarred from them. The prospect of enduring time in a self burdened by these frustrated energies is enough to make one wonder "how much must that poor heart endure!"

These sensibility poems creatively put to use their fascination with the psychology of the foundering self, in its baffled inner colloquy, which opens up so much scope for inherent interest, affective power, and thematic subtlety. The self thrown back on itself by the loss or discreditation of its external objects is in a critical predicament; it is then forced to think, and to do much work that will likely be fruitless. This theme introduces a significant degree of refinement in the description of subjectivity, as the uneasy mind (or "heart"—choose your metaphor) reflects upon its condition, dreads it, and is driven to odd, moving, delicate struggles for adjustment. Perturbation of this kind drives such romantic crisis lyrics as "Dejection," "Tintern Abbey," and the Intimations Ode.

As a poet of psychological deadlock, Charlotte Smith was even closer to Wordsworth and Coleridge than Bowles was. Wordsworth described her as an innovative writer of considerable influence.[7] I have quoted two Bowles sonnets that show some degree of urgency; however, Bowles generally writes within the tradition of a more muted meditative poetry— the mood poem of quiet nature and somber reflection, which the early romantics also reprised. Smith, on the other hand, works to portray psychological crisis dramatically; she concentrates on evoking the emotions of anguish and claustrophobia, and the entanglement of the self in the burdensome persistence of its energies. Compare Bowles's "To Time" with Smith's sonnet on the "hope" of forgetfulness:

> Forgetfulness! I would thy hand could close
> These eyes that turn reluctant from the day;
> So might this painful consciousness decay,
> And, with my memory, end my cureless woes.
> Sister of Chaos and eternal Night!
> Oblivion! take me to thy quiet reign,
> Since robb'd of all that gave my soul delight,
> I only ask exemption from the pain
> Of knowing "such things were"—and are no more;
> Of dwelling on the hours for ever fled,
> And heartless, helpless, hopeless to deplore
> "Pale misery living, joy and pleasure dead:"
> While dragging thus unwish'd a length of days,
> "Death seems prepared to strike, yet still delays."

Bowles's reflective musings give way before this passionate, importunate mode.[8] Now the self is in a state of emergency; it recognizes that its condition is "cureless," "heartless," "helpless," and "hopeless," but it cannot take refuge in patience and resignation. It cannot rest in, accept, or endure its condition, but cannot get out of it, either. The self has grown uncomfortable within itself, impossibly afflicted by its own "painful consciousness," a consciousness painful because aware of its own peculiar futility as it broods over its "cureless woes" (or what Smith elsewhere repeatedly describes as "fruitless anguish" and "vain regret"). The mind is putting in great effort, which it bizarrely knows will not issue in any progress, purpose, or end. This dilemma legitimizes the poem's air of urgency and its fervid apostrophes. Smith broods over a psychological impasse similar to that sketched out in some of Bowles's sonnets; but, in advance of the romantics, she has raised the impasse to the status of a full-fledged crisis. The self's predicament is intolerable; and the very insistence on its intolerability opens the way to an involved discourse of psychological disaster. As it happens, Smith's treatment of crisis tends to be impacted rather than expansive, because she made it her aim to distill emotions, and chose the foreshortened form of the sonnet precisely because it seemed to her "no improper vehicle for a single Sentiment."[9] Yet the drama of her turbulent, unresolved emotions solicits expansion.

In her concentration on "cureless" despair, Smith compellingly portrays the subject faced with a "blank void"[10] where the future ought to be. Her halted or stymied subject links previous eighteenth-century poetry with that of the early romantics. This continuity is evident in the opening lines of "To the South Downs," one of her many poems on the familiar theme of nostalgic homecoming:

> Ah! hills belov'd!—where once a happy child,
> Your beechen shades, "your turf, your flowers among,"
> I wove your blue-bells into garlands wild,
> And woke your echoes with my artless song.
> Ah! hills belov'd—your turf, your flowers remain;
> But can they peace to this sad breast restore;
> For one poor moment soothe the sense of pain,
> And teach a breaking heart to throb no more?

Smith retraces the springs of disturbance in the classic poem of "revisitation": the contrast of childhood ease with adult unhappiness, the exacerbation of the contrast through the identity of the site, the awakening of awareness to, and hence, the heightening of that unhappiness, the alienation or discomfort of consciousness. But a subtler common idea also emerges: the evocation of nostalgia and regret colored with the apprehension of self-diminishment. (Naturally, Smith quotes from Gray's Eton College Ode.) The adult is not just unhappy, but unhappy because she is unhappy, downcast to find herself among the fates that did not thrive.

The glamour has gone; the self undergoes an irreparable shrinking in its own eyes, and mourns for itself, that it has fallen away. Out of the poem's cloying nostalgia this more exquisite loss emerges.

Gray, Collins, Cowper, Bowles, and Smith share the theme of the "adult-hood" of the self, in which it has its own discredited being on its hands, and for this reason feels aimless and ensnared. Though addicted to cliché, these poems show what is compelling about the subject of the self foundering in its restlessness and desperation. Wordsworth and Coleridge drew on all these sources, and openly adopted their nostalgic, anxious, melancholy themes. But it was not simply these poets' pathos or bleak notions of adulthood that the early romantics reprised: Coleridge and Wordsworth perceived that in these portraits of discouragement lay the potential for considerable sophistication in the delineament of psychological life. The later poets grasped the intellectual and aesthetic potential of the problematic broached in the "self-elegy" (as we might call it) of the later eighteenth century. The sensibility theme of the abject self came to play a formative role in the development of the representation of subjectivity and the emerging literature of psychological naturalism. But the cliché preceded the fresh and seemingly authentic expression; and in fact the cliché worked as an incentive to its own vivification.

Coleridge probably responded to these intimations from late eighteenth-century melancholy before Wordsworth did.[11] He seems to have been the first of the two to write first-person poems on the subject of disappointment. Coleridge had the autobiographical interest in the phenomenon of demoralization, perceiving himself to be a disappointed (and disappointing) man, thwarted in his marriage and in his vocation. William and Dorothy Wordsworth were shocked by his plaintive "Verse Letter to Sarah Hutchinson" (the first draft of "Dejection: An Ode"). Richard Holmes implies that it was both Coleridge's frankness and his pessimism that disturbed them.[12] "Dejection" is manifestly continuous with Gray, Bowles, and Smith in its themes of conscious self-depletion and stagnation in an "empty now." And though "Dejection" may be said to reply to the evocation of disappointment in the first four stanzas of the Intimations Ode, Coleridge had already, some time before, begun to write about the self-disenchanted self.[13] He may have bequeathed his project to Wordsworth.

His earlier, less emphatic, conversation poems, "This Lime-Tree Bower My Prison" and "Frost at Midnight," are infused with an elusive sadness which arises from the speaker's conviction that he has squandered the promise of his life. However much hope he may hold out for others, he hardly projects any future for himself. Paul Magnuson has aptly characterized the temporal impasse faced by the speaker of "Frost at Midnight," for whom both childhood recollections and adult dreams have been exposed as fantasy: "The transition from one moment or period of life to another in 'Frost at Midnight' is either a reversal or a repetition. His imprisoned school days reverse entirely his free childhood, and his adult reveries merely repeat his school dreams by the fire."[14] The avenues to both the past and the future being blocked, the speaker can envision no adequate employment for his residual imaginative energies. This is a classic Coleridgean theme, and if we attribute the invention of the conversation poem to Coleridge, then it was likewise his innovation to have discovered in its flexible form a promising venue for the exploration of disappointment.[15]

Coleridge's early experiments in conversation poems—first-person poems on the theme of disappointment, such as "The Eolian Harp" and "Reflections on Having Left a Place of Retirement"—date from 1795.[16] If we take "Tintern Abbey," written in 1798, to be Wordsworth's earliest poem on disappointment in the first person, then we can agree with Holmes's judgment that Coleridge led the way in using his frustrations as a serious subject for first-person poetry. Of course, Wordsworth was primed for this innovation, being like Coleridge an admirer of the sensibility poets and, like Coleridge, having recently suffered his own political and cultural defeat.

As it happens, Wordsworth began his career writing elegiac poetry. In *Wordsworth and the Poetry of Human Suffering*, James Averill points out that Wordsworth's first poems all deal with tragic (and sentimental) subject matter. In "A Ballad," Wordsworth quotes what his teacher had actually said to him on his deathbed: "my head will soon lie low." As Averill analyzes it, "The adolescent Wordsworth imports these words into the text of "A Ballad" because he wants to exploit their deep, if personal, emotional significance. He wants to give the poem added power and calls in the language of real life, even this early, to endow a conventional and imitative fiction with tragic emotions."[17] He was already in search of the persuasive elegiac note, as if from the start he conceived of loss and failure as the appropriate topics of poetry.

The search for tragic feeling led to the discovery of the resources of autobiography. Or, as Averill puts it, somewhat more cautiously, "The impulse toward the 'poetry of experience,' whose genesis Robert Langbaum has located in Wordsworth and the romantics, would seem, then, to stem from late-eighteenth-century efforts to discover a literature which could be both 'sentimental' and 'simple.'"[18] This is a tantalizing observation: it is as if the taste for the tragic (sentimental, maudlin, whatever we want to call it), which was first explored in artificial forms—odes, pastoral elegies, fake ballads—*produced* the impetus toward the poetry of personal experience, melancholy experience in particular. Once sadness was identified as the affect poetry ought to evoke, *then* the use of personal experience materialized. A sense of that discovery inhabits Gray's Elegy, and that may be part of what made the poem so popular. It is also active in Bowles and Smith, which is why Wordsworth and Coleridge were so keen on them. Wordsworth and Coleridge were not impressed merely by the elegiac emotions in the sonneteers, nor by the "simplicity" and "earnestness" of their style. They were excited by the direction in which these sonnets pointed: toward a poetry for which experience was the *perfect* source. Through elaboration on the history of their own frustrations, Wordsworth and Coleridge were then able to revitalize lyric pathos.

The most immediate basis for Wordsworth's interest in the theme of disappointment was the failure of the French Revolution and of the millenarian hopes it had generated. This failure was widely understood to have created a severe malaise of discombobulation and paralysis among a generation of young radicals. Critical convention supposes that Wordsworth emerged out of this malaise by evolving his personal philosophy of imaginative renewal. For example, in *Wordsworth and Coleridge: The Radical Years*, Nicholas Roe argues that Coleridge's disillusionment and guilt over the deterioration of the Revolution led to a crisis that destroyed his creativity, whereas Wordsworth managed to reinvent his values and so disentangle himself from implication in the collapse of radical hopes. He harmonized "revolutionary idealism with subjective experience" by relocating the arena of renewal; "human regeneration has become the prerogative of the individual mind in communion with nature, and, introspectively, with itself."[19]

M. H. Abrams made a similar argument about Wordsworth's buoyant recovery in his classic account of the effects of the Revolution on romantic poetry. Abrams contends that the constant theme of disillusionment refers ultimately to the breakdown of the Revolution and the crisis of feeling it precipitated: "Pervasively in both the verse and prose of the period, 'hope,' with its associated term, 'joy,' and its opposites, 'dejection,' 'despondency,' and 'despair,' are used in a special application, as shorthand for the limitless faith in human and social possibility aroused by the Revolution, and its reflex, the nadir of feeling caused by its seeming failure."[20] But Wordsworth, according to Abrams, found his way out of the impasse and emerged stronger than ever, by giving up the poetry of public interest, which leads to "declamation," and adopting a more fruitful, introspective mode. In his search for alternative subjects and sources of inspiration, he discovered his signature project: in *Lyrical Ballads*, Wordsworth gave up "the hope of revolutionizing the social and political structure," and replaced this hope with a new "radical poetic vocation"—to communicate his "revelation of the more-than-heroic grandeur of the humble, the contemned, the ordinary, and the trivial."[21]

Two questions need to be raised about this account of Wordsworth's poetic development. First, how completely is his disappointment with the Revolution displaced by new hopes and projects? In other words, to what extent does Wordsworth really represent himself as triumphing over disappointment? And second, how late (or how early) in his poetic development did Wordsworth begin to work out his paradigm of disappointment? Was it only with the defeat of the Revolution that he did so? Abrams takes at face value Wordsworth's brashest claims to recovery and re-creation of self. By contrast, Abrams characterizes the hope raised in the closing lines of *Prometheus Unbound* as hope "now hard to distinguish from despair."[22] This insightful characterization might serve, as we shall see, to characterize the uncertainty of hope in Wordsworth too.

But if hope is uncertain in Wordsworth, then his new poetic project is not so new, nor so free; in fact, it continues to reecho his old disheartenment. He had become fascinated with the psychology of disappointment through his education in late eighteenth-century poetry, and his major poems never leave the topic behind.

In fact, Wordsworth's political frustration gave him autobiographical material out of which to elaborate a persuasive paradigm of disappointment, and so to fulfill the call of the morose poetry of sensibility.[23] In an early poem, "Lines Left upon a Seat in a Yew-Tree" (1797), he portrays a revolutionary whose life has been foreshortened by the collapse of his sphere of action. As Roe points out, the solitary is Wordsworth's own "barren alter ego," scorched by political disillusionment that has progressed into a state of despair: "The poignancy of his isolation stems from his awareness of a genial possibility that is withheld. . . . He is an inarticulate visionary who has withdrawn from 'the world' to exist in a limbo between the potential politics had once seemed to hold and an alternative communion he cannot attain."[24] In this limbo of disappointment, one suffers from the agitation of one's own powers, which have no use now that their potential objects have been placed off limits by the mind in its exercise of those same powers. The solitary is at one remove from his capacity to imagine reengaging with the world and recovering generous hopes; he can empathize with others able to do so, but he cannot do so himself:

> Nor, that time,
> When nature had subdued him to herself,
> Would he forget those Beings to whose minds
> Warm from the labours of benevolence
> The world, and human life, appeared a scene
> Of kindred loveliness: then would he sigh,
> Inly disturbed, to think that others felt
> What he must never feel: and so, lost Man!
> On visionary views would fancy feed,
> Till his eye streamed with tears.   (38–47)

The recluse is driven back on "visionary views" because the proper objects of his emotion have been evacuated by his own wary mind. The closing lines propose an alternative to what we might call this "self-vexing" state:

> True dignity abides with him alone
> Who, in the silent hour of inward thought,
> Can still suspect, and still revere himself,
> In lowliness of heart. (61–64)[25]

"Suspicion" of oneself is proposed as an antidote to pride and solipsism; "reverence" of oneself (in lowliness of heart) is offered as an antidote to the self-hating paralysis of disappointment. Humility is to parry humiliation. Wordsworth's contorted syntax suggests that this cure would require a difficult balancing act. The dubious phrasing thus reflects his hidden misgivings about the moral therapy he proposes, and suggests that disappointment is not to be corrected through moral piety, but represents a genuine psychological impasse.

Jacobus acutely observes that "The recluse is not merely another study in wasted sensibility but the first of Wordsworth's explorations of the introspecting mind."[26] Thus, Wordsworth's capacity for complex representation of "the introspecting mind" emerges in relation to the theme of disappointment. The "introspecting mind" *is* the disappointed mind, in which the experience of blockage yields a typically Wordsworthian psychological subtlety. It is Wordsworth's interest in "wasted sensibility" and "morbid disappointment" that motivated him to enlarge his representation of "the introspecting mind." Both Jacobus and Roe contrast the "Yew-Tree," a first experiment in psychological representation, with Wordsworth's later successes in the mode. They attribute the failure of the early poem to its evasive use of the third-person point of view. We may say at least that Wordsworth remained dedicated to the subject of disappointment, but between "Yew-Tree" and "Tintern Abbey," he shifted his voice from third to first person and gave the subject a frankly autobiographical treatment. This line of development is notably counterintuitive: the interest in disappointment as a poetic topic comes first, then the mode of introspection, and then the recourse to autobiography.

Wordsworth pursued the theme of political disillusionment in *The Excursion* and *The Prelude*, to which this discussion will return after studying his major autobiographical meditations and lyrics. He also represented the plight of disappointment in a number of his narrative poems—in "Simon Lee," "Michael," "The Ruined Cottage," and "The Brothers,"

for example. Clearly, this form of suffering engaged Wordsworth's attention. But a poem about disappointment in the third person differs from
such a poem in the first person: the topic itself changes, for the point is
no longer to represent "the introspecting mind." When a poem portrays
disappointment in the first person, it portrays a subjective experience
that is precisely felt to be solitary and unshareable. The question raised
in third-person poems—how the disappointed figure appears to others,
and how these others react to the spectacle of suffering—is quite distinct
from the questions raised by subjective experience[27] (unless the third
person is a euphemism, as in Stevens and Ashbery).[28] Wordsworth is at
his most innovative in his poetry of subjective experience, in the mimesis of self-disenchantment, or the representation of the experience from
within.

What we might call the deflation of the self is the subject of Wordsworth's major crisis lyrics. Though these poems may seem to portray
disappointment with the external world and its fading glories, such losses
fundamentally compromise the self's relation to itself, and for this damage no remedy is found. It might be countered that, though Wordsworth
emulated the eighteenth-century poem of "personal loss and the effort
of recovery," he had the merit of transcending the genre, precisely by escaping the deadlock of hopelessness. In the last chapter of *Preromanticism,*
Marshall Brown argues that the discovery of "hope" freed the romantics
from the impasse of melancholy and confusion in late eighteenth-century
poetry. To an extent, this is true. Wordsworth did expand the psychological narrative of "hope," and this represented a signal, and fruitful,
departure from the later eighteenth century's obsession with an impacted,
static "melancholy." But the discovery of "hope" actually functioned paradoxically; for it allowed Wordsworth to create a more extended and persuasive representation of the psychology, not of hope and "self-renewal,"
but of their opposite—the longing for them—and of all the complexities
arising from the restiveness of longing. In other words, it allowed him to
work out the means to an affectively charged but nuanced portrayal of
disappointment, yearning, and humiliation. In this way, Wordsworth
reprised the sensibility poets'—and then Coleridge's —concentration on
the humbled, self-sorrowing self.[29] Rather than reject or transcend these
themes, Wordsworth played them out in the arabesques of the "crisis

lyric." The emergence of "hope," resolution, and recommitment in his major poems of psychological crisis represents not a transformation but a refinement of self-elegy, in which the striving for and the decision to embrace new sources of confidence constitute maneuvers in the struggle to escape from disappointment.

In *The Prelude*, book 6, Wordsworth contrasts "Dejection taken up for pleasure's sake," moods in which there remained "an underthirst of vigour," with his chagrin when he crossed the Alps without knowing it: "A deep and genuine sadness then I felt" (492). Wordsworth's poems are more forlorn than they have been taken to be, for their aim is to perfect the evocation of "genuine sadness" on behalf of eighteenth-century verse, cased in its stilted sorrows. And Wordsworth's poems—at least his autobiographical poems—do this in part by intertwining disappointment with the tentative explorations of hope—for these explorations are really just wishes, produced by the disappointment that at the same time enfeebles them. Jacobus has described "Lines written in early spring" as "a poem not so much of belief as of the wish to believe"; and from this, she adds, comes "its poignancy."[30] In fact, Wordsworth's major autobiographical poems all join in this frailty of hope or belief; they do not end with resolution or self-renewal, but with their shadows, with compromise, hunger, and dream, which rather enhance than dispel the initial melancholy.

Perhaps it is common consensus that "Tintern Abbey" (1798) is a sad poem; but it is worth identifying the source of its sadness and showing how the poem tends to sustain its despondency, rather than dissolving it. Wordsworth already improves on the eighteenth-century tradition of self-elegy by making his speaker so much more indirect. The speaker is more open in his invocation of personal experience, not hedging it about with generality, but he is more evasive about saying that he is sad or what it is he is sad about, as if he were reluctant to bring it out in the open and make it real. This internal resistance makes the sadness seem all the more "deep and genuine." An atmosphere of disorientation and anxiety gradually emerges through the first few stanzas, but it is not until the fourth that their causes are identified. Still, we know something is wrong from the beginning because of the urgency in the first stanza, with its emphatic demonstratives ("These waters," "these steep and lofty cliffs," "this

dark sycamore," and so forth) and its air of desperate determination. The
speaker has come to this place with certain expectations he really *needs* to
be fulfilled; he is counting on it, having shifted some emotional burdens
by appealing in thought to the consolations this place represents. His
consciousness of need comes out in the second stanza:

> These beauteous forms,
> Through a long absence, have not been to me
> As is a landscape to a blind man's eye:
> But oft, in lonely rooms, and 'mid the din
> Of towns and cities, I have owed to them
> In hours of weariness, sensations sweet,
> Felt in the blood, and felt along the heart;
> And passing even into my purer mind,
> With tranquil restoration. (23–30)

A great deal depends on whether the speaker can still see those beauteous forms as worthy of the idealization he held them in during his absence. Their memory was an antidote to the "wearying" disappointments
of his early adulthood; was it a true antidote or a fiction created out of his
yearning, a temporary anodyne? They stood for contact with something
valuable and real and thereby bestowed on the speaker who treasured
them a confidence in his substantiality—in the truthfulness of his feeling
—against all the nihilistic effects of "lonely rooms" and "the din of towns
and cities," which show the individual that his fate is obscure and that
continuity of every form—including that represented by history and by
understanding—is mere appearance. To retain confidence of this kind
against the fear that it is unwarranted will seem a notable gain, yet in another light such confidence offers only a slender thread to cling to. Quite
a bit is already granted to the subject's despair by this means of characterizing his hope. Wordsworth hints at an ebbing of expectations in his
rather grim definition of what constitutes "that best portion of a good
man's life": "His little, nameless, unremembered acts / Of kindness and
of love" (33–36). He has already made a major concession to pessimism
in suggesting that to be "a good man" means to want to show "kindness
and love" in spite of their relative insignificance—their ingloriousness—
and their failure to be so much as "remembered." He says outright in the

next breath that in the "blessed mood," "the heavy and the weary weight / Of all this unintelligible world, / Is lightened" (39–41). It is this "unintelligibility" of experience for which the meaningful landscape is to provide an antidote. The "heavy and the weary weight" of unintelligibility describes a certain species of disappointment: the doubt of continuity, the dread of things happening to no particular purpose, and experience proceeding without any kind of accumulation—any progress or learning. The promise of teleology has gone slack, or vanished.

The speaker faces the familiar plight of being separated from the forward momentum of time and left to occupy "an empty now." Against this threat he will later make his prayer for continuity with a chipperness that turns macabre:

> My heart leaps up when I behold
> A rainbow in the sky;
> So was it when my life began;
> So is it now I am a man;
> So be it when I shall grow old,
> Or let me die! ("My Heart Leaps Up," 1–6)

The lines that follow, used as an epigraph for the Intimations Ode, show how much he recognizes this desire for continuity as an anxious and critical one, a need whose very self-consciousness compromises it:

> The Child is father of the Man;
> And I could wish my days to be
> Bound each to each by natural piety. (7–9)

It might seem inevitable to put the stress on the notion of "natural piety"; but perhaps it ought rather to fall on the "wishing" and the "binding." The wish is only a tentative one ("I could wish"), held in check by what? A kind of suspicion about it? A twinge of wistfulness, or an apprehension lest the wish should be defeated? We may call it, at least, a self-consciousness (and so a doubt) about wishing, a wishing at one remove, comparable to Jacobus's "not believing, but wishing to believe." The speaker of "Tintern Abbey" hesitates this way when he calls into question the promise of contact and continuity represented in and by his memories: for he concedes that the "trust" he placed in the renewing power of these memories may reflect nothing but a "vain belief." The line, "If this / be but a vain belief," constitutes the turning point in the poem, the point at which the speaker acknowledges the nature of his anxiety, even if he does immediately reiterate the strength and efficacy of his "trust." His admission changes the nature of his claim, for now he concedes that the iteration of his "trust" is an expression of his need and innocence and desire:

> If this
> Be but a vain belief, yet oh! how oft—
> In darkness and amid the many shapes
> Of joyless daylight; when the fretful stir
> Unprofitable, and the fever of the world,
> Have hung upon the beatings of my heart—
> How oft, in spirit, have I turned to thee,
> O sylvan Wye! thou wanderer thro' the woods,
> How often has my spirit turned to thee! (49–57)

He has retreated a step away from characterizations of what he "owes" to "these beauteous forms," and a step toward the description simply of his faith and longing. For he clearly perceives that the affirmation of his trust, though it reveals something about his sadness, says nothing about the validity of his consolation. This is a major reverse, for now he is back where he started, in a world of "unintelligibility" where the self is left to fumble about on its own, negotiating between its desire, its heartbreak, and its underconfident mythologies.

We now have a more refined description of the sadness in the poem: it comes from the apprehension of being thrown back on the self, but a self which has in the process of discovering its loneliness, lost conviction of its singularity, resourcefulness, and importance. Not even his suffering makes him special. The sufferer feels he has endured a permanent disheartenment, but also feels that it came over him accidentally. He might have gone on thinking as he did; he might have been better off; and others, after all, have been spared. Isolated by his sadness, he must suffer the additional mortification of reflecting that it has been inflicted capriciously. He regards himself as the victim of haphazard misfortune and therefore as stripped of his uniqueness—his metaphysical aura of singularity—through which, perhaps unconsciously, he has taken it for granted that he would succeed and thrive: he was the star, he would be protected. Disappointment has dealt a blow to that expectation. In this way, the subject sustains a grave narcissistic wound. He loses an elemental form of self-regard, an assumption about the privileged ontology of his fate.

Though this narcissistic ideal of uniqueness should not be equated with egotism, the humbled subject is only too willing to make the equation, and to (try to) adopt a stance of gratitude, going along with the claim that he has been morally edified. Wordsworth stakes such a claim in "Tintern Abbey," or still more chillingly, in *The Prelude*, when he affirms "I bowed low / To God who thus corrected my desires" (11.373–74). It is precisely at the point of such a considerable erosion in self-esteem that you would not want to rely on yourself alone for solace and encouragement. For this reason, the speaker consoles himself at the end of "Tintern Abbey" with promises that reconstitute his trust that there is something good *outside*. (Compare Coleridge's appeal to God, the "Great universal Teacher," in "Frost at Midnight.") He announces that he is

> well pleased to recognise
> In nature and the language of the sense,
> The anchor of my purest thoughts, the nurse,
> The guide, the guardian of my heart, and soul
> Of all my moral being.
>   Nor, perchance,
> If I were not thus taught, should I the more
> Suffer my genial spirits to decay:
> For thou art with me here upon the banks
> Of this fair river; thou my dearest Friend.   (107–16)

He generates two alternatives for something besides himself to put his faith in, and that external thing of value has continuity, he insists, so he can rely on its being there to sustain him. (He imagines that he might die and leave Dorothy to remember him, but not the reverse!) And so the future opens out again, time regains its fluidity, and he is released from his "empty now." But the gain is slighter than it looks, for the self has not recovered its dignity and pride; quite the reverse. The speaker has settled for the humility of partial, extrinsic consolation.

Having willfully adopted a hopeful perspective, though without putting his hope in himself, the speaker of the poem predicts that he will deteriorate. He makes no effort to defy this conclusion; in lieu of struggle, he embraces the solace of natural beauty and its recollection, here figured as a gift from external sources, nourishing an enfeebled or empty self:

> While here I stand, not only with the sense
> Of present pleasure, but with pleasing thoughts
> That in this moment there is life and food
> For future years. And so I dare to hope.   (62–65)

Marshall Brown has stressed the boldness in "daring to hope"; but one should note its self-consciousness and doubtfulness. This is a forced hope, a hope that has contrived itself, and so is delicate and dangerous, and knows it. Yet only after fortifying itself with this tottering, prospective "hope," can Wordsworth's "deep and genuine sadness" permit itself to be articulated: his regret that he is "changed, no doubt, from what I was when first / I came among these hills" (66–67). He has lost the glamour of his "passion" and become an aimless, obscure soul. The harshness of his self-contempt ought not to be slighted, in spite of the mild-sounding pieties to which it gives rise. For their humility is a symptom of his desperation. He may assure us that he is reconciled to his losses

> Not for this
> Faint I, nor mourn nor murmur; other gifts
> Have followed; for such loss, I would believe,
> Abundant recompense.   (85–88)

but his assurances reflect his very demoralization: he is too convinced and too shaken to "Faint" or "mourn" or "murmur," all reactions that reflect a spirit of rebellion, or what the eighteenth century called "impatience," which he is too sad to feel. Thus, his determination to hope betrays the completeness of his disappointment rather than any recovery or self-renewal.

He consoles himself that his loss represents a necessary and inevitable development, and thus, that "Nature never did betray / The heart that loved her" (102–3). He professes to himself, in other words, that there is still something benevolent in the world, and something real, even if one's contact with it is doomed to diminish over time. That he would welcome these humbling thoughts indicates how much his self-regard has been reduced. The "recompense" and "resolution" of "Tintern Abbey" must be measured in light of their failure to mitigate the speaker's humiliation. The deliberateness of his hope and trust testify to his fear that in himself he has no resources to cope with his disappointment. His dejection holds no "underthirst of vigour." Through the acceptance of his humility, the speaker is made conscious of his helplessness and is debarred from pursuing sublimity or making grand gestures.

The prospect of a vacant future adumbrated in "Tintern Abbey" makes a dramatic appearance elsewhere, especially in book 1 of *The Prelude*, in which Wordsworth represents himself as struggling with a form of writing block he figures as "vexation" but also as "blankness." The "discouragement" of his hopes and "defrauding" of his "harp" leave him with no "aim" with which to "brace" himself (1.134, 104–5, 124). Experience has lost its teleological structure. He has nothing to do, but rather than being at leisure, he feels entrapped and uneasy; he is once again imprisoned in an "empty now." In a crucial description of this state, Wordsworth emphasizes the discomfort of the self-confinement that follows from his anxious, estranged relation to time:

> Thus from day to day
> I live a mockery of the brotherhood
> Of vice and virtue, with no skill to part
> Vague longing that is bred by want of power,
> From paramount impulse not to be withstood
> A timorous capacity, from prudence;
> From circumspection, infinite delay.
> Humility and modest awe themselves
> Betray me, serving often for a cloak
> To a more subtle selfishness, that now
> Doth lock my functions up in blank reserve,
> Now dupes me by an over-anxious eye
> That with a false activity beats off
> Simplicity and self-presented truth.
> Ah, better far than this to stray about
> Voluptuously through fields and rural walks

> And ask no record of the hours given up
> To vacant musing, unreproved neglect
> Of all things, and deliberate holiday.
> Far better never to have heard the name
> Of zeal and just ambition than to live
> Thus baffled by a mind that every hour
> Turns recreant to her task, takes heart again,
> Then feels immediately some hollow thought
> Hang like an interdict upon her hopes.
> This is my lot; for either still I find
> Some imperfection in the chosen theme,
> Or see of absolute accomplishment
> Much wanting—so much wanting—in myself
> That I recoil and droop, and seek repose
> In indolence from vain perplexity
> Unprofitably travelling towards the grave,
> Like a false steward who hath much received
> And renders nothing back.   (238–71)

This passage pays acute attention to the even and inexorable passage of time, as emphasized by phrases such as "day to day," and "every hour." Being conscious of the progress of time is oppressive because though time is moving forward, Wordsworth is not. He is in a curious way isolated from time, frozen, "liv[ing] as a mockery," with his "functions lock[ed] up in blank reserve." Not even his hopes are allowed to stir, for "some hollow thought / Hangs like an interdict" upon them. Naturally, he images his aphasia as claustrophobic, but it is particularly so because it has substituted vacant repetition (day upon day and hour upon hour) for the advance of time. When Wordsworth imagines an alternative to this malaise, he imagines having a different relation to time, one not characterized by panic and rigidity, but rather by acceptance and relaxation. He would still be idle, but he would not feel suffocated. He would be freed up, fluidified, so as to move with passing time instead of chaffing against it: he would

> stray about
> Voluptuously through fields and rural walks
> And ask no record of the hours given up

> To vacant musing, unreproved neglect
> Of all things, and deliberate holiday. (252–56)

As it is, he unsuccessfully "seeks repose" in an "indolence" that knows no ease but only tension and dissatisfaction, with a "vexed" or burdensome self close at hand and time as its enemy. For time moves forward all the same, though he can make no use of it, and is desperate when he finds himself "Unprofitably travelling towards the grave." The passage of time brings with it no sense of accumulation or progress, but is instead exposed as meaningless iteration, a failed economy in which Wordsworth is "Like a false steward who hath much received / And renders nothing back."

The poem departs from all these images of blockage, enclosure, and rigidification with the next line, as Wordsworth relinquishes the present and "strays / Voluptuously" back into the past where he will find his subject. This release begins with the image of a river, "the fairest of all rivers," the liquid speaker who joined his voice to others', "lov[ing] / To blend his murmurs with my nurse's song" (272–73). Blending, flowing, communication, interchange; freedom from paralysis and self-confinement. Movement is both imaged by this river and, in the poem's terms, initiated by it. Teleology is restored. For teleology brings unidirectional forward momentum, like the line or course of a river. Now the progression of Wordsworth's task is in sync with the linearity of time. These submerged metaphors of teleology remain through the end of the book, where he declares that because he has found his subject, "The road lies plain before me" (1.668).

The prospect of a "plain road" is reassuring although it entails a cost in self-circumscription. In this way, Wordsworth extends the eighteenth-century description of the psychology of disappointment to include more of its struggle: its bewilderment, its humility, and its casting about for moderated hopes like the hope of a "plain road." This disappointed self must cast about because it is entrapped, alone, and adrift in time. From adumbrations in Gray, Bowles, Smith, and Coleridge, Wordsworth has pursued the idea that disappointment discombobulates one's relation to time. The disappointed figure is frozen, cut off from "the progress of life."

In his discussion of romantic hope, Marshall Brown quotes from the phenomenological speculations of Gabriel Marcel, with whom he concurs that hope is a form of patience, an openness with respect to the future, that enables one not to "stiffen" nor "rebel" but rather to "take one's time." Marcel forcefully summarizes the contrasting attitude of the desperate:

> In face of the particular trial, whatever it may be, which confronts me and which must always be but a specimen of the trial of humanity in general, I shall always be exposed to the temptation of shutting the door which encloses me within myself and at the same time encloses me within time, as though the future, drained of its substance and mystery, were no longer to be anything but a place of pure repetition, as though some unspecifiable disordered mechanism were to go on working ceaselessly, undirected by any intelligent motivation. But a future thus devitalized, no longer being a future for me or anybody else, would be rather a prospect of vacancy."[31]

Or in another, even more succinct formulation Marcel notes: "It is as much as to say we are here in a world where time no longer *passes*, or, which comes to the same thing, where time merely passes without bringing anything, empty of material which could serve to establish a new truth or inspire a new being."[32] Clearly, this is the threat haunting poems like "Tintern Abbey" and the Intimations Ode: the speaker has fallen out with his own time and lost his purposes. A vacuum of pointlessly unfolding days confronts him. The function of the hopes by which he strives to cheer himself is to restore a pattern of logic and purposiveness—a structure of teleology—to time.

Marcel is an apologist for hope. He argues that its "true character" exhibits "humility," "timidity," and "chastity"; and, in a traditional way, he contrasts these qualities of hope with the egotism of despair. Knowing that he opposes common prejudice, he defends hope against its association with naiveté and self-deception. Wordsworth also can be interpreted as an apologist for hope, and therefore has been subjected to some tacitly contemptuous readings in which he is accused of a willingness to be mystified and a fondness for "enabling fictions." But in fact he had a more sophisticated understanding of the psychology of hope. The antithesis of hope in Wordsworth is not despair, an affect long codified through its religious associations, but the more recent invention, disappointment, in which one suffers a severe blow to fundamental narcissism, and therefore exhibits as much "humility" and "timidity" as hope does; humility leads directly to the embrace of piety and hope.

Wordsworth's hopes are faint and delicate, arising out of anxiety and doubt, and so tinged by them. His hopes seem so airy because they represent a merely intellectual or psychological shift. The material situation that necessitated them, the world they attempt to reengage, remains the same. Only one question is left: whether or not the speaker can readjust his attitude, so as to mollify himself. All the activity, and all possibility of movement, occurs within his own mind, which is at once the seat of his trouble and the only available source of a remedy. What makes the struggle so fine, and so tricky, is that paradox. The speaker confronts an insoluble dilemma: how are adequate hopes to be found that shall coexist with, and even emerge from, the same material as the despairs that they are needed to counteract?

Wordsworth firmly acknowledges that those hopes are compromised. He regards them as necessary, crucially necessary, but only for practical purposes. (He would presumably agree with Johnson that "it is necessary to hope, tho' hope should always be deluded, for hope itself is happiness, and its frustrations, however frequent, are yet less dreadful than its extinction."[33]) This equivocal attitude comes out in an arresting pair of lines from "The Old Cumberland Beggar," in which we are exhorted to "Reverence the hope whose vital anxiousness / Gives the last human interest to his heart" (177–78). Wordsworth does not say that the beggar's hopes are warranted; they obviously are not. But they keep him alive, at least for our "interest." They keep him from becoming a ghoul. This quotation demonstrates how closely yoked hope and disappointment are in Wordsworth. Hope releases the future; it allows one to participate again in the progress of time, or, in Marcel's terms, it constitutes a "memory of the future" with "the power of making things fluid." But it is only an emotional stirring, based on nothing and confined to the world of thought and feeling. It offers a small shift in attitude; and if that shift is regarded as therapeutic, it makes no difference, in this bleak view, whether the hope is justified or fulfilled or not.

Disappointment is a catastrophe that changes one's relation to time; it cuts off future possibility but also severs one from the "past self." The distinctive pathos of disappointment in "Tintern Abbey" and the Intimations Ode springs from the speaker's surprising failure to de-idealize his earlier self. Such a de-idealization is characteristic of disillusionment, which can then regard itself as having transcended a condition of naiveté, and in this way moved on, improved, and kept up with "the progress of life." But if the subject does not repudiate the earlier self from which he has diverged, if he continues to regard that earlier self with substantial nostalgia, then his new state will appear to be one of insufficiently compensated devolution. One tendency in Wordsworth criticism is to read "Tintern Abbey," and especially the Intimations Ode, as providing narratives of necessary development, that is, of a spiritual evolution with its rewards. This interpretation draws its support partly from analogy with poems like the later "Elegiac Stanzas," which definitely does reject the solipsism of the earlier self, as well as from the Intimations Ode's deference to "the philosophic mind." In these moments, the speaker regards himself as having made intellectual progress and gained a kind of spiritual maturity. But if we read candidly, we will find that the speaker of the Intimations Ode is no more genuinely heartened by these developments than the speaker of "Tintern Abbey" was genuinely gladdened by his education in the "still, sad music of humanity."

At the beginning of the Intimations Ode, the condition of isolation, which Magnuson identifies as the theme of "Frost at Midnight" and "Tintern Abbey," is still more vividly realized than in those works. The plight of isolation is a given in the representation of disappointment, from Gray's elegy for Richard West through Bowles and Smith to Wordsworth and Coleridge: for the disappointed subject finds himself or herself in a private pocket of dismay, exiled from others who give the appearance of entering together into the current of time. These unafflicted others have not been brought to a halt by a mistrust of time, whereas the disappointed feel they have been overtaken by a calamity that was all along in time's treacherous power to inflict. Their own purposes dissolved, they find themselves adrift in a new time robbed of the tension of promise.

Early stanzas of the Intimations Ode register a panicked insistence on

an experience of community, though the declaration of unity is constantly interrupted by reminders of fracture and unease:

> Now, while the birds thus sing a joyous song,
> And while the young lambs bound
>> As to the tabor's sound,
> To me alone there came a thought of grief.　　　　(19–22)

Unlike the speaker, the animals join in a celebration of seasonal change,
for they move with time and it holds for them no terrors ("And with the
heart of May / Doth every beast keep holiday" [32–33]). The speaker
protests that he can "see" and "hear" and even "feel" their joyful ease,
but these verbs serve to call attention to the fact that his participation is
not immediate. The speaker continues to know separation from others
compounded by an apprehension of temporal difference, a radical dis-
similarity between now and then. The world of the present has been reduced to a sign of its difference from the past:

> —But there's a Tree, of many, one
> A single Field which I have looked upon,
> Both of them speak of something that is gone:
>> The Pansy at my feet
>> Doth the same tale repeat:
> Whither is fled the visionary gleam?
> Where is it now, the glory and the dream?　　　　(51–57)

In this version of being cut off from "the progress of life," the world of
sights does not offer an antithesis to the speaker's frozen solitude, but
rather reiterates its own emptiness; it stutters instead of advancing. In
Gray's elegy for Richard West, the speaker was alienated and depressed
by the indifferent fertility of the natural scene, from which his friend
was missing, but here the natural scene is itself the site of change, and instead of standing out in sharp contrast to the speaker's paralyzed sorrow,
it reechoes his sentiments.

The world looks exactly the same as it always did—as it does objec-
tively—and it is only in a subjective sense that it is changed. The second
stanza testifies to this subjective difference with its nursery rhymes, whose
very banality reflects the speaker's sense of loss:

> The Rainbow comes and goes,
> And lovely is the Rose,
> The Moon doth with delight
> Look round her when the heavens are bare,
> Waters on a starry night
> Are beautiful and fair;
> The sunshine is a glorious birth;
> But yet I know, where'er I go,
> That there hath past away a glory from the earth.   (10–18)

Naturally, the speaker faces the same predicament as in "Tintern Abbey": he is shocked by an apprehension that the world, which has remained identical, and continues the same for everyone else, has been robbed of its interest and vitality *for him*; and insofar as the loss is subjective, it cannot be remedied by the internal powers that are responsible for it. In the Intimations Ode, Wordsworth unknots this impasse, notoriously, by concocting a wonderful myth of mechanical devolution; the invention of this myth has the virtue of universalizing his loss and of relieving him of the apprehension that the loss was accidental, but at the cost of forcing him to accept the prospect of irreversible degeneration.

Wordsworth adopts a grandly impersonal language in stanzas 5 through 9, as he explains the terms of his myth; it is only in stanza 9 that he reverts to the first-person exploration of disappointment. The consolation offered by the elaboration of the myth is minimal. The modesty of this consolation can be measured by the qualifications of stanza 9, which come across as severe in spite of the triumphant exclamation points:

> O joy! that in our embers
> Is something that doth live.   (130–31)

> Which neither listlessness, nor mad endeavour,
>   Nor Man nor Boy,
> Nor all that is at enmity with joy,
> Can utterly abolish or destroy!   (158–61)

In the end, the disappointed self remains just as isolated as it was at the beginning; it is still merely "seeing" and "hearing," as from a distance, vital experiences it cannot participate in, even if the experiences now have a truly transcendental character:

> Hence in a season of calm weather
>   Though inland far we be,
> Our Souls have sight of that immortal sea
>   Which brought us hither,
> Can in a moment travel thither,
> And see the Children sport upon the shore,
> And hear the mighty waters rolling evermore.   (162–68)

The fate of the disappointed subject, in this life at any rate, has not been reversed or exalted; he is to accept the permanence of his loss and to take consolation in a highly refracted assurance of its necessity. He is to be plunged back into the progression of time that remains empty for him, but whose emptiness he must stoically embrace:

> What though the radiance which was once so bright
> Be now forever taken from my sight,
>   Though nothing can bring back the hour
> Of splendour in the grass, of glory in the flower;
>   We will grieve not, rather find
>   Strength in what remains behind.   (176–81)

It is here, in stanzas 10 and 11, that the poem fully returns to the plaintive lot of the disappointed subject, in his uneasy present, whose want of promise has not been rectified by the conclusion that it had to be, or that it is part of a richer story. Nothing has been added; the subject must still patch up an existence out of a sorry residue, the sloughed skin of a faded transcendental hope. The comfort of contact with the transcendental, with that which elevates an individual existence, has been permanently redefined as a comfort which the forlorn adult can only draw upon in the form of a memory of disorienting experiences ("Fallings from us, vanishings") now no longer actually experienced. The transcendental is replaced by the mundane ("human suffering" and "the philosophic mind"), whose unsatisfying character is subtly registered in the grim collective "we" of these homiletic formulae. This "we" replaces the "I" of the opening stanzas, that "I" which still felt entitled to raise its lament and express its bewilderment. For the loss is a loss to self-conception and is not repaired by the appeal to the "strength" of "what remains behind."[34]

Wordsworth's note to the poem makes it sufficiently clear what primitive narcissistic certainties were involved in his apprehension of transcendental glory: "Nothing was more difficult for me in childhood than to admit the notion of death as a state applicable to my own being. . . . [I]t was not so much from feelings of animal vivacity that *my* difficulty came as from a sense of the indomitableness of the Spirit within me. I used to brood over the stories of Enoch and Elijah, and almost to persuade myself that, whatever might become of others, I should be translated, in something of the same way, to heaven"³⁵ The "intimations of immortality" offered by the poem's myth ought to have restored some confidence to the speaker, with his faltering sense of having a unique and transcendental destiny, but they have not because the hope they offer is tentative and remote and because they do not assure the speaker that he is different from others, or that his ease, or sense of power and pleasure, will return in the present (he is certain that "nothing can bring back the hour / Of splendour in the grass, of glory in the flower" (178–79)). He is reduced to a plea that he be not further reduced:

> And O, ye Fountains, Meadows, Hills and Groves,
> Forbode not any severing of our loves!
> Yet in my heart of hearts I feel your might;
> I only have relinquished one delight
> To live beneath your more habitual sway.   (188–92)

He anticipates and accepts the prospect of a darkened existence, permanently "subdued" and "chastened":

> The Clouds that gather round the setting sun
> Do take a sober colouring from an eye
> That hath kept watch o'er man's mortality.   (197–99)

Once again, he identifies his new role as that of the witness or observer, a passive role and perhaps superfluous. He joins the anonymous crowd of the experienced, those who know themselves to be unelected. The conviction that the possibility or power or significance in existence has passed to other hands is reflected in the enigmatic, somehow regretful, line, "Another race hath been, and other palms are won." Read together with the lines that follow, this humbled expression casts a shade over the speaker's apparent gratitude.

Another race hath been, and other palms are won.
Thanks to the human heart by which we live,
Thanks to its tenderness, its joys and fears,
To me the meanest flower that blows can give
Thoughts that do often lie too deep for tears.   (200–4)

Despite his words, he does not really give thanks in these lines, but rather surrenders to necessity by acknowledging the mundane, even demeaned provenance of his new alliances. He assumed these alliances somewhat reluctantly, and now he feels them to be inescapable. That their prospect gives rise to thoughts "too deep for tears" testifies not so much to the profundity of these thoughts as to the fact that such thoughts—nostalgia, astonishment, and regret—revolve around circumstances that are beyond alteration, and thus beyond the reach of protest or drama.[36]

"Tintern Abbey" and the Intimations Ode contain some equivocal praise for "the philosophic mind," but only in the service of making the best of things. Essentially, they do not represent the speaker's loss as laudable, nor as attended by any truly desirable intellectual or moral change. The speaker goes on longing to be what he once was. In other poems, Wordsworth firmly disclaims his former self. "Elegiac Stanzas Suggested by a Picture of Peele Castle" characterizes the past self as obtuse in contrast to the present, enlightened by loss and suffering. Yet even "Elegiac Stanzas" participates in the psychology of disappointment. The poem is especially vivid in its assertions of moral improvement, precisely because it is a poem of mourning: written in 1806 to commemorate his brother John's drowning the year before. Wordsworth represents his grief over John's death as a trauma that shocked him out of his complacency. To all appearances, this poem transcends the narcissistic concerns of the disappointed subject. But in fact, what it reveals is the way in which mourning for loved objects entails mourning for the self.

Earlier in this chapter, several elegies from the sensibility period were grouped with poems of disappointment; what follows will clarify why these subjects of grief and disappointment should fall in together so naturally. The connection lies in the fact that bereavement inflicts a narcissistic wound. This is made clear most readily in the signal passage from

Wordsworth's elegy for his drowned brother. His loss has altered his estimation of his own capacities and his sense of his relation to the greater forces of the world: "I have submitted to a new control: / A power is gone, which nothing can restore" (34–35). He has suffered that catastrophe of humiliation definitive of disappointment, having been compelled to resign his will.

Hartman rightly points out that "Elegiac Stanzas," like "Tintern Abbey," and more subtly, the Intimations Ode, is a poem of revisitation. The first eight stanzas are devoted to describing the "naive" state before Wordsworth's perspective was irrevocably altered. His return (through representation) to a scene frequented before the change reveals the depth of his transformation. In the earlier time, he would have posed the picturesque Peele Castle beside "a sea that could not cease to smile," whereas he now approves of Beaumont's stormy painting, with its intimation that natural reality is precarious and cruel.

In his naive state, he trusted to the benignity of nature and of his own experience. He anticipated no disasters; indeed, he trusted implicitly that none would ever come, and he trusted that his confidence was firmly rooted in the character of reality. He knew the truth; it was not relative, and it would not be revised. Wordsworth associates this condition of unreflective confidence with a mental lull, or hypnotic state. But he also conveys its great felicity:

> So pure the sky, so quiet was the air!
> So like, so very like, was day to day!
> Whene'er I looked, thy Image still was there;
> It trembled, but it never passed away.
>
> How perfect was the calm! it seemed no sleep;
> No mood, which season takes away, or brings:
> I could have fancied that the mighty Deep
> Was even the gentlest of all gentle Things. (5–12)
>
> Such, in the fond illusion of my heart,
> Such Picture would I at that time have made:
> And seen the soul of truth in every part,
> A steadfast peace that might not be betrayed. (29–32)

The last sentence is key; in his naive state, he would have projected his own sense of "peace" onto the picture, and a large part of that "peace" consisted of his expectation that it would continue. He trusted that his trust was not of the sort ever to be "betrayed."

"Betray" is a significant term in Wordsworth's vocabulary—a word charged with the current of essential wishes and anxieties. In "Tintern Abbey," he hopes that "Nature never did betray the heart that loved her," though he fears she did and does. Betrayal in Wordsworth is always the betrayal of hope and innocence, and so it always involves a self-betrayal. In "Elegiac Stanzas," Wordsworth finds himself foiled by his own simplicity and his failure to anticipate loss. His trust in the benevolence of experience—which must not be considered naiveté, but a virtue of sorts, or related to virtue—has been turned to his disadvantage. He has been surprised by a malignity in the world, and then surprised by his own surprise.

The sudden death of Wordsworth's young brother has not only brought him grief, but also caused in him a catastrophe of self-loss. He has been humbled by this death, which has shown him that what he holds dear is not to be spared, that both he and his own have been classed as contingencies, and relegated to the world of accident. The canopy of narcissistic security has been swept away, and he has had to surrender a large portion of reliance on his volition and his autonomy. His previous state of illusion was violently eradicated by the intervention of a "new control," an external force by which he feels himself to have been crushed. He has *submitted* to this new control; he has been rendered helpless, and worse, has been made to perceive himself as such. He sees himself as broken and sapped: acknowledging this passivation is the final blow to elemental narcissism.

His "power" is gone—not his mere poetic power but confidence in his will, which surprise and dismay have permanently destroyed. It is hard to do without the exuberance of ontological self-esteem. The difficulty of doing without it is made clear in the rest of the poem, as Wordsworth struggles to right and to console himself. He tries to find some substitute for self-sufficiency by establishing a relation to external powers that can fill the void left by the newly experienced weakness of the self.

"A deep distress hath humanized my Soul," he says. This is a highly equivocal remark. In one light, it is normative and approving; but in another, it is merely descriptive and sad. His characterization of himself as "humanized" obviously contains a polemical, religious claim. He professes implicitly that his suffering was necessary to his moral development, insofar as it lessened his arrogance and his solipsism: he was forced to give up his self-oriented obsessions and his sublime aspirations in order to accept his part in the common fate and so begin to share in the common life.

It must be emphasized that, whatever claims these passages make for a compensatory gain in understanding and compassion, they nonetheless associate "humanizing" with reduction and humiliation; to join humanity is to join all that is small, powerless, and pitiable. This is where the equivocation enters in. For to say that "A deep distress hath humanized my Soul," is to say that the Soul has lost contact with its own divinity. It has shrunk and faltered into the merely human. Thus, "humanization" does not mean, foremost, that the Soul has been made more humane, but rather that it has been permanently "chastened" and "subdued" through resignation to its ontological diminishment. Diminishment of this kind cannot be combated or reversed.

Wordsworth argues that certain good things follow from this chastening—that his solipsism was tempered and so forth. But this very line of argument offers a refined measure of his sadness: he must try to be good, and to rationalize his losses. He cannot afford to give himself over to sadness, nor does he even quite feel entitled to be dejected—much less to feel envy or resentment. He can only seek some source of consolation by which to sustain himself, at least temporarily, even though he knows his own motives, and must consequently suffer the subtle degradation of seeking to be consoled.

As usual, the consoled state is really rather close to the unconsoled. Wordsworth declares that "The feeling of my loss will ne'er be old; / This, which I know, I speak with mind serene" (39–40). But what can be the content of this "serenity"? It is not the serenity of the naive state, when "So like, so very like, was day to day!" The new "serenity" can hardly be confounded with peace and contentment; it appears instead to share in the somber artificiality of the "fortitude" and "patient cheer" invoked in the poem's last stanza.

But welcome fortitude, and patient cheer,
And frequent sights of what is to be borne!
Such sights, or worse, as are before me here.—
Not without hope we suffer and we mourn.   (56–60)

It is the formal, studied character of this determination to fortitude that gives the poem its pathos. There is nothing else for the speaker to do but adopt this fixed stance. He is acutely aware of having no alternative. His deliberateness arises from his hopelessness; for he realizes that he has been completely cut off from his earlier self. He mourns not only his dead brother, but also, as in "Tintern Abbey" and the Intimations Ode, a lost relation to himself and the world. He must begin again and seek a new accommodation, but one in which he will not be given, and will not be allowed to desire, the grounding of self-interest and self-satisfaction.

He must shift his focus of interest and allocation of energy to something else, something outside himself. But it can hardly be another person because the security of the individual is precisely what has been called into question. So his new alliance will have to be with that vague "humanity," "the Kind," with whose helplessness he has identified his misfortune. He embraces his subsiding into what he still defines, at some level, as an inglorious order because his devastation is so complete as to eliminate the potential for resistance. He accepts the justice and the necessity of his humiliation. But the close relation between the eagerness of his renunciation and the depth of his sorrow makes the poem's compensatory scheme as well as its optimistic resolution seem improvised. The poem's concluding line, "Not without hope we suffer and we mourn," is especially strange. Unless Wordsworth refers to the hope of an afterlife, which we have no reason to believe, it is hard to say what object this hope could have. The poem cannot summon up a credible form of hope at this point because, at bottom, disappointment does not believe that it has been recompensed with the acquisition of strength or negative knowledge. But it may undertake to describe itself as such, out of humility, because it is not permitted to be grand, or give itself over to postures of impatience and self-importance.

If Wordsworth could be uniquely subtle and self-conscious in his examination of the psychology of disappointment, he could also become programmatic and obtuse. The delicacy of Wordsworth and Coleridge's invention—the elaboration of a psychological reality out of a formula inherited from sensibility—can be measured by the fact that, even within their works, the invention could degenerate into cliché again. This is precisely what happened in *The Excursion*, the much-scorned magnum opus for which Wordsworth had had such high hopes and ambitions. The poem has a patent didactic intention. The central books of *The Excursion* are called "Despondency" and "Despondency Corrected." Wordsworth had made it his project in this poem to "correct" disappointment; his hero, the Wanderer, enters into debate with the "disgusted" Solitary, in order to provide inspiration and argument against his pessimism.

The difference between this didactic approach and the descriptive, exploratory character of Wordsworth's autobiographical poems should be clear enough. Yet it is in *The Excursion* that Wordsworth first uses the word "disappointment" with a sense of its importance as a theme.[37] However, what Wordsworth now explicitly calls "disappointment" is not what he once had in mind, when he first became fascinated with the sensibility poets. It is as if Wordsworth had lost track of his own idea, or flattened it out, as often happens to writers when they become fully conscious of their ideas and are able to articulate them masterfully. The Solitary suffers the intimate losses and personal grief of one of the figures in the narrative poems, such as "The Ruined Cottage" or "Michael"; but Wordsworth then goes on to combine this cause of "disappointment" with several other sources of demoralization. The Solitary becomes a compendium of disillusionments.[38] By lumping together these sources of disappointment (personal, political, existential), Wordsworth produces a young man with a general philosophical problem that, insofar as it is discursive, can be countered discursively—by the Wanderer's orthodox pieties. The Solitary is supposedly a figure in crisis, but for him all the questions have become abstract.[39]

Wordsworth is at his most acute in narrating the effects of political disillusion when he explores its modulation into the self-loss of disappointment. He portrayed this modulation in the recluse of "Yew-Tree," but it emerges at its fullest and clearest in the late books of *The Prelude*, in which he describes his own experience of malaise upon the failure of the Revolution. Book 11 begins with a summary of the story behind his discouragement and "moral crisis":

> Long time hath man's unhappiness and guilt
> Detained us: with what dismal sights beset
> For the outward view, and inwardly oppressed
> With sorrow, disappointment, vexing thoughts,
> Confusion of the judgement, zeal decayed—
> And lastly, utter loss of hope itself
> And things to hope for.   (11.1–7)

His mental self-division here should be compared with his episode of blockage in the first book of *The Prelude*, when his mind "vex[ed] its own creation." In the aftermath of the Revolution, he also experienced an intellectual and emotional paralysis in which his mind became its own tormentor, impeding access to any objects of its attention except itself and its own workings. Out of self-disgust, it deprived itself of "things to hope for."

Wordsworth quickly reassures us that he will not halt at this impasse: "Not with these began / Our song, and not with these our song must end" (11.7–8). He turns instead to praising nature, whose

> ministry it is
> To interpose the covert of your shades,
> Even as a sleep, betwixt the heart of man
> And the uneasy world—'twixt man himself,
> Not seldom, and his own unquiet heart.   (11.15–19)

Nature restored his morale, but at first only in the muted and minimal form we have come to associate with the "hope" of the disappointed subject:

> The morning shines,
> Nor heedeth man's perverseness; spring returns—
> I saw the spring return, when I was dead
> To deeper hope, yet had I joy for her
> And welcomed her benevolence.   (11.22–26)

Like the recluse of the "Yew-Tree" and the speaker of "Tintern Abbey," he has a vicarious experience of someone else's emotional freedom. Tentative to the end of this verse paragraph, Wordsworth hints that he has suffered a permanent impairment:

> Her I resorted to, and loved so much
> I seemed to love as much as heretofore—
> And yet this passion, fervent as it was,
> Had suffered change; how could there fail to be
> Some change. (11.35–38)

Though he will sound more confident in describing his emergence from his "eclipse" (11.96), Wordsworth's vocabulary of hope in the late books of *The Prelude* confirms the suspicion that he was acutely conscious of its equivocality. Wordsworth is scrupulous about recording the multiple orders of hope: there are "depths" of hope, hopes which take the form of being consciously deferred, and curiously doubled hopes: hope, and things to hope for; hope, and hope to find hope.[40]

Even his description of finding his vocation (in books 11 and 12) shows its continuity with the elegiac themes of "Tintern Abbey" and the Intimations Ode. For Wordsworth makes it manifest that despite his ecstatic embrace of his discoveries and his declaration that he was thence "renewed" and "restored," what he really feels is gratitude at having been vouchsafed any "hope" whatsoever and any "things to hope for," though their sources be of a retrospective and fading character. Here, as in the Intimations Ode, he "gives thanks and praise" for the influxes of the past, and the memory of them—in other words, for sources of creativity, trust, and hope that are already on the wane.

Wordsworth has not been able to rework or reinvent his hopes. Instead, he wants to leap back over the onset of disappointment, in an effort to disinter his earlier capacities. But such time travel will prove impossible if disappointment is what he fears it may have been—an irreversible catastrophe. Hence he arrives at his glorification of memory, whereby the recollection of stirring moments in the past—"spots of time" —infuses the present with an old affective power. His mind has to go *backward* to *recover* the sense of hope: "through the weary Labyrinth" "Nature's self . . . Conducted me again to open day" and "Revived the feelings of my earlier life" (10.291 ff.). He struggles to heave the same weight of the present figured as "the dreary intercourse of daily life" in

"Tintern Abbey." And again, it is memory that he summons to counteract the present's burden of emptiness and restore the fluid motion of
teleology: the "spots of time" revive him when he is

> depressed
> By false opinion and contentious thought,
> Or aught of heavier or more deadly weight
> In trivial occupations and the round
> Of ordinary intercourse.   (12.259–63)

But there is a price to be paid for a therapy found in the "revival" of earlier feelings. The backwards displacement of energy jeopardizes the future, by making it depend on the elusive, departing past. How long can
energy that is receding continue to be accessible? Even as he formulates
his praise for the "renovating virtue" of the "spots of time," Wordsworth
laments that its influx, uncertain to start with, is growing ever more
sparse. The autonomy of memory is what makes it both magical and
treacherously ungovernable:

> The days gone by
> Come back upon me from the dawn almost
> Of life; the hiding places of my power
> Seem open, I approach, and then they close;
> I see by glimpses now, when age comes on
> May scarcely see at all.   (11.333–38)

No wonder he is anxious to "enshrine the spirit of the past / For future
restoration" (11.341–42); it is a precious elixir, volatile, and evanescent.
The way Wordsworth has constructed the new paradigm of inspiration
has made his decline inevitable.

In the last "spot of time," Wordsworth chastises himself for the "anxiety of hope" (371) he indulged in as he eagerly anticipated a school va-
cation. His father died while he was at home, and so, as Wordsworth
conceives it, he was punished for having too much hope. In keeping
with this superstition, his hopes are now circumscribed; he has a cheerful new program, yet the fact remains that he has preserved only a dwindling memento, or what Shelley would call a "fading coal," out of the
detritus of his former and more powerful self. That he would settle for

so little—and celebrate so little—shows that he is still working within the psychology of disappointment, even in these last books of *The Prelude*, which putatively celebrate "The Imagination, How Impaired and Restored."

It will not seem novel to argue that Wordsworth made a considerable advance in the representation of psychology, or that he did this by means of expanding the themes of loss, confusion, and temptation to despair. But Wordsworth is in most cases interpreted as a didactic poet, who offered, or attempted to offer, solutions for bewilderment and consolations for loss. Or, more boldly, he is understood to describe patterns of genuine "self-renewal." Hartman takes the later view in his formidable account of Wordsworth. Such poetry as "The Solitary Reaper"[41] and the later books of *The Prelude* appear to support this view. Wordsworth would seem to have taken heart in the "Imagination," and to have believed his own tale of how it came to be "Impaired and Restored." Scholars who accept this development at face value consider that Wordsworth's optimism distinguishes him from the other romantics. Once he is described as optimistic, his optimism can either be treated sympathetically and turned to his credit (as in Hartman and many others) or it can be denigrated and treated as an embarrassment.[42]

Historicist scholars adopt this characterization of Wordsworth as an optimist in faulting him for what they term his retreat from politics into a happy celebration of self. Critics such as Marjorie Levinson, Jerome McGann, and Alan Liu have argued that Wordsworth evolved his faith in the redemptive power of imagination as a substitute for the energies he had once invested in political radicalism but had since abandoned out of disillusionment and growing timidity. This reading of Wordsworth recapitulates Abrams's view, discussed above, which was formulated as early as 1962. According to Abrams, revolutionary disillusionment produced a vacuum in the face of which former dissidents retreated to self-concern and "spiritual quietism."[43] This very retreat paved the way for the creation of "the great romantic poems."[44]

Levinson and McGann espouse the same notion that Wordsworth successfully transumed his political disillusionment. But rather than exalting "the great romantic poems" on these grounds, Levinson, McGann,

and Liu take them to task for their "elision of history" (McGann) and
"transcendence of reference" (Liu). Drawing on Levinson's controver-
sial interpretation of "Tintern Abbey," McGann roundly asserts that in
this poem "the mind has triumphed over its times."[45] Levinson uses a
similar language of triumph and satisfaction, writing of the poem's
progress in finding "solution" and "capable consolation" through its
"mysticism" and its "transcendentalizing impulse."[46] Such representation of the poem borders on caricature, but the historicist critique of
Wordsworth does not end here. Liu argues more radically (though there
are hints of this argument in Levinson as well) that not merely the
poem's philosophy of spiritual development, but its very concentration
on the experience of the self renders it reprehensibly ahistorical (for it
was thus that Wordsworth "learned to digress into his own mind"[47]).
Apparently, Liu believes that to focus on psychological experience auto-
matically aggrandizes the self, or so he implies in his prejudicial account
of Wordsworth's "godly" first person: "'I' am everywhere in history,
Wordsworth's Spirit declares, and yet nowhere in particular in history.
'I' am the empire of the light of the setting suns, of the round ocean and
the living air, of the blue sky, and of the mind of man. 'I' am the com-
mander of motion and spirit that impels—indeed, *coerces*—all thinking
things, all objects of all thoughts, and rolls through all things."[48]

It is obvious that Wordsworth's political disillusionment played a role
in the sadness of "Tintern Abbey" and the other autobiographical poems
treated in this chapter. But these poems preserve the feeling of disheartenment they start from; in fact, they portray the collapse of precisely that
narcissistic satisfaction Liu so mockingly describes. In the end, they offer
no credible "solutions" and no "capable consolations"; the speakers remain mired in the psychological quandary wherein they began, and any
experiments with the "mystical" rhetoric of "transcendence" belong to
the desperate wish fulfillments by which these figures try but fail to reverse their discouragement. To the argument that Wordsworth substitutes the nourishment of "nature and the language of the sense" for the
claims of history,[49] it may be countered that no gratifying transferal of
this kind—and no relief from disillusionment—takes place in "Tintern
Abbey." Moreover, the poem can be characterized as "ahistorical" only
by means of a restricted definition of history because psychological expe-

rience is in fact one of the forms and manifestations of historical experience. "Tintern Abbey," along with the Intimations Ode and "Elegiac Stanzas," studies the irreversible effects of time and the experience of being miserably steeped in time. These poems seem to take place in a void precisely because they narrate the dilemma of being stalled in a lonely present, cut off from others who move forward in a fresher and more vital relationship to time.

This account of "Tintern Abbey" and the Intimations Ode departs from the general trend of both Yale school and historicist interpretation, which view these poems as descriptions of (pretended) "self-renewal." But in the reading given here, the context of isolation and "vacancy" prevails, and Wordsworth's interest lies in conveying the deterioration in self-concept that has created the need for "self-renewal." The renewal, on the other hand, emerges as feeble and transient. Wordsworth wants to portray not the overcoming but the afterlife of disappointment—though he may sometimes have forgotten this ambition, and mistaken himself for a poet with a didactic mission. But he did not "discover" grounds for hope; he was not a savior and writer of inspirational literature, even if his contemporaries tempted him to think he was.[50] He found a use for the representation of hope, as an extension of the representation of disappointment.

Wordsworth discovered how dexterous and compelling a poem about disappointment could be, enfolding as it does the story of deadlock and unease and the struggle to escape them. Poems like "Tintern Abbey," the Intimations Ode, and "Elegiac Stanzas" do not seek to devise and affirm hope, but to elaborate the evocation of disappointment through the portrayal of its longings. Hope is already undermined—imperiled and diminished—in the context of each poem, not by incoherence or inauthenticity but because of the psychological situation of which it is a part. Wordsworth took it as his task to detail the psychology of this impasse. Certainly many standard accounts of Wordsworth, including Hartman's, attend to the pathos in his tenuous efforts at "self-renewal." Under the adjustment of perspective proposed here, Wordsworth no longer has to seem wishful or naive: he emerges as an experimentalist in a new sense.

He and Coleridge worked on the remaking of the lyric into a site for the depiction of the foundering self, that is, into a species of crisis lyric, but not the crisis lyric as it has usually been described. For the source of trouble in the poem of disappointment goes deeper than the sources usually ascribed to the crisis lyric. The speaker does not descend into extremity simply because he finds himself at the threshold of an unenticing maturity, or because he has lost or fears losing his inspiration, or has reached some other crux of doubt about his vocation, or has succumbed to an episode of pessimism about his prospects; these truly are narcissistic or self-absorbed concerns. Rather, he has lost confidence in the very promise of selfhood—the innate conviction that the self is the locus of vitality and meaning, or of insight and authority over experience. His loss is a fundamental one, a loss at the level of concepts. And it is not a loss which, in the course of the poem, he comes to accept or transcend, as in the model crisis lyric, in which crisis eventually brings forth a resolution (or at least the poet's attempt to create one). The speaker in poems of disappointment does not emerge with a newly confident self precisely because that self, so severely undermined in its self-conception, cannot simultaneously become the spring of its own renewal.

2 | SHELLEY

A Love in Desolation Masked

SHELLEY WAS the most perspicacious of Wordsworth's immediate heirs, for he recognized that Wordsworth's power and chief claim to innovation lay in the refinement of elegiac feeling. In his early sonnet "To Wordsworth" (1816), Shelley characterizes his influential predecessor not as a refashioner of spiritual optimism, a celebrant of natural beauty or of self-realization, but as a prophet of loss and sorrow:

> Poet of Nature, thou hast wept to know
> That things depart which never may return:
> Childhood and youth, friendship and love's first glow
> Have fled like sweet dreams, leaving thee to mourn.   (1–4)

Though this tribute may be somewhat equivocal, insofar as its language is sentimental, Shelley clearly thinks that Wordsworth's poetry is distinguished by its frank emphasis on the experience of privation. The sonnet goes on to censure Wordsworth for subsiding into conservatism, and thus betraying not only his radical principles but the depth he achieved in his songs of departure.

Shelley's indebtedness to Wordsworth's ideas is well known. In one understanding of this legacy, critics have represented Shelley as riveted by the dark thesis of devolution adumbrated in "Tintern Abbey" and the Intimations Ode. He is said to have brooded over it throughout his career and elaborated it into a despairing existential vision. As Harold Bloom has summarized the argument of *The Cenci*, "[Shelley's] overt theme becomes the universal triumph of life over integrity, which is to say of death-in-life over life."[1] According to this interpretation, Shelley only gradually and reluctantly accepted the thesis in full, but when he did, late in his career, it was with a fierceness that outdid Wordsworth's timorous reflection and pious optimism. To quote Bloom again, "By the time Shelley had reached his final phase, of which the great monuments are *Adonais* and *The Triumph of Life*, he had become altogether the poet of this shadow of ruin."[2]

This chapter argues that Shelley's existential philosophy varied less dramatically than such a view supposes: moments that look like vacillation among different philosophical stances were actually moments in which Shelley was testing psychological possibilities. His interest in disappointment, moreover, does not reflect simply a personal obsession or an attachment to the ideas of a precursor; instead, his work pursues a powerful and rational extension of an older poetic theme, a theme first explored by the sensibility poets, and then isolated and enhanced by the early romantics. Yet Shelley played upon, explored, and expanded the fascinations of this theme with a greater range, and perhaps, a greater dexterity than any of his forbears. In his hands, the paradigm of disappointment became the leading concept in a theory about human psychology. He took the paradigm absolutely seriously, and deepened, or more significantly, generalized its application.

From the first, Shelley was intent on fathoming the collapse of hope, that is the discrediting of the self's innate capacity for idealizing and its frustration over the unattainability or inadequacy of the objects it has chosen to idealize. (Other critics have thought he simply lamented these reverses, rather than that he set himself to studying them.) The struggle with the specter of disinvestment is the subject of Shelley's major long poems, including "Alastor," *Julian and Maddalo, Prometheus Unbound, Epipsychidion*, and "The Triumph of Life." Because the outcome of the struggle differs in these poems, it has been assumed, somewhat inaccurately, that the variation reflects Shelley's own movements from optimism to pessimism and back (culminating in the climactic and undeniable gloom of "The Triumph of Life"). But he was engaged in investigation as much as in expression; he tracked the means by which self-regard is decimated and surveyed the extent of its effects. Like Melanie Klein, he appears to have regarded deidealization as the signal catastrophe of psychological experience and to have wondered whether it is either escapable or reparable.

When such a state perceives itself as irreversible, it qualifies as disappointment in our sense. Early on in his career, Shelley had made tentative gestures toward portraying and analyzing this condition of disappointment. Adumbrations of the permanently passivated and deflated spirit appear in any number of his poems, but it was not until he wrote his late lyrics to Jane Williams that Shelley chose to concentrate on the representation of this state in unredeemed isolation. Though always fascinated with tragic affect and seeking elegiac intensities—even in his juvenilia identifying like Wordsworth the elegiac as the premier literary project —it was not until the last stage of his career that he began to write poems of disappointment per se. Only then did he work out an original and effective rhetoric of disappointment. In the novel style of his late lyrics, he found a mode of enacting (rather than merely describing) the uncommanding plight of self-disenchantment. The self-conscious quality of this experiment can be measured by the striking contrast between the style of these lyrics and the fierce rhetoric of disillusionment he was continuing to write, simultaneously, in "The Triumph of Life."

Before focusing on the late lyrics and the contrast in style between the two rhetorics of the late poems, this essay will unearth the compelling and subtle analysis of disappointment that Shelley pursued from moment to moment in his earlier work. Among his first important poems, "Alastor" most clearly traces the fate of disappointment, but that fate— and the means of escaping it—are also at issue in such major works from his middle phase as "Ode to the West Wind" and *Prometheus Unbound*. Shelley displays the same keen and precise understanding of the psychology of disappointment in all these poems, though he does not always put it to the same use.

"Alastor" was the first of Shelley's poems to concentrate on adapting Wordsworth's fascination with an inner life that finds itself cast adrift and foundering, without an object of love. What Shelley has done with the theme in "Alastor" is to eroticize it explicitly—that is, to locate the source of the Poet's demoralization in his inability to discover a satisfying erotic object. This failure renders his world as disturbingly "vacant" as that which the speakers of "Tintern Abbey" and the Intimations Ode have woken, in a panic, to behold—the world as a desert, "a waste and solitary place," with no more nourishment to offer this particular, re-maindered self. And, as in "Tintern Abbey" and the Intimations Ode, the subject's psychological impasse cannot be said to result from simple disillusionment: the Poet does not move from naiveté to clarity, or suffer from being disabused of a cherished faith. Yet Shelley's analysis already differs subtly from Wordsworth's, for the Poet has been alerted to the absence of something that he had not known to be possible as a presence, whereas in Wordsworth's poems, the speaker had simply taken the presence for granted.

In his preface, Shelley introduces the story of the unnamed "Alastor" Poet as one of deep and generalized frustration, calling this plight "one of the most interesting situations of the human mind." The "Alastor" Poet "seeks in vain for a prototype of his [ideal] conception. Blasted by his disappointment, he descends to an untimely grave."[3] Shelley is more direct than Wordsworth at bringing out the psychological quandary this situation involves, with the self's apprehension that the vacancy of the external world has thrown it back on a vacancy within. In Shelley's pre-cise phrasing, the Poet's spontaneous imaging of an erotic ideal creates material that was not there before, not there intrinsically: the "vision on his sleep" represents "a dream of hopes that never yet / Had flushed his cheek" (150–51). This "dream of hopes" immediately assumes the com-promised character not of eagerness but of anguished desperation: "The insatiate hope which it awakened, stung / His brain even like despair" (221–22). "The mystery and the majesty of Earth / The joy, the exulta-tion" (199–200) abruptly vanish, replaced by a void of silence, not only without, but within, in mirrored emptiness: "His wan eyes / Gaze on the empty scene as vacantly / As ocean's moon looks on the moon in heaven" (200–1).

The landscapes through which he now aimlessly wanders also become "wide and melancholy waste[s]" (273). Their "waste" reflects his feeling of the "waste" in him, which denotes not only his sense of inner emptiness (boredom, panic, and fatigue), but also his consequent apprehension that he has lost his use for time (he has no more aim) and consequently, all his hours are "wasted." The poem now begins to use this word (and some of its cognates) obsessively and in all its permutations—to mean arid, bare, withering, dissipating, misapplied, or tragically misused:

> where the desolated tombs
> Of Parthian kings scatter to every wind
> Their wasting dust, wildly he wandered on,
> Day after day, a weary waste of hours. (242–46)

With his paralyzing discovery of inner desolation, the Poet's curiosity about the world fades; he drifts about and finally pines away in a kind of anorectic phantasmagoria. In the language of Shelley's preface, the Poet "perishes" when "the vacancy of [his] spirit suddenly makes itself felt."[4]

An emptiness in the external world evacuates the internal world as well. With a psychological understanding parallel to Klein's, Shelley has shown that discovering the inexistence of the ideal poses a threat to self-conception, or to the experience of occupying a particular self whose own pride of wealth and resourcefulness is diminished by the disappearance or de-idealization of its erotic objects. To put it in Kleinian terms, the extinction of the external good object eclipses the good object within. One is abandoned to a lonely psyche stripped of its "glamour" and capacity for self-nourishment. This is clearly a more complex psychological condition than the "narcissism" to which critics have usually attributed the Poet's malaise.

Paradoxically, though the Poet experiences his own interiority as barren and resourceless, this grim torment and the intensity of his self-entrapment become a fierce and devouring source of energy. He

> Bear[s] within his life the brooding care
> That ever fed on its decaying flame
> . . . .
> Life, and the lustre that consumed it, shone
> As in a furnace burning secretly
> From his dark eyes alone. (246–47, 252–54)

The self-vexing anguish of disappointment is in fact an expression of energy and a tragic obsession; but by definition it cannot be experienced as powerful by the disappointed subject, who feels him or herself to be, on the contrary, faded and aimless.

The Poet emerges as a kind of hero, inspiring even a certain degree of awe—at least in the narrator, who likens the Poet's "frail and wasted human form" to that of "an elemental god" (350–51). Reproducing the Poet's own experience of bereavement, the narrator complains in the final lines that when "some surpassing Spirit, / Whose light adorned the world around it" (713–14) departs, he leaves "those who remain behind, not sobs or groans, / The passionate tumult of a clinging hope; / But pale despair and cold tranquillity" (715–17). The Poet may be heroicized in this way, but only by outsiders, by the narrator and the reader. Third-person perspectives on disappointment, like this one and the later *Julian and Maddalo*, necessarily cannot explore the unique enervation of that psychological state in the same way as first-person perspectives. When Shelley writes first-person poems of disappointment, there is no occasion for this awkward and confusing species of idealization.

In fact, the long, somewhat tedious description of the "waste" landscape in "Alastor" seems to result from the mode of third-person narration; it substitutes for an account of the Poet's interiority—a prolonged, lightless, passive, and resourceless state. The Poet's passivity, like Prometheus's, reflects psychological impasse. Shelley may have wanted to convey the atmosphere of this impasse through the lonely, haunted landscape, full of moving waters, odd, still scenes, silent groves of trees, and images of self-absorption. The infamous blooms gazing at their reflection in the water have been taken to image narcissism, but it would be more precise to interpret them as an image of self-enclosure. The Poet's surrealistic fading away represents the fate of disappointment. At this stage Shelley can only represent the experience of this state by analogical means. The Poet has been dismissed to a self that is figured as a "waste" place, a desert to occupy.

One does not have to look far to find other Shelley poems that concern either the collapse of self-approval or the resistance to it. They are major themes throughout his work. He consistently represents the reverses of life and the processes of maturity as a threat not only to purpose, action, and idealism, but also to what in his view makes them possible: a certain nobility of self-conception. In "Ode to the West Wind," Shelley experiments with a first-person lament in the mode of Wordsworth by adopting Wordsworth's thesis of the spirit's inevitable devolution—and, more importantly, its enervating consciousness of this decline. The poem's much-mocked lines offer a classic formulation of disappointment:

> If even
> I were as in my boyhood, and could be

> The comrade of thy wanderings over Heaven,
> As then, when to outstrip thy skiey speed
> Scarce seemed a vision; I would ne'er have striven

> As thus with thee in prayer in my sore need.
> Oh! lift me as a wave, a leaf, a cloud!
> I fall upon the thorns of life! I bleed!   (47–54)

These lines evoke a condition of disappointment by means of a familiar dichotomy: a fall from a youth energized by its unchallenged narcissism and its absence of self-doubt into a maturity crippled by actual reverses and by what they inspire—the conviction of one's weakness and insufficiency. The pain of this condition lies largely in its self-consciousness; it is humiliating to have to represent oneself to oneself, not only as having devolved since boyhood, but also as now "striv[ing]" in "sore need." The awareness of being in need is itself a burden. And to compound this burden, the speaker recognizes that his "striving" has constituted a defensive but unsuccessful attempt to show that he still has resources, that he is not in need. But he recognizes that at the same time his struggle has also represented an attempt to challenge the energy of transcendence, and so to absorb some of that energy he has thereby shown he needs.

He wants to assert his autonomy as well as to claim the consolations of dependence; and he has detected his weakness. He has surprised himself, pining in contradictory desires. Such bad faith and self-division are major liabilities of his unenviable adulthood. (Bad faith follows from the splitting of the self: from the repudiation of one self-characterization by another aspect of the self generated for the purpose of this repudiation. As Sartre defines it, it is "A lie to oneself within the unity of a single consciousness."[5]) To "bleed" from the pricking of the "thorns of life" means in part to endure this sense of failure, of stumbling and helplessness, compounded by the humiliation of catching oneself in an act of bad faith.

The next lines, echoing the Intimations Ode, reiterate that the blow dealt by "life" is a blow to self-conception: "A heavy weight of hours has chained and bowed / One too like thee: tameless, and swift, and proud" (55–56). He has been "bowed" or humbled by his awareness of no longer being "tameless and swift, and proud." Here, "pride" means not "conceit" but "a sense of one's own proper dignity or value; self-respect." With the speaker's loss of self-respect comes an odd sort of sorrow and shame at losing it—at the dwindling or diminishing from within. The speaker suffers from that feeling of shame. His self-conception is too corroded for him to dream of rivaling the transcendent force in spirit; and he is saddened when compelled to look upon his demoralization and his new timorousness.

The poem ends with a kind of rhetorical upswing, a burst of vigor which offers an escape—in mood, at any rate—from the impasse of disappointment portrayed in the fourth stanza. It seems that Shelley had no desire to resign the poem to that paralyzing atmosphere. Yet his contrived solution is equivocal because it depends not on reversing the conclusions of disappointment but on carrying out the death-wish promoted by them. The speaker eludes his shame and self-sorrow by resigning his residual attachment to autonomy. He prays to be made instead an agent of the wind, like the "withered leaves" of autumn; and this means embracing his own dying or "autumnal" status and the "dead" character of his thoughts. In this way, he will become a medium for vitality, though he will not himself be revitalized. From this ambiguous ending we may conclude that, though Shelley had already worked out a keen understanding of the psychology of disappointment, he did not quite wish to explore it in itself—whether because he was dissatisfied with the rhetorical limitations of such a project, or because he sought to investigate other permutations that the psychology of existential humiliation might take.

Shelley portrays many forms of despair in *Prometheus Unbound*, the major poem of his middle phase, yet it is also in this work that he most acutely anatomizes the harmful stasis of disappointment; and then he goes further, seeking to imagine a means by which it might be overcome. The specter of disappointment is at the heart of the pessimistic fears and visions that threaten Prometheus with paralysis in act 1. The Furies, who articulate his fears, introduce themselves as "the ministers of pain and fear / And disappointment and mistrust and hate" (1.452–53). At the beginning of the climactic passage of Prometheus's torment and temptation, they taunt him with his fear that humanity is so weak and self-divided as to be incapable of reformation. What will forever forestall such reformation is the erosion of confidence and courage—an erosion that they represent as an inevitable concomitant of experience. In their confident, chilling analysis, this ruin is insidiously penetrating; it occurs within each individual psyche, where episodes of loss, discouragement, and dread survive their occasion to deposit a legacy of trepidation and self-doubt. As in "Ode to the West Wind," the reverses of maturity create a kind of rippling effect of weakness and consciousness of weakness. One becomes convinced of one's vulnerability and helplessness; one begins to be afraid and so takes refuge in hypocrisy, inaction, and denial.

> In each human heart terror survives
> The ravin it has gorged: the loftiest fear
> All that they would disdain to think were true:
> Hypocrisy and custom make their minds
> The fanes of many a worship, now outworn.
> They dare not devise good for man's estate
> And yet they know not that they do not dare.
> The good want power, but to weep barren tears.
> The powerful goodness want: worse need for them.
> The wise want love, and those who love want wisdom;
> And all best things are thus confused to ill.
> Many are strong and rich,—and would be just,—
> But live among their suffering fellow men
> As if none felt: they know not what they do.   (1.618–32)

"Terror survives / The ravin it has gorged"; the predations of anxiety and sadness have a lasting effect on the psyche. They leave not merely a scar but a festering wound because they make one reconceive oneself as imperiled, and yet incapable and small. They are (or can be) permanently chastening. With this notion of aftereffects—the "survival" of terror in the form of self-denigration—we have entered into the realm of disappointment, whose secondary damage to self-conception proves to be its most significant as well as most subtle complication.

Prometheus does not reject the Furies' pessimistic view of experience as devolution, though it may be belied by the utopian imaginings in the later acts of the play. In this act, even in the inspiring reminiscences of the six Spirits of the human mind, the specter of disappointment remains. Here it is disappointment in the classical sense, as the frustration of hope, ambition, and desire. But the name Shelley gives to it is "Desolation." The fifth Spirit sees a "planet-crested Shape" sweep by on "lightning-braided pinions," "Scattering the liquid joy of life from his ambrosial tresses" (1.765–66). This glorious shape, like the "shape all light" in "The Triumph of Life," resolves into an image of delusion and defeat.

> as I past 'twas fading
> And hollow Ruin yawned behind. Great Sages bound in madness
> And headless patriots and pale youths who perished unupbraiding,
> Gleamed in the Night I wandered o'er.   (1.767–70)

This dark conclusion is confirmed and rephrased more abstractly in the beautiful speech of the Sixth Spirit:

> Ah, sister! Desolation is a delicate thing:
> It walks not on the Earth, it floats not on the air,
> But treads with silent footsteps, and fans with silent wing
> The tender hopes which in their hearts the best and gentlest bear,
> Who soothed to false repose by the fanning plumes above
> And the music-stirring motion of its soft and busy feet,
> Dream visions of aerial joy, and call the monster, Love,
> And wake, and find the shadow Pain, as he whom now we greet.
>   (1.772–79)

The "tender hopes" thus defeated are not only the hopes of lovers, but also the hopes of "sages," "patriots," and "youths," each of them with his or her own particular object of idealization. All these dreams are doomed to be met with a harsh reversal (at least until Prometheus fulfills the "prophecy" that "begins and ends in" him). The awakening to "find the shadow Pain" is very bleak; and the whole process of disillusion seems cruel and grim. Yet Shelley describes this "desolation" as "a delicate thing." Presumably he means that both hope and disillusion transpire on the most rarefied plane; they are at once most crucial—as the authors of attitudes and revolutions in attitude—and most subtle, individual, and arbitrary. The process of desolation is profound but invisible ("It walks not on the Earth, it floats not on the air"), even by contrast to other affects, which can be both manipulated and observed more readily. For hope and disillusion relate not to external objects, but to one's inner representation of them (one's idealization of or disappointment with them), and then, in turn, to relations within the self that are affected by the fate of these representations. (Of course, the failure of ideals need not be quite so intangible: the patriots, after all, have lost their heads. But the process of inner transformation—the turning from hope to disillusion—remains "delicate.")

Shelley regards the threat of such a major disappointment, or "desolation," as the crux of life—the potential turning point that can wreck an existence. It makes him all the more uneasy that this catastrophic event is so inner and arbitrary; life is brutal, in his view, yet it can only inflict disappointment if the psyche (mind, heart, and attitude) cooperates; it might have resisted, or felt otherwise. (This is the theme of "The Two Spirits: An Allegory.") And yet the psyche cannot will itself to resist. It might do so spontaneously and therefore mysteriously, but it cannot do so deliberately. For this reason, Prometheus's recovery is tenuous and optative. He is rescued from his bitterness and disappointment by the intervention of Asia, who reflects his own capacity for creative and hopeful feeling, yet she is represented as a separate and estranged part of him, an independent agent in a fragmented consciousness who arrives from elsewhere to be reunited with him. He and she make their discrete intellectual and emotional advances, but there is no single consciousness to will, effect, and oversee its self-transcendence. Thus, the means of Prometheus's integration and renaissance remain obscure. This is because Shelley does not quite believe in the power of positive thinking; that is, though he repudiated the authority of fatalism and pessimism,[6] especially with respect to political theory, he does not really think that an individual can recover from disappointment through sheer determination. Any such notion would be something of a paradox, for disappointment would lose its constitutive character if it could be overcome at will.

Thus far, we have been looking at third-person poems in which Shelley treats the theme of disappointment from an abstract or analytical point of view.[7] Later in his career, Shelley comes more often to use the paradigm of disappointment in explicitly autobiographical moments, in which no general questions are clearly in play. In these later poems, he dwells especially on the strangely active but self-entangled and self-unaiding stasis of disappointment (the stasis in which *Prometheus Unbound* begins). When he portrays himself in *Adonais* (even if it is in the third person), Shelley calls the broken figure he describes, "A Love in desolation masked." The word "desolation" echoes the Sixth's Spirit's warning against the danger of demoralizing self-erosion. The Shelley figure in *Adonais* has clearly fallen prey to this fate, but still "delicately," which is to say, complexly.

"A Love in desolation masked" is a curious phrase: we might have expected a more complete figure of transformation, such as "A love in ruins," or a "A love replaced by desolation." In this phrase Love is only wearing the "mask" of desolation, which suggests that it has survived, though in a concealed form. What this might mean is made clearer by the following lines:

> A Love in desolation masked;—a Power
> Girt round with weakness;—it can scarce uplift
> The weight of the superincumbent hour;
> It is a dying lamp, a falling shower,
> A breaking billow;—even whilst we speak
> Is it not broken? (281–86)

The Love survives, but "masked" in its desolation, which implies that the old longings remain alive, in some form, because disappointment on their behalf is still experienced. Shelley is "a Power / Girt round with weakness," because force and feeling subsist at the core, ruing their haplessness and helplessness with respect to the object world. His disappointment entails a powerful experience of fragility—but paradoxically it is self-contained and issueless, so that it cannot mistake itself for power.

He goes on, in *Adonais*, to represent himself as a species of anachronism, an incongruous survivor, enervated and undone: he wears a garland of "overblown" pansies and "faded violets," and carries a spear which

> Vibrated, as the ever-beating heart
> Shook the weak hand that grasped it; of that crew

> He came the last, neglected and apart;
> A herd-abandoned deer struck by the hunter's dart.   (294–97)

He recognizes his weakness, yet has vitality enough to perceive that he is entrapped in his disintegration (like Wordsworth in the Intimations Ode). His insistent iteration and urgent query reflect how uneasily he bears the burden of his frustrated energies. He characterizes himself as a force nearing the end (but not at the end) of the process of depletion. So long as his disappointment pains him, he remains, not desolate, but haunted by residual longings, which wear the guise of desolation.

In his last major poem, "The Triumph of Life," Shelley adopts the mode of generalization with a vengeance, producing a panorama of disablement and despair. The victims of Life succumb to the malaise of disappointment as Shelley had anatomized it in earlier poems such as *Prometheus Unbound*. The pessimism of the poem is so transparent, and so forceful and grand in its rhetoric, that it has stirred many critics to passionate efforts of paraphrase. Stuart Sperry, for example, eloquently expatiates on the poem's theme: "In Shelley's *Triumph*, Life the conqueror prevails over himself. His victory is the triumph of actualization over potential, of life as process over life as inception. His conquest represents the defeat of hopeful instinct, the corruption of virtuous impulse, the decline and degeneration of life's vital energies to a shadowy procession of forms that mock and disfigure the light from which they once proceeded. The vision is more a life in death, a *danse macabre*, than a pageant of living."[8] This is compelling rhetoric, answerable to Shelley's own, but we may want to ask for a more precise explanation: how exactly does Life subdue us in Shelley's account? The specific nature of the malaise Shelley portrays, and the scrupulous analysis he gives of it, can be further elucidated, for the poem's exteriorizing allegory encloses a suggestive and intricate psychological paradigm.

The "Wise, / The great, [and] the unforgotten" (208–9) are chained to the car of Life, just as the anonymous multitudes—"Numerous as gnats upon the evening gleam" (46)—are swept up in the wake of the chariot; in some way they suffer the same fate as the famous and powerful. What experience can it be that is common to all, and spares none—that is absolutely rigorous and universal in its depredations? What inevitable defeat is Shelley thinking of? His account becomes more detailed toward the end of the fragment, when, expanding on his vision of life's "triumph" (now in "Rousseau's" words), Shelley describes the "grove [that] / Grew dense with shadows to its inmost covers" (480–81). These shadows are no malevolent interposition of the car of Life, though they are "wrought" upon by its "creative ray" (533), but rather they are emanations of the victims themselves—the departing ghosts of "beauty," "strength," and "freshness," or else something produced when those things are lost. Strangely, these shadows are compared to "masks"—"Mask after mask fell from the countenance / And form of all" (536–37)—but masks in multiples, whose disappearance seems to promote deformation rather than revealing the true face.

In one of his characteristic—and characteristically creepy—self-reflexive images, Shelley intimates that our "defeat" is self-generated. It comes from within, though that makes it no less fated or unavoidable:

> And [other shadows] like discoloured flakes of snow
>   On fairest bosoms and the sunniest hair
> Fell, and were melted by the youthful glow
>
>   Which they extinguished; for like tears, they were
> A veil to those from whose faint lids they rained
>   In drops of sorrow.   (511–16)

The defeat consists not primarily of spontaneous interior degeneration or of subjection to frustration from outside, but instead follows from emotions or ideas redounding upon themselves, like tears that are meant to be expressive but turn into a concealing or distorting "veil." This is a subtle difference because all these processes could be said to arrive at the same result, but the processes are not identical, and it is the process of second-order self-erosion that Shelley is intent on here. The succeeding lines make the nature of this process more clear. Shelley contrasts "hope" with its deterioration into "desire":

> I became aware
>
> Of whence those forms proceeded which thus stained
>   The track in which we moved; after brief space
> From every form the beauty slowly waned

From every firmest limb and fairest face
The strength and freshness fell like dust, and left
    The action and the shape without the grace

Of life; the marble brow of youth was cleft
    With care, and in the eyes where once hope shone
Desire like a lioness bereft

Of its last cub, glared ere it died.   (516–26)

What is the difference between "hope" and "desire"? Shelley's meta-phor suggests that desire is belated and nostalgic, that it is narrowed and vitiated by the certainty of its frustration. It is on the verge of dying out because it is threatened by despair of itself. This emotion is distinct from hope, which by definition holds out the possibility of its fulfillment; de-sire is instead a corrupted, painful craving, which anticipates defeat and so expresses disheartenment. Desire is the decadent form of hope. Shelley is fascinated in this poem with the mechanism by which hope wears it-self down into disappointment—and not quite because of actual frustra-tions. It was not failure, but the internalization of the sense of failure (so disturbingly described by the Furies of *Prometheus Unbound*) that he re-garded with anguish, as an evil fate of self-reduction promoted merely by "living."

"The Triumph of Life" reflects bitterly on how people are subdued, crippled, and undone by the psychology of disappointment. Disappoint-ment is its theme, and yet its fierce, driving style transcends a stance of disappointment, and so begins to reveal the distinction between the poem that analyses and the poem that enacts disappointment. The authorita-tive rhetoric of negativity in "The Triumph of Life" conveys an almost vertiginously panoramic perspective. Its correspondingly severe, sweep-ing generalizations are exhilarating; and they point back to a speaker who continues to experience the satisfactions of intellectual mastery and rhetorical grandeur. At the very least, this vitality of expression will be seen to contrast with the emotional state of the weary and desperate figures following in the train of Life.

Shelley recognizes the discontinuity between his subject and his style, for he does not allow his own speaker to enjoy the pleasures of his impersonal rhetoric and lofty disillusionment. When the speaker tries to strike a disdainful pose, the Rousseau figure rebukes him:

> "Let them pass"—
> I cried—"the world and its mysterious doom
>
> Is not so much more glorious than it was
>   That I desire to worship those who drew
> New figures on its false and fragile glass
>
>   "As the old faded."—"Figures ever new
> Rise on the bubble, paint them how you may;
>   We have but thrown, as those before us threw,
>
> Our shadows on it as it past away."   (243–51)

The first-person narrator is consistently represented as being, at crucial moments, willfully ignorant and evasive. He likes his role as spectator and does not want the moral of the spectacle to apply to himself. Yet in response to his eager questioning, "Rousseau" taunts him with the prospect of being forced to join in life's triumph. At the risk of caricature, we might say that the speaker regards the prodigy before him as an abstraction and a mystery, something for him to examine from a philosophical distance, even if it is with indignation and horror. But Rousseau corrects him:

> "But follow thou, & from spectator turn
>   Actor or victim in this wretchedness,
>
> "And what thou wouldst be taught I then may learn
>   From thee."   (305–8)

The narrator is not to rest complacently in his spectatorship; he is not to be allowed a general and axiomatic disillusionment. By means of his natural resistance to becoming a disappointed "victim" in place of a disillusioned speaker, he both articulates and betrays the poem's stern and commanding rhetoric. Shelley thus thematizes the artificiality, opportunism, and instability of the stance of disillusionment—at least as a psychological, if not a poetic, phenomenon.

Adonais also addresses the subject of disappointment thematically, and also diverges from the late lyrics rhetorically. The situation of the first-person speaker sounds very like a condition of disappointment, especially in his apprehension of an empty future:

> Why linger, why turn back, why shrink, my Heart?
> Thy hopes are gone before; from all things here
> They have departed; thou shouldst now depart!   (11.469–71)

Yet the rhetoric of the poem is a rhetoric of vigor and speed, and the contempt for life is balanced by an embrace of something else, a (pretended) enthusiasm for death and praise of what is transcendent ("That Light whose smile kindles the universe" [479]). The psychology of the speaker thus is not identical to that of the speakers in the late lyrics; and this distinction is made clear within the poem when it distinguishes between the impassioned first-person speaker and the incapacitated "Phantom among men." With its last stanza, *Adonais* ends on a note of excited liminality; there is a terminus ahead, a journey with an end (however negative), whereas in the late lyrics, the speaker collapses ever deeper into his original condition.

Naturally, Shelley's late lyrics and his last long poems tend to be regarded as expressing the same state of disillusionment. But they ought to be more carefully separated. The poetic forms of both *Adonais* and "The Triumph of Life" are forms that accommodate, even demand, a rhetoric of determination and disgust (to go with the vigor and speed), and they are visionary poems, not first-person lyrics that express exhaustion. It would be easy to misconstrue Shelley's late lyrics as representing the emotional condition experienced by someone who thought the dark thoughts set forth in the long poems. But though the late lyrics do portray sadness and depletion, it is not of a sort consonant with the ability or desire to formulate the generalizations of the long poems. The disappointment of the late lyrics does not grow out of the conclusions reached by *Adonais* or "The Triumph of Life" nor does it represent the natural fate of the spirit of skepticism, which has worked to arrive at those conclusions. This disappointment is not organically related to skepticism—which is part of its sadness: it lacks intellectual prestige, and therefore, ought not to be identified with disillusionment, since the idea of disillusionment over-laps with the concept of edification.

In contrast to the sublime high rhetoric of "The Triumph of Life," Shelley in his late lyrics experimented with a representation of disappointment from the inside and with it a complimentary, muted style, a style that eschewed climax and rhetorical majesty. These are ostensibly modest exercises, as befitting their subject—short, self-effacing lyrics that contrast with the verve and ambition of *Adonais* or "The Triumph of Life." The late lyrics are about disappointment that experiences itself as wanting even the dignity of having found out the truth, and so unen-titled to adopt the authority of crusade or manifesto. In fact, Shelley's last lyric, "Lines written in the Bay of Lerici," remains fittingly unfin-ished, trailing off without a climactic conclusion. This wandering form echoes the self-conception of the disappointed person, such as the pitiful Phantom among men, who "came the last, neglected and apart." Disen-chantment in the late lyrics does not involve the tonic pain caused but also recompensed by the clarity of knowledge; it is rather a lonely and unproductive state.

But it would be inaccurate to conclude that in his late lyrics Shelley finally realized an ambition to represent disappointment effectively and inaccurate, therefore, to see his career as evolving toward an accom-plishment fulfilled in his late lyrics though betrayed in his last visionary poems. He had no such ambition; he had not been seeking a fitting po-etic embodiment of disappointment all along. What he had been doing was weighing the forms and futures of defeated idealism, political dis-gust, failing self-confidence, and thwarted hope. He came upon the harsh embitterment of his late visionary poems and the sheer febrility of his late lyrics as divergent paths for these forms of existential frustration. The accomplishment of his late poems is thus to refine—by separating out and clarifying—two psychological possibilities and their rhetorical counterparts.

Shelley had experimented earlier with the lyric of impasse, and in fact, his "Stanzas written in Dejection," a poem of 1818, is closer to Byron's last poem, popularly known as "On This Day I Complete My Thirty-

Sixth Year," than to his own late lyrics.[9] It represents an early version of the first-person poem of exhaustion, but like Byron's speaker, Shelley's narrator for the poem paradoxically has some spirit leftover. "Stanzas written in Dejection—December 1818, near Naples" displays plenty of ennui, and yet it is still possible to distinguish between its mood or rhetoric and that of the late lyrics. Though all these poems might be grouped together as despairing, there is a subtle difference between the varieties of despair they portray, and "Stanzas" remains more nearly clichéd. Consider the lines:

> Yet now despair itself is mild,
> Even as the winds and waters are:
> I could lie down like a tired child
> And weep away the life of care
> Which I have borne and yet must bear
> Till Death like Sleep might steal on me,
> And I might feel in the warm air
> My cheek grow cold, and hear the Sea
> Breathe o'er my dying brain its last monotony.   (28–36)

It would be fair to say that "despair is mild" in the late lyrics too, and yet the speaker's voice is not the same: the declarations of the "I" here ("I could lie down," which "I have borne," "I might feel") still resonate with a sense of agency. The speaker may protest that his confidence in his capacity and his sense of worth—even his viability as a subject—have been evacuated, but the rhetoric still (unintentionally, perhaps) suggests something of the opposite—a persisting vitality. For "Stanzas" does not strike quite the same tone of surrender as the late lyrics; something demanding and dramatic remains in the speaker's complaints. He does not yet feel humbled to the extent that he has lost his right to indignation. Or to put it more accurately, Shelley did not yet know how to write a compelling first-person poetry of disappointment that remains true to the speaker's sense of his unworthiness and enfeeblement.

He found out how to write this kind of poem when he wrote his last lyrics. "The Recollection," "With a Guitar. To Jane," "Lines Written in the Bay of Lerici," and "The Magnetic Lady to Her Patient" all work to tease out complex states of self-humiliation. They indulge in self-conscious pastoral fantasy, in which the fantasist knows that his drifting thoughts are idle and regressive, and that he is debarred by his experience from entertaining them ingenuously. These poems dramatize the irreversible damage of disappointment—the intellectual self-defeat, nostalgia, ambivalence, and fear of deterioration. They dwell in particular on the paralysis of emotional aims, and the corresponding attractions of illicit regression. Like Byron's poem, Shelley's lyrics explore what they represent: an incurable weariness with life. This weariness presages death and imposes on its harborer the sense of drifting in an arrested, futile, posthumous existence. But, though such feelings of weariness and futility can follow from disillusionment of an exasperated, violent order, the malaise of Shelley's speaker clearly does not fall into that category. It is not that he rejects the things he used to believe in—he does not suffer from lost illusions in that sense. He has rather come to mistrust something in himself and his particular life.

If he has been disabused of illusion, it was the illusion that the things he believed in were available to him, that they were open for his entertainment and could naturally become intervolved with *his* life. This at once hubristic and ordinary assumption has been proven false; his arrow, shot from the bow, is sunk and gone. Others may confidently persevere in the ideals he once held; they still offer an infinite amount of hope, but not for him. Such is his humiliation, moreover, that he cannot regard his thwarted fate as a noble failure—or even as striking, pathetic, or unique. For the speakers of the late lyrics, "despair is mild" in the sense of having lost its distinction.[10]

The oppression of occupying a life that will not thrive pervades Shelley's late lyrics and is perhaps most interesting in its implicit form, but to make the point, here is a more explicit manifestation, as it appears in the fifth stanza of "The Serpent Is Shut Out from Paradise":

> Full half an hour, to-day, I tried my lot
>> With various flowers, and every one still said,
>>> "She loves me, loves me not."
>> And if this meant a Vision long since fled—
> If it meant Fortune, Fame, or Peace of thought,

> If it meant—(but I dread
> To speak what you may know too well)
> Still there was truth in the sad oracle.   (33–40)

The last lines hint that the elusive woman is Jane Williams; the earlier candidates are vision, fortune, fame, and peace of mind, all of which Shelley thus identifies as having abandoned him, without suggesting that they were simply delusory goals. This lamentation of exile, though it may seem self-pitying, is in fact intent on cultivating a particular element of the psychology of disappointment: the ineluctable recognition that one's own existence is wretched, unexalted, and void. This humiliation debars its sufferer from consoling thoughts. Hopeful wishes have to be set apart from the self's reality; they are relegated to fantasy and projection onto others. Even nostalgia provides no refuge because it is contaminated by ambivalence.

"The Invitation," "The Recollection," "The Serpent Is Shut Out from Paradise," "With a Guitar. To Jane," "The Magnetic Lady to Her Patient," "To Jane (The Keen Stars Were Twinkling,)" and "Lines Written in the Bay of Lerici" present themselves as indulging in fantasy, the empty game of a spirit with surviving energies of idealism and innocence, which it is forbidden to take seriously. The speakers in these poems can only toy with a continued power to conceive transcendence: Shelley treats the allegory of Ariel, Miranda, and Ferdinand as an excursus of fancy, and there is conscious qualification in the claim that when she plays the guitar, Jane's voice reveals "a tone / of some world far from ours." All of Shelley's late lyrics render desirable thoughts only in a wishful mode, a wishfulness all the more fragile to the extent that it is self-aware. For all express the need for self-renewal, along with the sense of its fragility; all acknowledge the ephemerality of the illusory flash of renovation stirred by Jane's presence. Shelley's paradigm is thus subtly and importantly different from Wordsworth's because the renewal is not presented as believed in, or longed to be believed in, by the speaker; it is instead entertained as conscious, temporary, artificial, gossamer. The speaker has already come out on the other side of this momentary brightening while it is happening and thus, knows its faintness and unreality.

The rhetorically anomalous character of these poems is reflected in the unconventionality of their theme: they are love poems of a sort, but of a very peculiar one because the love object is regarded not merely as inaccessible, but as completely informed, sympathetic, and uninterested, while the lover describes himself as moved but discouraged by his own passion. There is never any question of the love being fulfilled; the affair is to take place in the dual indulgence of a shadowed fantasy. This complex failed eroticism contrasts with the projected ecstasy of Shelley's disavowed love poem *Epipsychidion*, written at roughly the same time. Though it contains some elements of the late lyrics, *Epipsychidion* ends with a trite projection of erotic idyll. This long poem describes the beloved as the sole light in darkness, "Veiled Glory of this lampless Universe!" (26), and "A smile amid dark frowns" (62), "a gentle tone / Amid rude voices" (62–63), "The glory of [whose] being . . . stains the dead, blank, cold air with a warm shade" (91–92). This conceit will be repeated with greater elegance throughout the late lyrics, sometimes subtly and implicitly, sometimes explicitly, as in "The Recollection":

> And still I felt the centre of
> The magic circle there
> Was one fair form that filled with love
> The lifeless atmosphere. (49–52)

These extravagant claims highlight the speaker's isolation and desperation. But, whereas *Epipsychidion* imagines a happy reunion with the love object, his other late poems more powerfully devote their passion to constitutively inaccessible objects (including the dead Keats). And the speaker knows that they are inaccessible. This motif should not be interpreted merely as a reflection of Shelley's own despair, for it operates as a means of representing the self-consciously compromised yearnings of disappointment.

Because their erotic feelings are so damaged, the late lyrics cannot adopt the stances of conventional love poetry; they dwell instead on the anachronistic character of the love (if in its complex and fractured state, it still deserves the name). The apprehension of anachronism is a classic feature of disappointment, from Gray's elegy for Richard West to the Intimations Ode. The sense of anachronism adheres to the state of disappointment because the disappointed subject experiences his existence as evacuated and therefore posthumous: he suffers from an atavistic superimposition of states, in which he continues to harbor lingering energies but without objects, and feelings that have been discredited but still persist. He is out of sync with time, like "A Love in desolation masked."[11]

The theme of anachronism recurs in "The Serpent Is Shut Out from Paradise," when Shelley analyses the ambiguous combination of pleasure and pain he feels in Jane's presence; perhaps he should "fly" from her, for her "looks . . . stir / Griefs that should sleep, and hopes that cannot die" (19–20). The speaker unwillingly entertains a persistent capacity for desire that he wants to tranquilize. It is a burden to him, not because he is inhibited by conventional morality nor because his love is unrequited, but because he can no longer fully participate in his own capacity to love; he wants the energy or the conviction to invest in it. His predicament is like Byron's in "On This Day I Complete My Thirty-Sixth Year," except that Shelley's speaker is debarred from throwing his energies into anything else, debarred, that is, by the extremity of his paralyzing self-mistrust.

The situation in "The Magnetic Lady to Her Patient" epitomizes the complex character of the late lyrics' foundering erotic life. The poem begins from a bizarre conceit: it records the speech of the beloved to the absent lover, the center of the poem, who has vanished into a hypnotic trance. Her speech is addressed to some part of him, yet it is not his waking self. This conceit puts the reader in an unusual position with respect to the lover, the lyric subject: we are the accidental audience of his beloved's words, while he lies in haunted sleep. But Jane is not in any case the "real" speaker. The lover ventriloquizes her response, articulating through her refusal his defeated assessment of his life and his stern conclusions about his future.

The poem takes place in a forlorn echo chamber, where the lover drifts in a momentarily becalmed state that subdues but does not extinguish the pain of his unhappiness. Apparently, the lover desires to be put into a stupor, to escape his ills, but in reality he is already leading the life of a broken spirit in a self-willed trance. He is balancing his last energies in a melancholy daze. The idea of hypnosis serves to evoke what his real state of mind is—weak, careful, porous to sorrow. This fantasied scene accurately represents his sense of his own passivity and vain wishfulness.

In his isolation and hopelessness, he is comforted by shadows of his own making—though his comfort is faint. The imaginary voice exhorts him to

> "Sleep, sleep and with the slumber of
>   The dead and the unborn
> Forget thy life and love;
> Forget that thou must wake forever;
>   Forget the world's dull scorn;
> Forget lost health, and the divine
>   Feelings which died in youth's brief morn;
> And forget me, for I can never
>   Be thine."
>
> (19–26)[12]

The repeated injunction to "Forget" introduces the hypnotic rhythm, as of the "magnetic" lady's swinging watch, by which the lover is to be entranced and made to obey; but the "forgets" appear in so vivid a catalog of the evils to be forgotten that the effect is by no means soporific. The poem takes its structure and force from this sort of paradox: every "comforting" anodyne is a wounding reminder.

The lover cannot successfully evade his own consciousness, nor is he trying to: instead he surprisingly combines a will to indulge himself with a wakeful fatalism. He permits himself to freely dream the dreams that satisfy his self-pity, his desires, and his death wish. Yet his halcyon hour, his dream of nirvana, does not suppress the reality of his situation. His is a stern fantasy, determined to incorporate the truth—that of Jane's gentle disinterest, as well as of his own half-heartedness and ruin. He cannot or will not let himself be truly self-indulgent.

The nature of the psychological situation is defined by this tortured relation to fantasy. There are no more fond memories: even the pleasures of nostalgia belong to a happier past. Now reminiscence stings, for the present has invalidated the past, transformed its strength and joys, trusted at the time, to illusory nothings. The lover describes his youth as a resplendent bubble, sublime, obtuse, unsuspecting, irrecoverable—to be recollected in the ironical notice of its irrelevance: he is to forget "the divine / Feelings which died in youth's brief morn." Those hopes and expectations have been permanently marked with the x of anachronism, and therefore cannot be desired without an ambivalent melange of emotions—impatience, grief, longing, frustration, and self-contempt. Experiencing nostalgia provokes a double self-indictment: it seems shameful to have been what one was and to be what one has since become, shameful both to indulge this nostalgia and to refuse it. Recognizing the genuine obsolescence of his past, the lover turns to face two equally contemptible alternatives for his future: corrosive regret or anesthetized stupor.

From this impasse the poem swerves at its end into a still subtler one. Having woken, the lover recalls the irony enslaving him:

> What would cure, that would kill me, Jane:
> And as I must on earth abide
> Awhile, yet tempt me not to break
> My chain. (42–45)[13]

Presumably he has suffered irreversible debilitation and is now too frail to reenter the world of life and hope. It is all he can do to walk his rounds and endure, as tamely as possible, the time he must "on earth abide awhile." Why exchange this fragile torpor for anguish? (Yet he is not nearly as numbed as he could wish.) In helplessness, he puts aside the temptation to "break [his] chain." Restored from his trance, he adopts this third course, neither corroded nor stupefied, but severe. He is to wake, and live, and be silent. Or rather, he is to know just what he knows, to look on himself as remaindered and pathetic; and he is not to languish nor to desire distraction.

What is the emotion expressed in this poem? Oddly enough, it is not longing for the return of love. The love unrequited has itself grown familiar, almost welcome. Still, there is some wishing here, though it is highly muted and hard to identify. It is something like nostalgia for dreaming, of the kind Ashbery identifies in "Self-Portrait in a Convex Mirror," in which the "lapse" of dreams is compared to "a wave breaking on a rock, giving up / Its shape in a gesture which expresses that shape."

Shelley's most intricate and successful treatment of this theme appears in his unfinished last lyric, which was subsequently entitled by someone else "Lines written in the Bay of Lerici."[14] This poem is a portrait of someone who has reached an acute state of impasse with respect to his own imaginative energies. No use of his thoughts is absorbing and free; he is blocked at every turn, whether it is by the cruelty of realism, the torment of his inner "demon," or the transparent and compromised character of his fantasies. The poem consists almost entirely of his tentative effort to entrance himself in a circumscribed and barren reverie. But even this modest ambition is thwarted by his shrunken conception of his deserts and his capacities.

> She left me, and I staid alone
> Thinking over every tone,
> Which though now silent to the ear
> The enchanted heart could hear
> Like notes which die when born, but still
> Haunt the echoes of the hill:
> And feeling ever—O too much—
> The soft vibrations of her touch
> As if her gentle hand even now
> Lightly trembled on my brow;
> And thus although she absent were
> Memory gave me all of her
> That even fancy dares to claim.—
> Her presence had made weak and tame
> All passions and I lived alone,
> In the time which is our own;
> The past and future were forgot
> As they had been, and would be, not.—
> But soon, the guardian angel gone,
> The demon reassumed his throne
> In my faint heart . . . I dare not speak
> My thoughts; but thus disturbed and weak
> I sate and watched the vessels glide
> Along the ocean bright and wide,
> Like spirit-winged chariots sent
> O'er some serenest element
> To ministrations strange and far;

> As if to some Elysian star
> They sailed to for drink to medicine
> Such sweet and bitter pain as mine.   (7–44)

We see him try to take refuge, again and again, in "harmless" exercises of imagination, in all his dreamy and knowingly wishful evocations —of Jane's tenderness in memory, of "spirit-winged" ships sailing on a mission to save him, of this hour itself as a syncope and a reprieve. But he is endlessly inhibited in this quest for a modestly lulling imagination because he knows these exercises are artificial and idle. Seeing he has no other use for his circumvented powers, he flees from this impasse to the sheer sensual pleasure in the natural scene, in the "fresh and light" wind, "the scent of sleeping flowers," and "the sweet warmth of day":

> And the wind that winged their flight
> From the land came fresh and light,
> And the scent of sleeping flowers
> And the coolness of the hours
> Of dew, and the sweet warmth of day
> Was scattered o'er the twinkling bay.   (45–50)

None of this luxury offers a true escape, for his heart is not genuinely "enchanted," as he had tried to tell himself it was. His mind keeps coming back to the fruitlessness of his plight—to images of frustration and violence, and to a death wish finally rendered in the fate of the gullible fish, summoned by and killed in a blind light:

> And the fisher with his lamp
> And spear, about the low rocks damp
> Crept, and struck the fish who came
> To worship the delusive flame:
> Too happy, they whose pleasure sought
> Extinguishes all sense and thought
> Of the regret that pleasure [   ]
> Destroying life alone not peace.   (51–58)

He claims to envy the fish their neutralizing death, which happily "Destroy[s] life alone not peace." This envy is a measure of how thoroughly he has come to accept the verdict of his damaged self-conception, that the psychological deadlock he faces is indissoluble. In the prolonged twilight of his disappointment, he has no permissible hopes or aims for his intellectual and emotional capacities.

In a number of earlier poems, Shelley had used the figure of Actaeon to represent the state of mental self-entrapment and self-enclosure. The most well-known of these appear in his self-portraits, first in *Epipsychidion*:

> Then, as a hunted deer that could not flee,
> I turned upon my thoughts, and stood at bay,
> Wounded and weak and panting.   (272–74)

And then in *Adonais*:

>   he, as I guess,
> Had gazed on Nature's naked loveliness,
> Actaeon-like, and now he fled astray
> With feeble steps o'er the world's wilderness,
> And his own thoughts, along that rugged way,
> Pursued, like raging hounds, their father and their prey.
>   (274–79)[15]

These are figures not merely of being trapped in, but of being betrayed by, one's own mind, consumed by thoughts that have no object or aim. In this specifically Shelleyan trope of disappointment, the subject, having lost viable outlets for its energies, is thrown back upon itself in a vicious circle of isolation and self-contempt. This is his intense and sophisticated version of the Wordsworthian predicament, now powerfully enacted in "Lerici." In "Lerici," the speaker has only two alternatives: perturbation or distraction, yet he cannot succeed in distracting himself —at least not for long—because distraction cannot be deep if it is willed and self-conscious. His wishful fantasies are undermined by their acknowledged emptiness, by the fact that they do not spring from hopes or ambitions the speaker feels entitled to hold, or which he does hold. He has no effective application for his energies but to suffer and torment himself.

The extent of the speaker's debilitation is evident in that he is not able to convert his bitterness into a satisfying rhetoric of disillusionment;

he cannot put his energies even to this use. For he is not in fact bitter; nowhere in the poem does he hint that he has suffered unjustly or met with a malicious fate. That he does not protest or struggle in the net, but seeks only a sort of rarefied and temporary mental accommodation to the uncomfortable situation is the index of his disappointment. He has nothing to say against life; his own existence has somehow failed, but failed in such a way that it has deprived him of the authority, or perhaps of the desire to generalize. Along with much else, a kind of literary zest —a zest for rhetorical opportunity and rhetorical strength—has been exhausted. Here we need to make a significant distinction between Shelley and his speaker because the poem itself can hardly be said to want literary ambition. Nevertheless, it is not an ambition after literary command. This poem has the strange and fascinating aim of representing a voice or psyche that has lost the "narcissistic supplies," the wherewithal of pride in the self, to aspire after expressive force. The poem seeks to bypass the usual routes to rhetorical authority and to achieve literary power by subtler means.

Did Shelley then have the gratification of fulfilling his literary aspirations, and did he thus escape the fate of disappointment himself? "Lerici" was composed on the reverse of one of the draft sheets of "The Triumph of Life." He knew this lyric to be the antithesis and the shadow of the larger poem, as he construed his own failing life to stand in the shadow of his poem's fierce rhetoric. In the manuscript of "The Triumph of Life" he had written "Alas, I kiss you Jane,"[16] inscribed in a small, shaky hand after the line: "And some grew weary of the ghastly dance / And fell, as I have fallen by the way side" (540–41). This is Rousseau speaking, but it is obvious enough that Shelley would have felt the autobiographical resonance of these lines especially since he had already written "Lerici"—a poem which tells how he is weary and fallen by the wayside —earlier in the manuscript. This sad little scrawl, self-consciously inapt or obsolete (hence the small hand) bears the same relation to the manuscript of "The Triumph of Life" that the text of "Lerici" itself does: both are the self-consciously anachronistic interpellations of an erring, lost life. In their confluence, they suggest the displacement or disappearance of Shelley as the subject who might take satisfaction in his own persuasive representation of disappointment.

Last Thoughts of the Unfinished Thinker

LIKE HIS ROMANTIC predecessors, Stevens meditates on the interplay of what Heather Glen has called "vision and disenchantment." He studies the complex history of the longing to believe or love, its disillusionment, its self-contempt, its hesitations, and its renewal or will to renew itself. Described this way, he sounds like the Shelleyan poet that he is, and yet this comparison draws on an incomplete interpretation of Shelley and of Stevens as well. For in both Stevens and Shelley, following the cycle of vision and its failure, another phase ensues, a phase of disappointment when the subject stands humbled before his participation in an irresolvable dialectic and the defeat of his will to be ennobled.

Shelley's "Lines Written in the Bay of Lerici" expresses this kind of self-resignation, though it will seem surprising to say of any first-person poem that it should do so. Poems of disappointment require feats of rhetorical subtlety; that is one reason why poets are drawn to write them, and one reason why it took time for Shelley and Stevens to work out how they might be written. Checked by his reticence and stern temperament, Stevens was late in his development before he was ready to write a poem of unbraced submission. But gradually, over his last several volumes, and culminating in the luminous lyrics of *The Rock,* he abandoned his façade of strength in favor of a quieter verse confessing the diminished provenance of the self.

This chapter explores the relinquishments of Stevens's late work. Of course, he never came to write poems of disappointment exclusively, any more than Wordsworth or Shelley did. Only some poems can be poems of disappointment because, despite its guise of permanence, disappointment is not a sustained condition. The intense but fitful moments of disappointment transfix the poets of the romantic and postromantic tradition; these are the moments to which Wordsworth, Shelley, Stevens, and Ashbery keep returning imaginatively, and which they most want to interpret. Something in the state of disappointment—that state of unforeseen self-dismay—insists on being faithfully described and construed.

Helen Vendler and Harold Bloom are the students of Stevens most attentive to his themes of self and self-definition. Although some of their readings will be cited to supplement the interpretation presented here, there are fundamental differences between their views and my interpretation. In *Wallace Stevens: The Poems of Our Climate,* Bloom makes the case for Stevens as a descendent of Emerson and Whitman, concerned like them to protect the largesse of the transcendental self. In Bloom's view, Stevens is in his most natural or happy vein when he is expressing confidence in the solitary imagination and expatiating in his imaginative powers. Though he was frequently frustrated in his aims and succumbed to doubt or experienced tragic reversal, he intermittently rebounded and continued seeking to recover a brave Emersonian idealism of the self. This determination is the bedrock of his thought, whereas his episodes of disappointment are its epiphenomena. Even his more muted late poems still partake of this determination; the dejected "Madame La Fleurie" "is not characteristic of Stevens's final phase, but rather of the ebb that dialectically keeps crossing the Transcendental influx dominating the phase."[1] Although this version of Stevens sounds almost bluffly affirmative, Bloom's nuanced readings actually pay eloquent tribute to the varieties of elegiac feeling in Stevens. This book argues with Bloom's interpretation in its main outlines, taking the opposite view: it was the pressure of disappointment that cradled Stevens back into poetry, in early middle age, and he toyed with idealism only in reaction to his underlying dejection.

In general terms, my understanding of Stevens is close to the one Vendler advances in her incisive monograph *Wallace Stevens: Words Chosen out of Desire.* Vendler says her aim is to "tether Stevens's poems to human feeling" so as "to remove him from the 'world of ghosts' where he is so often located, and to insist that he is a poet of more than epistemological questions alone."[2] "He has been too little read as a poet of human misery."[3] This book is indebted to Vendler's recovery of the pathos in Stevens, particularly the pathos of the disarmed self. Taking as her epigraph the phrase, "Desire without an object of desire," Vendler devotes her first two chapters to the plight of the subject with a continuing need for emotional investment but no objects in which it can any longer persuade itself to invest. Reading Stevens's oeuvre as a chronicle of the aftermath of the loss of love, she catalogs the forms of this inevitable loss in one forcible paragraph:

> Many of Stevens's poems—read from one angle, most of the best poems—spring from catastrophic disappointment, bitter solitude or personal sadness. It is understandable that Stevens, a man of chilling reticence, should illustrate his suffering in its largest possible terms. That practice does not obscure the nature of the suffering, which concerns the collapse of early hopeful fantasies of love, companionship, success, and self-transformation. As self and beloved alike become, with greater or lesser velocity, the final dwarfs of themselves, and as social awareness diminishes dreams of self-transcendence, the poet sees dream, hope, love and trust—those activities of the most august imagination—crippled, contradicted, dissolved, called into question, embittered. This history is the history of every intelligent and receptive human creature, as the illimitable claims on existence made by each one of us are checked, baffled, frustrated, and reproved—whether by our own subsequent perceptions of their impossible grandiosity, or by the accidents of fate and chance, or by our betrayal of others, or by old age and its failures of capacity.[4]

Although it is difficult to quarrel with the content of this description, one could add to—perhaps even alter—Vendler's definition of what constitutes disappointment. Hers is a catalog of palpable losses; as she says, she wishes "to remind readers that Stevens's poems concern the general emotional experiences common to us all."[5] Later, she dwells particularly on the failure of romantic love, which she takes to be the prototype, and most important instance, of all disappointments. The themes Vendler identifies are pertinent; but Stevens's disappointment may be assigned even deeper sources. For his losses include a decline of confidence in the meaningfulness of art, a collapse of belief in destiny and in the self's purchase on the supramundane, and an ebbing of the pleasure the mind takes in its own powers, in as much as it perceives it does not have authority over experience and thus that it has no higher vocation. These disappointments occur in what Vendler calls the (putatively remote) "epistemological" field. But it is crucial to recognize that for Stevens epistemology is tied to "human feeling"; that is, the loss of hope for the self and its knowledge is as dispiriting as any more tangible erotic loss. Rather than taking the miscarriage of erotic love as the template for disappointment, Stevens treats it as a subspecies of the failure of idealism, the self-destruction of "romance." The most elemental romance for Stevens is the romance of the self, or mind, with its inflated view of its being and destiny. Its deflation is a painful, many-layered surprise. Stevens gathers all his losses under the rubric of this disappointment, which may be called either epistemological or ontological, for in him they come down to the same thing: he is disappointed with the inadequacies of knowledge insofar as they impoverish the status of the subject.

With its dramatic adjectives and vigorous rhythm, Vendler's sweeping rhetoric attributes the authority of demystification both to the Stevens who beheld the chaos of disillusion and to the critic who beholds it in him. But the strength of this presentation belies the true condition of disappointment that the passage describes. For no deep disappointment such as that expressed by Stevens would leave such a residue of gusto. Whereas it would be unfair to fault Vendler for not enacting the enervation of disappointment, her vigor fails to reflect the modulations of Stevens's own rhetoric, and particularly the unique sadness of his late poems in which the equivocal form of his knowledge—the knowledge of having acquired incompletable knowledge—gives him no pleasure. It is not merely his fate—his personality and his individual experience—with which he is disappointed; rather, he comes to relinquish the general promise of selfhood. Just as Bloom presents an exaggerated version of the transcendental Stevens, so does Vendler present a monumentally melancholy Stevens, settled in his tragic apprehension as Bloom's is content in his transumptive solipsism. These hyperbolic renditions of Stevens and of his romantic inheritance are large and mythy models at opposite ends of the spectrum. What follows presents an alternative, a third moment, in which the language and tone of Stevens's late poems follows from a

disheartenment of the self that turns him back, uncertainly, upon an irredeemable world.

Stevens noted in May 1954 that he expected his *Collected Poems* to be his
last work, "though I shall probably go on writing cheerful poems on
good days and cheerless ones on bad."[6] With this plain remark, Stevens
registers a subtle sense of failure in the endowment of poetry and, what
was for him so closely allied to it, the potency of thought. He recognizes
that he is not to gather his forces in a final perfected system. He is not to
arrive at a conclusion, but to go on vacillating, by the whim of his moods,
between fortitude and discouragement. As he put it in "July Mountain,"
we are "Thinkers without final thoughts." His poetry becomes not the
path to a resolution but the sensitive record of mental accidents. Stevens
had unhappily noted the fickleness of thought before:

> In the metaphysical streets, the profoundest forms
> Go with the walker subtly walking there.
> These he destroys with wafts of wakening.
> ("An Ordinary Evening in New Haven," 473)

> And yet what good were yesterday's devotions?
> I affirm and then at midnight, the great cat
> Leaps from the fireside and is gone.
> ("Montrachet-le-Jardin," 264)

With the admission that thought is driven to mutability, Stevens confronts a species of epistemological disappointment: after other hopes have
been defeated, the mind itself, last locus of value, is found to fall short of
its claim to authority. He had hoped thought itself would exert a mastery
that would compensate for his more general helplessness because even
when it takes the tragic view, the understanding affects to rise above all
in panoptical perspective, like a king on his throne. In the face of ordinary frustrations, one holds out the hope, or as Stevens calls it,

> the idea
> That merely by thinking one can,
> Or may, penetrate, not may,
> But can, that one is sure to be able—

> That there lies at the end of thought
> A foyer of the spirit in a landscape
> Of the mind, in which we sit
> And wear humanity's bleak crown.

("Crude Foyer," 305)

As this poem sums it up, thought is "False happiness"; its promise of a redemptive intellectual mastery is delusive because the mind is forgetful, changeable, and confused. We cannot achieve the dream of seeing *sub specie aeternitatis*. As Stevens sadly commented in "Esthetique du Mal": "It was the last nostalgia: that he / Should understand" (322).

This dream expresses the hope of incorporating something eminent into the constitution of our subjectivity, and Stevens repeatedly makes short work of such longings. Yet there is a difference between an expression of anguish at the failure of this dream, and the sobered, matter-of-fact language of his self-description in May 1954. Stevens's plainness represents another stage in the incorporation of disappointment. It reflects surrender rather than reconciliation, for as Stevens in his severity consistently pointed out, the rhetoric of tragic sorrow bears the traces of self-congratulation. Many of his late poems share the strange, equivocal tone of unassuming accommodation. They pay homage to the mind's ambition, the last refuge of transcendental hope, while confessing its failure.

Though a few of his late poems are clearly bleak (such as "Madame La Fleurie"), others seem at first to be more tranquil and happy. "Final Soliloquy of the Interior Paramour" strikes an apparently exultant note:

> Here, now, we forget each other and ourselves.
> We feel the obscurity of an order, a whole,
> A knowledge, that which arranged the rendezvous.
>
> Within its vital boundary, in the mind.
> We say God and the imagination are one . . .
> How high that highest candle lights the dark.   (524)

The last sentence in particular professes confidence that something transcendent has been wrested from the vacuum of existence. And yet, as Bloom boldly asks, "How high does any single candle, even the highest, light the dark?" He justly concludes: "the passage, and the poem, assert less than they seem to assert."[7] Stevens's glad rhetoric champions what turns out to be a minimal claim, and the poem is shot through with the pathos of this self-circumscription.

Jahan Ramazani notices a similar shade of diffidence in the opening lines of Stevens's poetic self-assessment, "The Planet on the Table." The poem's title is evidently an allusion to his own *Collected Poems,* published in 1954. The poem might be taken as a straightforward expression of Stevens's satisfaction with his work, but Ramazani finds more nuances in it and subtler evocations of disappointment: "Looking back on his poems, Stevens modestly sees them as personal utterances, utterances that now satisfy him although they recorded only his own sights and likings."[8] For someone who believed in the cultural importance of poetry, it cannot have been gratifying to conclude that his poems merely "were of a remembered time / Or of something seen that he liked" (532). He does not take a despairing stance, or brusquely dismiss his achievement, but characterizes that achievement with constraint. He takes genuine pleasure in a limited accomplishment; and that is the sign that he has curtailed his hope.

Many of Stevens's late poems relinquish the larger promises of the intellect, while continuing to marvel at the aspiring industry of thought, which perseveres in its own void after it has lost hope of fulfillment and productivity. Consider the last lines of the beautiful "The World as Meditation," in which Penelope, figure of the ambitious mind, is forever suspended in expectation of Ulysses' arrival—the time when thought will achieve the perfect authority it strives for and settle on the height it regards as its provenance. For the mind has often been tantalized with intimations of what Kant called its "higher destiny":

> It was Ulysses and it was not. Yet they had met,
> Friend and dear friend and a planet's encouragement.
> The barbarous strength within her would never fail.
>
> She would talk a little to herself as she combed her hair,
> Repeating his name with its patient syllables,
> Never forgetting him that kept coming constantly so near. (521)

According to Bloom, Penelope as "interior paramour" is "subdued to a continuous process edging toward the little beyond of a possible transcendence."⁹ Though Bloom is circumspect in his wording—the muse is "subdued," the process is only "edging" toward a transcendence, and the transcendence is only "a little beyond"—still, it seems that he has overstated the degree of contentment in this passage. Continuing this line of argument, he says that they manifest a "triumphant tenderness." It does appear that Stevens is kind to thought's aspiration and its longing to join the transcendent. But this is a poem about an unfulfilled hope. The powerful feeling of these lines springs not from continued participation in the dream of transcendence but from continued sympathy for it, which is not the same. Stevens commemorates the dream at a distance. He is moved by the fierce persistence of the mind's aspiration, which never relents one measure in the whole course of life. Even in an old man like himself, "the barbarous strength . . . would never fail."

In its vacuum of isolation, the mind stirs itself with its own vivacity. It sings to itself, to use a Stevensian locution. The dove in "Song of Fixed Accord" stands for the interior life, which inspires itself whether its thoughts are impassioned or depressed:

> Day's invisible beginner,
> The lord of love and of sooth sorrow,
> Lay on the roof
> And made much within her.   (520)

Thought is self-consuming, like time, of which it is a form, and therefore it never seems to itself to have finished its task. In fact, it is always on the verge of embarking. It is perpetually beginning again. Stevens as an old man finds that, though he has come to the end of many things, he has not come to the end of thinking. He feels himself to be a novice at it still.

As he says in "Long and Sluggish Lines," another poem about thought's passionate self-renewal, he is "not born yet." This recognition modulates the initial gloom of the poem into a more enigmatic affect. Stevens begins with a desolate account of the tedium of old age:

> It makes so little difference, at so much more
> Than seventy, where one looks, one has been there before.
>
> Wood-smoke rises through trees, is caught in an upper flow
> Of air and whirled away. But it has often been so.

> The trees have a look as if they bore sad names
> And kept saying over and over one same, same thing.   (522)

Life has exhausted its panoply. And because nothing is ever new, time has lost its forward momentum. As Vendler points out in characterizing other of Stevens's late poems, he has come to occupy a prematurely post-humous existence, and his grief is that of Tithonus, "that one can neither die nor live, as one endures the last protests and affirmations of desire."[10] In other words, the poem up to this point conforms to the emotional logic of disappointment as it was anatomized by the sensibility poets. Stevens' portrayal of grief echoes Gray, who lamented, "In vain to me the smiling mornings shine."

But soon the poem takes a turn through a comic diversion, and reemerges in what seems to be a different, a happier place:

> Wanderer, this is the pre-history of February.
> The life of the poem in the mind has not yet begun.
>
> You were not born yet when the trees were crystal
> Nor are you now, in this wakefulness inside a sleep.   (522)

These lines seem to hold out hope for a rebirth of intellectual experience, a revivification of its relation to the object world. And yet, rather than anticipating a change in the perception of the object, they recall the volatile character of thought itself, which can never cease its permutations.[11] Even in the face of experiential exhaustion, thought remains active, by dint of necessity. In consequence, Stevens realizes that his sense of having attained to a depleted maturity is misguided, for like the "child asleep in its own life," he still dwells within the unbreachable confines of the understanding. He is alert but dim-sighted "in this wakefulness inside a sleep," still wrongly imagining he has emerged into clarity. In fact he has it all to do over: "The life of the poem in the mind has not yet begun." Rather than "shak[ing] off the crushing weight of repetition,"[12] Stevens stumbles upon it in a stranger form. He finds that thought is incorrigibly self-confident; it is perpetually emerging from its haze and thinking to start again. And though Stevens can observe this species of delusion, he can do nothing to put a stop to it. Thus, the condition of disappointment in which the poem began has been transmuted but not reversed.

Earlier in his career, Stevens had written that "It can never be satisfied, the mind, never" ("The Well-Dressed Man with a Beard"). In this
apothegm, the incessant activity of the mind is attributed to its own force
and volition, whereas in "Long and Sluggish Lines" that same activity is
experienced as automatic. The thinker is passive with respect to the urgent industry of his thought. Stevens observes the power of necessity
hastening the mind on in its strange, unstinting, futile quest. But—to be
exact about the tone in which he makes these observations—his view is
not heartening; he is impressed by this necessity, touched even, but he is
hardly exalted.[13]

The poems discussed so far study the work of thought, and in their
muted way sometimes show a fondness for it, despite its failure to achieve
its aims. In fact, these poems evince a curious quiet, a subsiding of urgency, that stems from the recognition that the mind's project will now
never be fulfilled. With the prospect of death, Stevens's respect for the
fervor of thought becomes musing and valedictory. Yet his awareness
that the work of the mind is soon to be scattered, that its fraught life has
led to nothing, sometimes spikes, and he expresses his frustration with
anguish. The life of the mind is really all there is to life, as far as he is
concerned, but the volatility of thoughts condemns them to evanescence,
both within the mind and within the world of which they make so significant but so intangible a part. For this reason, as he begins miserably
in "The Rock," "It is an illusion that we were ever alive" (525); it is as if
we had never been. What remains of the past does not include us: "The
houses still stand, / Though they are rigid in rigid emptiness" (525). With
this image Stevens may be recalling the house of "The Auroras of Autumn," in which mother and child were "together" and it was "warm."
The house may still stand, but what it was, the memory of it, is bound to
mortality along with the child:

> Even our shadows, their shadows, no longer remain.
> The lives these lived in the mind are at an end.
> They never were. (525)

But though the past and the body, which lodges its memory, may fail in
this way, do not Stevens's poems record his thoughts indelibly? In his
present mood, he thinks his poems frail and inadequate as an embodi-

ment of life: "The sounds of the guitar / Were not and are not" (525).
They are trivial; their promises are "absurd."

In "Madame La Fleurie," the darkest poem in *The Rock*, Stevens
gives a fuller statement of his conviction that his life has vanished into
the smoke of the past, into "illusion." He was brought forth in order to
nourish a fertile, arduous, passionate inner experience that will merely
die with him. For now his real intellectual achievement—what travail has
brought him to know and understand—is to be swallowed up in earth,
from which he came.

> Weight him down, O side-stars, with the great weightings of
>   the end.
> Seal him there. He looked in a glass of the earth and
>   thought he lived in it.
> Now, he brings all that he saw into the earth, to the waiting
>   parent.
> His crisp knowledge is devoured by her, beneath a dew.   (507)

Earth is the malevolent mother who has cruelly designed him to suffer
his worst frustration at her hands. She has made him live, struggle, and
achieve knowledge—including the knowledge of her treachery—only
in order to extinguish his history in the end, returning his body to its
inert, material uses:

> His grief is that his mother should feed on him, himself and
>   what he saw,
> In that distant chamber, a bearded queen, wicked in her
>   dead light.   (507)

In place of this unrelieved angst, Stevens in his late lyrics usually adopts
a more modulated tone of acceptance that still manages to convey as much
pathos. "Lebensweisheitspielerei" will be the last example of this complicated effect. The poem laments the irretrievable loss of the grandeur
of life, submerged in a miasma of mediocrity. (As he had put it in "The
Plain Sense of Things": "The great structure has become a minor house.
/ No turban walks across the lessened floors.") The conviction of diminishment appears to be final, and Stevens is consequently sorrowful rather
than exasperated. He grieves that he has no access to the transcendental,

that glimpses of the "inhuman" and sublime no longer visit him. He finds himself now in a simply "human" world.

> Weaker and weaker, the sunlight falls
> In the afternoon. The proud and the strong
> Have departed.
>
> Those that are left are the unaccomplished,
> The finally human,
> Natives of a dwindled sphere.
>
> Their indigence is an indigence
> That is an indigence of the light,
> A stellar pallor that hangs on the threads. (504–5)

This "stellar pallor" is a light of common day, to be contrasted both with Wordsworth's celestial gleam and with the varieties of astral promise in Shelley. But like Wordsworth in "Elegiac Stanzas," Stevens finds something to recoup out of the devastation of his hopes for a vital destiny. It is only that what he recoups is so small. He takes comfort in the ordinariness that is left, in persons without wings, because he is touched by the forlorn persistence of the real.

> Little by little, the poverty
> Of autumnal space becomes
> A look, a few words spoken.
>
> Each person completely touches us
> With what he is and as he is,
> In the stale grandeur of annihilation. (505)

This is Stevens's version of embracing "the Kind," though Stevens does without Wordsworth's deceptive piety. He had pursued the same strategy, an alliance with the commonplace, in "Wild Ducks, People and Distances," when, abandoning his old contempt for "the grand ideas of the villages," he conceded that "the villages" brought him aid and comfort; they "Held off the final, fatal distances, / Between us and the place in which we stood" (328–29). He is sincere, but it is clear that he takes his reconciliation at a price, and knows it, in relinquishing his loftier ambitions. In the lyrics of *The Rock*, Stevens surrenders his tenacious hope for existential resolution; and his surrender seems profound because he has ceased to keen and protest.

There is, then, a late Stevens—a Stevens who like Shelley came to articulate disappointment in a way he could not earlier—whereas there is not a late Wordsworth. Yet Stevens did not discover a new subject matter in his last work. Remaining consistent in his themes, his poems instead evolved in rhetoric and tone, so as to alter, subtly, his familiar thoughts. The study of Stevens's earliest mature work shows it to be thematically continuous with the lyrics in *The Rock*, while it is poetically divergent.

Stevens had reflected on the pain of disappointment in his first volume, *Harmonium*, and had continued to do so ever since, sometimes in unhappiness, sometimes analytically, and sometimes with a vigorous rebuff. Only rarely did he take a specific personal disappointment as his subject ("Le Monocle de Mon Oncle," on the discontent of his middle-aged marriage, is an example). Rather, he expressed his sorrow in more general or abstract terms: he rued the poverties of life as they are—to use Shelley's language—unveiled one after another. Finding fault with the nature of life and the condition of being a subject, he expresses disappointment that is immediately and explicitly ontological.

Stevens's chagrin over the terms of existence is fanned out in a variety of themes, some finer and more original than others. The mind must come to grip with a number of losses: the failure of erotic idealization ("Le Monocle de Mon Oncle"), the decline of belief in God and the comforts of traditional religion ("Sunday Morning"), the rebuke to ambition and the discouragement of vocation ("The Comedian as the Letter C"), the withdrawal of glamour and promise from ordinary life ("Banal Sojourn"), and the collapse of hope that the self shares in the nature of the transcendent ("The Man Whose Pharynx Was Bad"). After *Harmonium*, Stevens's themes of disappointment become more sophisticated, but they are not transformed.

It is artificial to make sharp distinctions among these themes because they are continually regathered under the same wave of existential dismay. All follow from Stevens's surprise at discovering that his deep assumptions of ontological security have been overturned, though he hardly knew he harbored them until he found them to be false. He dwells implicitly on the thought Shelley enunciated, "Alas, this is not what I thought life was."[14] And, like Wordsworth and Shelley, he finds it a difficult, obsessing task to say how exactly he has been disappointed. So he follows the topic through its branching variations, seeking sometimes to make it elemental and other times, rarefied.

A covenant, a promise, a certainty of value have been stripped away. The world turns out to be naked and poor. It is not merely a world without God and the immortality of the soul but altogether without a telos— a bounded, temporal world in which our actions have no claim beyond their moment. As Stevens puts it in "Sunday Morning":

> We live in an old chaos of the sun,
> Or old dependency of day and night,
> Or island solitude, unsponsored, free,
> Of that wide water, inescapable. (70)

Experience without a transcendent origin and destiny is pitiful, aimless experience, in which we are hard pressed to know what to want or how best to employ our forces. There is something fateful about this pared-down existence. Platonic and Christian dualism tell of a grander world, which touches upon ours and ratifies its meaning. But the singleton world is lonely, "unsponsored," "inescapable"—all ours and nothing more. Yet it is also "free," and Stevens will sometimes make much of this potential value. "Evening without Angels" assures us

> Bare night is best. Bare earth is best. Bare, bare,
> Except for our own houses, huddled low
> Beneath the arches and their spangled air. (137–38)

For many, this is the characteristic Stevens—the Stevens who wrests, or aims to wrest, a positive conclusion from his secular anxieties. Though it is tempting instead to regard these genial episodes as inauthentic, that judgment might also be reflexive. The truth is, as Stevens said, that he wrote both sad and cheerful poems. On his cheerful days, he wrote poems like "Notes toward a Supreme Fiction," in which he is excited by the promise of poetry. But his cheerfulness always exerts itself in contrast to his disappointment, whereas his disappointment stands alone. It is to the apprehension of a sad reality that he continuously responds, whether his response is colored by submission or resistance.

A recoil typically follows the burst of humanist elation, springing from the fear that the glamour of an "unsponsored" existence cannot last. The immanent sublime fades. If the world is mediocre, then the self deprived of transcendent provenance will come to know itself as mundane. It will repine at its imprisonment and feel nostalgia for the lost thrill of sighting the exalted, for lost feelings of power and self-delight. Stevens wrote many such elegies for the compromised self, and many poems of nostalgia for its deluded hours. Experience subsides into the routine; the self cased in "the dreadful sundry of this world" ("O, Florida, Venereal Soil," 47) sorrows at its cheerless fortune.

Several short poems in *Harmonium* exemplify these themes. "Banal Sojourn" and "Depression before Spring" both lament the withdrawal or decay of transcendent feeling and a consequent miring in the mundane. In the Intimations Ode, Wordsworth lamented that the natural world. though still beautiful, had lost its filiation with otherworldly greatness. Stevens expresses this same disappointment in a modern idiom:

> The hair of my blonde
> Is dazzling,
> As the spittle of cows.
> Threading the wind . . .
>
> But ki-ki-ri-ki
> Brings no rou-cou,
> No rou-cou-cou.
>
> But no queen comes
> In slipper green.

("Depression before Spring," 63)

"Banal Sojourn" immediately precedes "Depression before Spring," and makes its theme clear in the title: we find ourselves to be lodged in a tedious habitation.

> Pardie! Summer is like a fat beast, sleepy in mildew,
> Our old bane, green and bloated, serene, who cries,
> "That bliss of stars, that princox of evening heaven!"
>   reminding of seasons,
> When radiance came running down, slim through the bareness.

> And so it is one damns that green shade at the bottom of the
>   land.
> For who can care at the wigs despoiling the Satan ear?
> And who does not seek the sky unfuzzed, soaring to the
>   princox?
> One has a malady, here, a malady. One feels a malady.   (62–63)

Stevens's malaise is the malaise of Wordsworthian recollection: he used to be bewitched by the real, and now, without willing it, he has been disenchanted.

Yet some poems in *Harmonium* express the opposite point of view; they maintain a continued confidence in the transcendent powers of mind and imagination. In "The Place of the Solitaires," for example, or the last lines of "Stars at Tallapoosa," intellectual severity paradoxically restores the promise of intense apprehension, "Making recoveries of young nakedness / And the lost vehemence the midnights hold" (72). It took time for Stevens to arrive at the impressive fusion of moods in his late poems, which combine chagrin and accommodation under the general aegis of unresolved disappointment. In *Harmonium,* Stevens is still separating out and schematizing these attitudes.

In "The Man Whose Pharynx Was Bad," the self is more elaborately caught up in the "malady of the quotidian." It feels itself to be, as Kierkegaard would put it, steeped in time—unable to rise above the conditions of immediate experience so as to see and think *sub specie aeternitatis.* The speaker hears the wind blow on "the shutters of the metropoles" and the bell tolling "the grand ideas of the villages." This is the contemptible round of the transient and ordinary, figured in terms of complacent bourgeois routine: if only the self could pursue a challenging intensity; if only it could find the resources within itself to transcend the dimming life fosters; if only there were some element of experience to encourage this ambition. Even harsh trials calling forth an Emersonian defiance would be preferable to this disheartening captivation by the mundane. But the self cannot stop time and create a pause in which to feel free. Instead, it is perpetually demoralized by its subjection to what Ashbery calls "the waterwheel of days":

Perhaps, if winter once could penetrate
Through all its purples to the final slate,
Persisting bleakly in an icy haze,

One might in turn become less diffident,
Out of such mildew plucking neater mould
And spouting new orations of the cold.
One might. One might. But time will not relent. (96)

Stevens's thinking takes an interesting turn here: the declining magic of experience is no longer blamed on the banality of the given world, but found to inhere in the self's own insufficiencies, which it perceives with mortification. Time may be charged with checking the self's aspirations, but it is clearly a weakness in the self's constitution that has made it the prey of time.

In "Anatomy of Monotony," the "spirit" is "aggrieved" because of its mortality and its nothingness, both products of a real indifference in the order of nature. It is also ashamed of its willingness to be duped in this matter, to construe the world sentimentally, as a world of love and change:

The body walks forth naked in the sun
And, out of tenderness or grief, the sun
Gives comfort, so that other bodies come,
Twinning our phantasy and our device,
And apt in versatile motion, touch and sound
To make the body covetous in desire
Of the still finer, more implacable chords.
So be it. Yet the spaciousness and light
In which the body walks and is deceived,
Falls from that fatal and that barer sky,
And this the spirit sees and is aggrieved. (108)

"Aggrieved" carries a double meaning. The spirit is "aggrieved" in that it feels insulted or wronged by nature's stinginess, coupled with her deceit. But, more powerfully, it is unhappy on its own account, seeing itself as paltry, ill-fated, and eager to be beguiled.

In "Anglais Mort à Florence," a poem from his second volume, Stevens gives the emotional history of someone who is shrinking in his own eyes, like the spirit of "Monotony." Whereas Stevens in these comparatively early poems adopts a vigorous and stern attitude when he writes about disappointment in his own voice, he permits the "Englishman" to be genuinely enfeebled, subsiding in his pride and strength. The opening theme of diminishing élan, wherein desire loses its objects, might belong to an account of simple disillusionment. But already there are hints that something more than the objects of the object world has lost its luster. The Englishman mourns not merely the poverty of diversions but a poverty felt within the self.

> A little less returned for him each spring.
> Music began to fail him. Brahms, although
> His dark familiar, often walked apart.
>
> His spirit grew uncertain of delight,
> Certain of its uncertainty, in which
> That dark companion left him unconsoled
>
> For a self returning mostly memory.   (148)

This self is dwindling in its experience of itself; its vital narcissism now a thing of the past, it is becoming numb, losing its hold on both the immediate world and the vista of the future. The Englishman finds that the gloss of existence is wearing thin—the moon now appears "naked and alien, / More leanly shining from a lankier sky" (149)—but he braces himself to accommodate this diminishment. He must undertake a struggle (out of despair) to accept a lessened life and a lessened self-conception.

> He used his reason, exercised his will,
> Turning in time to Brahms as alternate
>
> In speech. He was that music and himself.
> They were particles of order, a single majesty:
> But he remembered the time when he stood alone.
>
> He stood at last by God's help and the police;
> But he remembered the time when he stood alone.
> He yielded himself to that single majesty;
>
> But he remembered the time when he stood alone,
> When to be and delight to be seemed to be one,
> Before the colors deepened and grew small.   (149)

These final lines sum up a dramatic change in self-conception and its complex aftermath: the development of a new self-contempt and nostalgia for an earlier self, combined with an opposing spirit of humility and resignation. The Englishman has a consciousness, not of having fallen from himself in some general way, but of having deteriorated precisely in so far as his estimation of the self's powers has shrunk. (For "self-conception" in this case means not his view of himself in particular, but of *the* self—that is, of the ontological status of the self.) The Englishman grasps at straws, like Wordsworth, and nominally, at least, defers to an impersonal "order" that is to take the place of a lost perception of self-sufficiency, which is seen in retrospect to have been both illusory and enabling. In fact, the poem's central line could stand as a parody of the pieties that conclude "Tintern Abbey" and the Intimations Ode: "He stood at last by God's help and the police." He has accepted that the self has no autonomy and no grandeur; he acknowledges the need for a higher power (anything beyond himself, God perhaps, or just some regulatory institution like the police), and he gives up the fantasy of "standing alone." But he is ashamed of making this accommodation, for he suspects there was a species of honor in maintaining the abandoned fantasy.

Stevens wrote "Anglais Mort à Florence" in the third person, and for once this strategy is truly distancing (as opposed to his use of "one," or "we," or "he" when he means himself). He was not quite ready to identify with the pitiable victim of disappointment. But he came close to writing the self-portrait of disappointment in "The Comedian as the Letter C." George Bornstein compares "The Comedian" to Shelley's "Alastor" and that comparison seems apt on a number of counts.[15] Like Shelley, Stevens wrote "The Comedian" during a phase of frustration early in his career; and like "Alastor," "The Comedian" details the way in which the inner and the outer world conspire to defeat poetic vocation. Crispin begins in a "green brag." He is a "marvelous sophomore," like Wordsworth's Chatterton, the "marvelous boy" whose glorious beginning and sordid end exemplify the baffling of the poet's self-excitement:

> I thought of Chatterton, the marvelous Boy,
> The sleepless Soul that perished in his pride;
> Of him who walked in glory and in joy

Following his plough, along the mountain-side:
By our own spirits are we deified:
We Poets in our youth begin in gladness;
But thereof come in the end despondency and madness.

(Resolution and Independence, 43–49)

Crispin's fate is not the dramatic one of the "Alastor" poet's strange death
or of Chatterton's and Burns's "despondency and madness." It is the modernist equivalent: a life foreshortened by its submission to mediocrity.
Crispin feels the persistence of vocation (the desire to write) in the face
of decay in his self-confidence and a disintegration of his subject matter.
His disabling takes place stage by stage: interest in the transcendent is
revealed to be merely "romance" while the "realist" comes to recognize
his insignificance vis-à-vis the real. Writing seems not to add anything to
the real—nor does the story of this loss itself seem worth telling (see v—
"Was he to bray this in profoundest brass / Arointing his dreams with
fugal requiems? / Was he to . . . Scrawl a tragedian's testament?" [41]).
Pinched by these discouragements, Crispin hears the call of the sensual
and immediate, "the ready and easy way":

In the presto of the morning, Crispin trod,
Each day, still curious, but in a round
Less prickly and much more condign than that
He once thought necessary. Like Candide,
Yeoman and grub, but with a fig in sight,
And cream for the fig and silver for the cream,
A blonde to tip the silver and to taste
The rapey gouts. Good star, how that to be
Annealed them in their cabin ribaldries!
Yet the quotidian saps philosophers
And men like Crispin like them in intent,
If not in will, to track the knaves of thought.   (42)

Sorry immediate comforts jolly Crispin out of his adolescent intensity.
Thus his "green brag" is eroded by experience.

One hears anger and self-disdain in this and many comparable passages from "The Comedian" in which the speaker decries Crispin's fall.
Stevens spurns the banality of experience with a force that recalls Shelley's commanding asperity:

After brief space,
From every form the beauty slowly waned;

From every firmest limb and fairest face
The strength and freshness fell like dust, and left
The action and the shape without the grace

Of life.   ("The Triumph of Life," 518–23)

Stevens's attitude toward the perils described in "The Comedian" is acrimonious and uncompromising; like Shelley in "The Triumph of Life," he rejects existence on its terms. His disgust is conveyed in the poem's famously rebarbative style—its expectorant clusters of *c* sounds and torturously esoteric diction. Stevens's indignation is also, somewhat paradoxically, reflected in a gloomy fatalism through which he spurns milder and more accommodating views. Crispin is summarily entombed:

The curtains flittered and the door was closed.   (42)

        So deep a sound fell down
It was as if the solitude concealed
And covered him and his congenial sleep.
So deep a sound fell down it grew to be
A long soothsaying silence down and down.   (42)

But day by day, now this thing and now that
Confined him   (40)

The very man despising honest quilts
Lies quilted to his poll in his despite.   (41)

This is the wounded extremism of impatience. It hardly matters to Stevens if the life steeped in the apprehension of its mediocrity has any distinct shades. The self and the world are faulted and expelled, spat out.

Because the force of this rejection communicates a surviving rigor, a strength and pride in the speaker, Stevens's rhetoric does not participate in the psychology he describes. His pretense of command distinguishes the speaker from the complacent Crispin, his specter, and alter ego. This evasion of identification prevents "The Comedian" from being a true poem of disappointment, in the sense of enacting it—as Shelley's or Stevens's late lyrics do. "The Comedian" is thus a poem of disappointment, thematically, while rhetorically, it is a poem of disillusionment. For neither psychological experience nor psychological understanding are at issue, but rhetorical skill. Stevens makes it clear in the ending of "Le Monocle de Mon Oncle" that he wishes to keep faith with the chastened accommodations of disappointment, yet he is unable to prevent his tone from swerving into a conventional pattern of recovery and affirmation. In this way, the poetics of *Harmonium* fails to keep pace with Stevens's finer intuitions.

In his second volume, *Ideas of Order,* Stevens continued to write poems of disillusionment in the rhetorical mode of *Harmonium*. Then, after divagating through the metapoieic themes of *The Man with the Blue Guitar,* and the mostly tired verse in *Parts of a World,* he began to evolve a new tonality in *Transport to Summer.* Of course, he still wrote poems of disillusionment as well, poems in which his stance is appalled and grim. "No Possum, No Sop, No Tatters" offers a powerful instance of what Vendler calls Stevens's "brutality," his savage utterance of despair. It presents the stark perspective of depression, using grotesque images to convey a paranoid horror of life.

> Bad is final in this light.
>
> In this bleak air the broken stalks
> Have arms without hands. They have trunks
>
> Without legs or, for that, without heads. (293–94)

There is no margin for humility in this frightening state; the encroachment of experience has to be repulsed.

But in another frame of mind, Stevens recalls that every conclusion is provisional. Bad is only final in *this* light; the certainty of having reached the last truth, however unwelcome, will soon be superseded by another certainty and another truth, which will also present themselves as final. As Emerson said, our moods do not believe in one another. This form of self-deception is particularly acute in the case of disillusionment, which considers itself to have rent all the veils of deception and arrived at the solid clarity of negation. It promises to settle the mind. But its promises

are spurious, in part because our capacity for investment remains un-
daunted and picks its nimble way to a new love. As Stevens put it in *The
Necessary Angel*: "we think that we have long since outlived the ideal.
The truth is that we are constantly outliving it and yet the ideal itself remains alive with an enormous life."[16] As if echoing the Japanese proverb
"Life is a bridge from dream to dream," Stevens says in "An Ordinary
Evening in New Haven" that our life proffers "Inescapable romance, inescapable choice / Of dreams, disillusion as the last illusion" (468). Our
penchant for idealization is intractable, and even disillusionment embraces its own form of the ideal.

Someone who has descried this fruitless round, will find himself in a
psychological quandary, divided between the inevitable will to idealize
and the expectation of its equally inevitable defeat, or between the authority of disillusionment and the anticipation of its collapse. This is the
quandary of disappointment. In Stevens it leads to an abandonment of
pride in the observing self, that is, to a rhetorical change in which he surrenders the pleasure of declaiming for the muted tones of regretful concession. He becomes weary, as in "Less and Less Human, O Savage
Spirit," in which, knowing that the longing for the transcendent—the
god—is obdurate, but knowing also that awareness of its incorrigibility
compromises the longing, he can only plead that it should become memorial and subdued:

> If there must be a god in the house, must be,
> Saying things in the rooms and on the stair,
>
> Let him move as the sunlight moves on the floor,
> Or moonlight, silently, as Plato's ghost
>
> Or Aristotle's skeleton. Let him hang out
> His stars on the wall. He must dwell quietly.
>
> He must be incapable of speaking, closed,
> As those are: as light, for all its motion, is;
>
> As color, even the closest to us, is;
> As shapes, though they portend us, are.   (327–28)

Life has failed to answer his desire for contact with the transcendent, but the desire lingers on, like the ineffectual god whom Stevens would wish to suppress but admits he cannot. Both the phantom of the god and the once enchanting qualities of the material world—light and color—continue beckoning to us while failing to satisfy us. For as Stevens characterizes it in the last line of this poem, our world is one of which "we are too distantly a part" (328).

"Less and Less Human" uniquely combines longing and resistance, insight and helplessness: this is the special pathos of disappointment in late Stevens. He appears to have found this new voice rather suddenly, in the lyrics of *Transport to Summer.* If, as a heuristic exercise, one were to identify the moment when this attitude emerges, it would be in "The Bed of Old John Zeller" when Stevens accepts his place in the family line. This acknowledgment comes at the same time that he gives in to the tenacity of wish-fulfillment. Rather than rejecting it as intellectual error, he owns his desire for what he cannot have, figuring it as a resurgence of the archaic, familial origin: "This is the habit of wishing, as if one's grandfather lay / In one's heart and wished as he had always wished" (327). The poignancy of these lines is naked; no brusqueness or severity protects the dignity of their author.

It is no accident that this note of compassion should be introduced along with a reference to Stevens's family. A defense against personal references was breaking down at this period. Stevens was beginning to think more about his family—both his immediate family and his ancestors (see "Dutch Graves in Bucks County"). As his metaphor from "Zeller" suggests, he had ceased to resist identification with those whom he had willfully escaped; the prospect of escape had grown less desirable, and, in any case, he saw that escape was impossible.

The pathos of the late poems often emerges through such sad reflections about his family. The disappointment of the family romance becomes a more intimate name for the failure of the self's aspirations. As we have seen, there are many ideas in Stevens through which he explores the theme of disappointment with the self, its powers, and its lot: there is, for example, his interest in the chagrin of mortality, the failure of access to the transcendent, the elusiveness of mastery through knowledge, and the artificiality of compensation. In a number of late poems, this complex of disappointments is figured in the lingering frustration of the family romance.

Stevens's most poignant lament for the end of the family romance appears in "The Auroras of Autumn," his only long poem that concentrates on the anatomy of disappointment. It is a poem of almost pure elegy, standing midway between the depression of *Harmonium* and the mysterious equivocations of *The Rock*. It portrays Stevens, speaking in propria persona, as he confronts a profound reduction in his view of the achievements and comforts available to the avid self.

Bloom has identified "The Auroras of Autumn" as the only one of Stevens's long poems that can be regarded as a crisis lyric. As befits a crisis lyric, it is set in a desperate present wherein even the subtler forms of ambition and expectation have lost their venue. Vendler points out that the sense of present personal urgency is stronger in "The Auroras of Autumn" (and its companion piece, "Credences of Summer") than it had ever been before.[17] Not just the use of the present, but the representation of an "I" floundering in an emergency, is unprecedented: "No previous long poem in Stevens's collections had ever placed a lyric speaker firmly in the landscape of the present moment: all had used the haziness of a past distancing or the impersonality of an invented persona."[18] Stevens's use of an authentic first person helps to make "The Auroras" a true poem of disappointment, an owning of the lessened fate he turned aside in "The Comedian." Just as when he confessed that his grandfather lay in his heart, so in his frank admission of crisis in this poem, Stevens permits an old pretension to collapse. He does so deliberately because his theme is the crumbling of the hope for the self's autonomy and distinction.

The present is the tense of disappointment because disappointment spells enclosure in the immediate and a grappling with the question: what to do now? In the opening lines of canto I, Stevens echoes the deictic urgency of "Tintern Abbey," in which Wordsworth is arrested by a particular visual scene: by "this dark sycamore," "These waters," "these steep and lofty cliffs," "these orchard-tufts," "these hedgerows." The radiant auroras naturally capture Stevens's attention. For both poets, the vividness of the present scene displaces the province of the mind, the work of memory and reflection, and so precipitates anxiety about the flowering of fantasy in solitude (each asks: "Have I dreamt up false hopes, to keep me company?"). The serpent of canto 1 embodies the false hope of living contentedly because powerfully in one's world. And yet unlike Wordsworth, Stevens's relation to his fantasy is already a vexed one: his poem begins in mature skepticism.

The serpent is malevolent because he is superior. He is "bodiless," un-like us—"*His* head is air" (411; my italics). He reproaches us with his re-moteness, for he images an escape from Cartesian dualism, or the anguish of having a material body that interferes with transcendent aspirations. Because he is free in this way, he fulfills a second, more rarefied but no less fundamental dream: the dream of having panoptical vision or per-fect clarity of mind, with eyes that "open and fix on us in every sky" (411). He has achieved intellectual authority, as "the master of the maze / Of body and air and forms and images / Relentlessly in possession of happiness" (411). Yet his image is its own critique, collapsing under the weight of its perfection. Therefore, the serpent's "poison" is to make us "disbelieve" in the fantasy he stands for. We know that his enviable ca-pacity may be unreal; he may be a wish-fulfillment, "Another image at the end of the cave / Another bodiless for the body's slough" (411)—and yet we go on beholding him, amazed at his brilliant display. His image is caught in the dialectic of repudiation and reinvestment.

With this perception, Stevens can only retreat into idle, if lyrical, reminiscence:

> His meditations in the ferns,
> When he moved so slightly to make sure of sun,
> Made us no less as sure. We saw in his head,
> Black beaded on the rock, the flecked animal,
> The moving grass, the Indian in his glade.   (411)

The shift into past tense shows that we have moved backwards, intellec-tually as well as temporally. Stevens recalls the pleasure of a contented mind, trusting in itself, and recalls this pleasure with especial love be-cause suspicion has blocked the road to it. He gives us his version of Wordsworth's hapless protest in "Tintern Abbey": "If this / Be but a vain belief, yet oh! how oft, / How oft, in spirit, have I turned to thee." (49 ff.). From this point on, through the next several cantos, Stevens abandons himself to nostalgia for his old ontological confidence, the confidence that made faith in the serpent possible. He devotes himself to reckoning his losses, describing his present disarmed state in canto 2, and the atrophy of his expectations—figured as the end of the family romance—in cantos 3 and 4.

The deserted beach of canto 2 images the internal landscape of emptiness—or, since disappointment is full of thoughts—the prospect of emptiness. "It is white" here, as we would expect—lonely and blank—but not the intense white of blazing adolescent alienation; it is "the white of an aging afternoon," which knows that it once was brighter and had a prouder spirit of defiance:

> The flowers against the wall
> Are white, a little dried, a kind of mark
>
> Reminding, trying to remind, of a white
> That was different, something else, last year
> Or before. (412)

Like Shelley in the "Ode to the West Wind," Stevens remembers that he used to have enough security about his participating in the transcendental to challenge the strength of nature, or fate. Stevens suffers a middle-aged version of Shelley's frustrating awareness that if he retained his former spirit he "would ne'er have striven / As thus with thee in prayer in my sore need" (51–52). There is no prayer in the austere Stevens, of course, but his musing entails the dark knowledge that the mind has no self-sustaining glory with which to counter the starkness of existence in the "natural" world. He had had such confidence when he was "visible," as a younger, "self-deified" poet; then, in his fervor and arrogance, he was of "the solid of white, the accomplishment of an extremist in an exercise." But he is not visible now; he "turns blankly on the sand," lingering in an atmosphere of increasing desolation:

> A cold wind chills the beach.
> The long lines of it grow longer, emptier,
> A darkness gathers though it does not fall. (412)

He measures his diminishment by observing the ever-renewable power
of the natural sublime:

> He observes how the north is always enlarging the change,
>
> With its frigid brilliances, its blue-red sweeps
> And gusts of great enkindlings, its polar green,
> The color of ice and fire and solitude.   (412)

But the countering "ice and fire and solitude" of his younger self have
been replaced by the apologetic longings of a middle-aged man.

Charles Berger points out that canto 3 describes the destruction of the
House, the classic subject of Greek tragedy, and that the end of Stevens's
nuclear family was much on his mind at this time (he was now the sole
survivor). He forcefully described his perturbation at the loss of the past
in a letter written soon after receiving the Bollingen prize, when his old
and forgotten friends from Reading had written to congratulate him:
"This has been a really moving experience. . . . But, also, this experience
reveals the occasionally frightening aspect of the past, into which so
many that we have known have disappeared, almost as if they had never
been real."[19] The language of this letter is echoed in the lament that
opens "The Rock," quoted earlier. But when Stevens says "farewell" to
his family and his past in "The Auroras," he says "farewell to an idea" as
well, that is, to what the family and the past and the memory of the past
represent, or rather, what the capacity not to surrender them yet would
mean.

In canto 3, Stevens describes an archaic loss, the loss of a sense of ontological security as represented by the exalted status of the "mother."

> Farewell to an idea . . . The mother's face,
> The purpose of the poem, fills the room.
> They are together, here, and it is warm,
>
> With none of the prescience of oncoming dreams.
> It is evening. The house is evening, half-dissolved.
> Only the half they can never possess remains,

Still-starred. It is the mother they possess,
Who gives transparence to their present peace.
She makes that gentler that can gentle be.

And yet she too is dissolved, she is destroyed.
She gives transparence. But she has grown old.
The necklace is a carving not a kiss.

The soft hands are a motion not a touch.
The house will crumble and the books will burn.   (413)

The "mother" (whatever else she may symbolize) is the locus of meaning and source of ontological comfort, that which keeps one company in
one's heart and saves one from feeling utterly cast adrift; she is the "interior paramour." The sense of enveloping security that a child may feel in
its mother's presence best evokes this "mother's" power to reassure. What
does it mean for her to have "grown old"? She has failed to be invulner-
able and thus to secure protection for her child. The parent's magic is
gone. "The necklace is a carving not a kiss. / The soft hands are a motion
not a touch." The figure and gestures of the mother lose their glamour,
their power to inspire, their divine aura of transcendence. They have
fulfilled their destiny of subsiding into the mundane.

Thus, though materially everything remains the same, the man loses
an idea that was a charm for him, and now he sees the life of which he
was a part as devoted to insignificance and death: "The house will crumble and the books will burn." He still loves his paramour, his mother, his
dream, but somehow she has worn through her power to solace him.
As he puts it in "Things of August," "She has given too much, but not
enough. / She is exhausted and a little old" (495). In the language of canto
3, they will still be together "here," where "it is warm" in the tranquil,
"half-dissolved" evening, but this idyll has revealed how incomplete and
insubstantial it will always be: "Only the half they can never possess
remains" (413). "They are at ease in a shelter of the mind" which takes
the edge off the fiercely "boreal night," but their refuge is consciously
delimited and temporary. Stevens knows that soon "A wind will spread
its windy grandeurs round / And knock like a rifle-butt against the
door" (414).

Here he has formulated a notably Kleinian view: union with the mother stands for the feeling that something in our existence is benevolent to us, and so for a time of being at peace in our world. Stevens thinks this is a faith native to childhood.[20] When the mother shrinks into a mortal thing, the illusion of the parent's power and freedom is disproved, and a major source of ontological confidence is vacated: for the parent's freedom is a gage of the child's own freedom. The loss is intellectual as well as emotional. It produces a change in the perception of the world because it includes forsaking the notion that experience is teleologically ordered—that is, ordered toward a transcendental aim. That is of course a major theme for Stevens. Even when he argues for acceptance of it, the loss is undiminished. Our world turns out to be a world of accidents, floating loose and free. And when, as in "Evening without Angels," Stevens chooses to be affirmative about this, he claims that one can match the revealed spareness of this world with the strength of one's own clarity. But the thought of this naked contingency is grievous; it represents the disappointment of a confidence that is instinctive to us and is perceived as necessary to our happiness. This confidence begins in the child's assurance that its parents are unique, and that their world is therefore of a "mythy," both dramatic and meaningful, order.

To give up this frail warmth in the world might seem like the end, but as canto 4 reminds us, "The cancellings, / The negations are never final" (414). The existence that has watched the mother "grow old" and that has accepted its solitude may find its way to a new self-affirmation. That is what the "father" represents: his severity (his "bleak regard"), his energy, his authority, and his self-possession stand for the mind's projection of its own solitary splendor, its intellectual command over experience:

> He assumes great speeds of space and flutters them
> From cloud to cloudless, cloudless to keen clear
>
> In flights of eye and ear, the highest eye
> And the lowest ear, the deep ear that discerns,
> At evening, things that attend it until it hears
>
> The supernatural preludes of its own.   (414)

The "father" is proud and self-congratulatory. But his stance undoes itself: for the mind is doomed eventually to recognize its impotence. Stevens deflates its fantasy of power at the end of the canto with a single impatient inquiry: "What company, in masks, can choir it with the naked wind" (415)? What intellect, with its theatrical content, can keep up the pretense of having mastered experience?

The mother brings us hope in the world of others; she "invites humanity to her house / And table" (415). The father gives us confidence in the revelations of the lonely intellect and in the comfort of knowledge; he "fetches tellers of tales / And musicians who mute much, muse much, on the tales" (415). But he is not able to impose a teleology on the chaotic nature of experience, which remains only a precipitate of the dissolving moment: "There is no play. / Or, the persons act one merely by being here" (416). The extravagance of life's display is sadly unmeaning:

> It is of cloud transformed
> To cloud transformed again, idly, the way
> A season changes color to no end,
>
> Except the lavishing of itself in change.   (416)

In canto 7, Stevens asks if the intellect can reassert its mastery through tragic apprehension, that is, if the idleness of experience be countered by the intensity of a skeptical mind, prepared to cast aside all illusions and crush its own hopes with its stern lucidity:

> Is there an imagination that sits enthroned
> As grim as it is benevolent, the just
> And the unjust, which in the midst of summer stops
>
> To imagine winter? When the leaves are dead,
> Does it take its place in the north and enfold itself,
> Goat-leaper, crystalled and luminous, sitting
>
> In highest night?   (417)
>
> It leaps through us, through all our heavens leaps,
> Extinguishing our planets, one by one,
> Leaving, of where we were and looked, of where
>
> We knew each other and of each other thought,
> A shivering residue, chilled and foregone,
> Except for that crown and mystical cabala.   (417)

The "grim" imagination, establishing its authority through harshness, dismisses the sentimental longings of the mother and her "humanity"; it makes "a shivering residue" of "where / We knew each other and of each other thought" (417).

Stevens had once expressed an esteem for this masculine austerity, for the "mind of winter"; but that fascination must have seemed in retrospect vainglorious.[21] He had already disposed of the intellect as self-fancying tragic poseur in "Crude Foyer." In canto 7 of the "Auroras," he subjects its failure to a closer analysis. The intellect that has crowned itself with melancholy grandeur must be uneasy. It cannot examine itself too closely, lest it unmask its pretension. And it will always be vulnerable to jokes on the part of experience, suffering from the impediment of the trivial and subversive.

> But it dare not leap by chance in its own dark.
> It must change from destiny to slight caprice.
> And thus its jetted tragedy, its stele
>
> And shape and mournful making move to find
> What must unmake it and, at last, what can,
> Say, a flippant communication under the moon.　　(417–18)

Stevens has reached a dead end: there is no means by which to redeem experience. Thus, the next canto opens with a radical disjuncture, an attempt to reimagine an ease of life on the earth, "a time of innocence." This innocence is related to the happiness of canto 3, though it is not identical, for here experience is trusted not to be benevolent but neutral. The lights of the aurora do not have to frighten; they may be taken as indifferent rather than intentful.

> So, then, these lights are not a spell of light,
> A saying out of a cloud, but innocence.
> An innocence of the earth and no false sign
>
> Or symbol of malice.　　(418)

And if the world were mild and discrete, instead of antagonistic, we might dwell in greater peace in the ever-moving present; we might

Lie down like children in this holiness
As if, awake, we lay in the quiet of sleep,

As if the innocent mother sang in the dark
Of the room and on an accordion, half-heard,
Created the time and place in which we breathed.   (418–19)

Stevens insists that this hope for easeful life should be regarded as legitimate, not dismissed as an errant or sentimental fantasy. "It exists, it is
visible, it is, it is" (418). The possibility of a respectable peace offers relief
even to those who cannot hope to share in it.

For the oldest and coldest philosopher,

There is or may be a time of innocence
As pure principle.   (418)

It is pure principle, bearing an equivocal relation to our life, tantalizingly lawful but inaccessible, from whence springs its sharp pathos for us:

Its nature is its end,
That it should be, and yet not be, a thing

That pinches the pity of the pitiful man,
Like a book at evening beautiful but untrue,
Like a book on rising beautiful and true.   (418)

Stevens tries to conceive his life in the "idiom" of this innocence in
canto 9, but because, as he has already said, innocence is a principle and
not a possession of "the oldest and coldest philosopher," his effort naturally breaks down.

We thought alike
And that made brothers of us in a home
In which we fed on being brothers.   (419)

This notion is a fantasy, one that perhaps recalls the way Stevens's mother
spoke of his childhood on her deathbed: "She wishes not to complain.
She said that she had had her 'boys' and asked, 'Do you remember how
you used to troop through the house?' "[22] One form of "innocence" would
be to embrace life, in this way, as a transient but meaningfully social phenomenon, or, as Stevens put it in "Wild Ducks, People and Distances":

> The life of the world depends on that he is
> Alive, on that people are alive, on that
> There is village and village of them. (328)

But no amount of wishing that he could take comfort in this gregarious view and live this way will make it so. In "Adagia," he had written: "Life is an affair of people not of places. But for me life is an affair of places and that is the trouble."[23] For life to be an affair of places means for it to be a life of solitary self-consciousness, divided longing, and nostalgia. The tranquillity of "innocence" is not for him.

Stevens has no choice but to acknowledge the malice of fate (the bizarre cruelty of death), so strangely incarnated in the indifferent resplendence of the natural world:

> Shall we be found hanging in the trees next spring?
> Of what disaster is this the imminence:
> Bare limbs, bare trees and a wind as sharp as salt?
>
> The stars are putting on their glittering belts.
> They throw around their shoulders cloaks that flash
> Like a great shadow's last embellishment. (419)

Because death is a necessary ally of these gorgeous northern lights, Stevens attempts to see it as kindly, in the etymological sense; it is natural to us, so that if it comes "tomorrow," it will come "Almost as part of innocence, almost, / Almost as the tenderest and truest part" (420). That signal qualification, "almost," shows that he recognizes his effort as wishful and knows that it has failed. But he is poor enough to entertain a consolation at one remove, as he also acknowledges. It would be a consolation to measure his suffering from a distance. Yet, how much comfort could such a distance really provide? And how sad must one be to take comfort—not in having such a perspective—but in imagining that there is such a one to be had?

In canto 10, Stevens recovers his verve and authority, largely by means of abandoning the first-person perspective. The plaint is given over, and now the language of impersonal generalization takes command. The reflective "rabbi" is exhorted to make the commentary, as canto 10 itself represents a commentary on the larger movement of the poem. The battered "I" of the first stanza retreats, to be replaced by an imaginary immortal mind, "the vital, the never-failing genius," who is able to fulfill "his meditations, great and small" (420) and, dwelling placidly in the bitter wind of the auroras, to achieve perfect knowledge, "The full of fortune and the full of fate, / As if he lived all lives" (420). The predicament of the lyrical speaker is not corrected, but abandoned in mid-disaster, as Stevens ends with this musing coda, this effervescent jeu d'esprit. Thus the poem ends without working out a resolution or finding a compensation for the losses it describes. Though Stevens had always been in the business.of repudiating earlier stances, he usually replaced them with a bold counterthought; "The Auroras of Autumn" is inconclusive in a new way.

In accordance with his insights about the restlessness of thought, Stevens's oeuvre presents a chronicle of ceaseless self-transumption. He is ever steeled to shed another layer of what has been revealed to be "illusion." As Bloom writes, "Stevens had said 'farewell' before in his poetry; indeed, in some sense he always had been saying farewell to some aspect of self or experience."[24] But not all farewells are of the same order. In his early poem "Farewell to Florida," Stevens is emboldened by his release from an old attraction. Excited and invigorated, he forges ahead:

> Go on, high ship . . . The moon
> Is at the mast-head and the past is dead.
> Her mind will never speak to me again.
> I am free.   (117)

And protesting perhaps a bit too much, he goes on: "How content I shall be in the North to which I sail" (117). We may suspect him of overcompensation in this assurance (especially when a note of regret glints through the last lines of stanza 3), but his eager anticipation of the stimulating north is genuine. Measure the distance between this refreshed if ambivalent farewell and the helpless nostalgia of "The Auroras." When Stevens says farewell to an idea in the later poem, his sadness is unmitigated because he is not replacing the "idea" he salutes with a more desirable alternative. The new idea does not promise renewal—not even in the form of shaking off illusion so as to attain a clean, hard mind like the "mind of winter." When he says good-bye to the warmth of the mother and the

promise of the father, to all the avenues of idealization he had represented in terms of the family romance, he says good-bye to everything by
which experience may be made fulfilling. To cancel the image of the
mother and father is to resign the hope that one's existence is in any way
irradiated. Stevens is alone in a different loneliness than he had dreamt
of in his earlier hymns to solitude: this is not the secular freedom of
"Sunday Morning" or the transcendental solipsism of Hoon. For he has
come to perceive a stark narrowness in the realm of the self. It could only
be a strange anachronism, a sort of joke, to call life in the company of
this perception "freedom."

It is not "freedom" because there is nothing left of the self's capacity
to take pleasure in its own motions. In "Waving Adieu, Adieu, Adieu,"
Stevens had imaged the elegiac but bracing perspective of a fully secu-
larized consciousness:

> In a world without heaven to follow, the stops
> Would be endings, more poignant than partings,
>   profounder,
> And that would be saying farewell, repeating farewell,
> Just to be there and just to behold.   (127)

The world without the promise of the transcendent is a world steeped
in the pathos of finality. Yet here, Stevens had imagined that the self
that awakens in this bare world will relish its self-sufficiency. It will discover its own pride, and thereby feel contempt for its diminishment,
"despis[ing] / The being that yielded so little, acquired so little, too little
to care" (127–28). It will be like Shelley's Rousseau, whose "disguise" of
material life "stain[s] that within which still disdains to wear it" ("The
Triumph of Life," 205). But the speaker of "The Auroras" does not set
his disappointment at defiance; he does not regard his worldly reduction
as one thing, and his true self as another. The loss of his ontological hopes,
the loss of his mother and father, are losses *in him,* permanent erosions
by which he has been decreated in his own eyes.

Stevens's "farewell" lacks the gusto of departure, for the old life has
not been superseded, though it has been rendered obsolete. Out of respect for the gravity of the change, Stevens chooses the word "idea,"

which here means a basic assumption or perception about the nature.of reality. Stevens does not judge his old idea to have been an illusion, even if it has vanished like one, being replaced by a colder perspective. An "illusion" can only be characterized as a "comforting" or "reassuring" anodyne, and summarily dismissed, by someone who still possesses a measure of compensating self-satisfaction. (Or talking as if he or she did, at any rate; for the distinction being made here is rhetorical). But Stevens does not pretend to retain any such spirit. He regards his old idea as simply another idea than he has now, a more generous and in some respects a more fruitful one. In his disappointment, he does not have the sense of forging ahead, and so of sloughing off worthless notions he has outgrown. He maintains a sense of respect for his former assumptions and an attachment to them, or to what in him they came from. When he says "Farewell to an idea," his nostalgia is full-blooded and his articulation of it is moving because he knows he will wrest no profit from his loss.

Stevens wrote two elliptical variations on his great requiem for the family romance in "The Auroras." These poems, "Debris of Life and Mind," and "World without Peculiarity," depict a fundamentally inconsolable state, a state wherein the capacity for restoration has suffered what seems to be permanent damage, as reflected in the end of the family romance. For when the imagoes of the parents lose their stature, the aggrandizement of the self, as the center of experience, fails too. The death of the family romance produces the apprehension—or what Stevens called "the coldest coil"—"that life / Itself is like a poverty in the space of life" ("Chocorua to Its Neighbor," 298–99).

"Debris of Life and Mind" begins with a careful qualification, which is really a lament: "There is so little that is close and warm" (338). What is "close and warm" is the immediate and intimate, known to be transient and to have no significance beyond itself, but nonetheless real and valuable. To feel that much is distant and cold instead is to feel that the world is emptied, or "Contracted like a withered stick" ("Two Illustrations That the World Is What You Make of It," 513). Since childhood is the preeminent time of reposing in the immediate, it is for this speaker "as if we were never children," and "it is as if we were never young"

(338). He is taking a stance one step further removed from the family romance than "The Auroras of Autumn," for the nostalgia of "The Auroras" reflects continued feeling for idealizations that have faltered. But the speaker of "Debris" also remains uninvigorated by the severity of his stance: he honors the "little" that is left, as if he were not proud enough or energized enough to make a bolder generalization.

If it seems "as if we were never children" at all (so dead are all those dreams), it must be because the resignation to emptiness has itself grown familiar and stale. Thus, not only the state of illusion, but even the pain of the disillusionment were preferable. The passion of disillusionment, with its germ of resistance and hope, is long gone. The words of the poem are plaintive yet grim:

> It is true in the moonlight
> That it is as if we had never been young.
>
> We ought not be awake. (338)

This is a ghastly nadir of feeling. After this suicidal moment, the poem swerves, to begin again, evoking a chastened reconciliation with things as they are:

> It is from this
> That a bright red woman will be rising
> And, standing in violent golds, will brush her hair. (338)

These lines are lyrical and promising, but their ascent is unsustained. For Stevens cannot overcome his chagrin at the dramatic decline he has known in the quality of experience. The "she"—who is the general subject, and who is Stevens—returns to the solace of the ordinary and the actual. Despite this attempt at resignation, Stevens is forced back to the persistent consciousness of the difference in the mind between then and now, the old Wordsworthian difference that demands to be articulated:

> She will speak thoughtfully the words of a line.
>
> She will think about them not quite able to sing.
> Besides, when the sky is so blue, things sing themselves,

Even for her, already for her. She will listen
And feel that her color is a meditation,

The most gay and yet not so gay as it was.   (338)

Though attempting to accept the consolations of the sensuous present, she continues to be conscious of that subtle but seemingly ineradicable discordance between its pale consolations and the heartier confidence of the past; thus, all is changed, and yet the world has itself remained exactly the same.

Rather than advancing upon the first, deadlocked, section, this second moment restates it. In fact, the poem seeks no way out of the impasse, but ends with a plea for temporary solace and distraction: "Stay here. Speak of familiar things a while." It is sad with respect to its own sadness. It does not seek to transcend the emotional crux it describes but accedes to the fact of it, wanting only amelioration rather than seeking escape or rebelling.

The disappointment of the family romance—and hence, of a whole set of hopes for the self—returns with all its pathos in "World without Peculiarity." This poem ends on what seems to be a note of resolution and affirmation. Joseph Riddell has written that "In the last three stanzas, Stevens effects a reversal, a transformation of grief into fulfillment."[25] The last line does invoke "a single being, sure and true," but the rhetoric of unity is deceptive. For the terms of the affirmation turn out to be quite limited. The speaker's sorrow remains unassuaged, and out of his demoralization he feels gratitude for a slight and rather refined mercy. The poem is in this way a descendent of "Tintern Abbey" and the Intimations Ode, except that Stevens is fully aware of accepting a poor compensation, and nonetheless accepts it, knowing its littleness. He is not defensive, and he does not make a greater claim for this consolation than it deserves.

As the poem begins, the transient serenity of the present is interrupted by the upsurge of memory. These memories are about the three central figures of any erotic life: the mother, the father, and the spouse. The thought of each of these figures brings unhappiness, perhaps partly because Stevens's relationship with each was unfulfilled, but largely because he feels a more general sense of mourning: mourning for the actual loss of his parents, for the ontological necessity of their and his own mortality, and for the inexorable translation of past strength into present humiliation. Against the weight of these memories and the melancholy of these thoughts, the pleasantness of material life can offer no significant antidote—and that very recognition becomes another source of sorrow:

> The day is great and strong—
> But his father was strong, that lies now
> In the poverty of dirt.
>
> Nothing could be more hushed than the way
> The moon moves toward the night.
> But what his mother was returns and cries on his breast.
>
> The red ripeness of round leaves is thick
> With the spices of red summer.
> But she that he loved turns cold at his light touch.
>
> What good is it that the earth is justified,
> That it is complete, that it is an end,
> That in itself it is enough?   (453)

Like "Debris of Life and Mind," this poem reaches a perigee halfway through, from which it seems to reascend but actually does not. The second movement of the poem proposes what turns out to be a sad alternative to the despair behind this anguished rhetorical question. The next lines begin hopefully enough. The "earth"—not sensual earth but our life in earthly reality— offers its moments of mitigation:

> It is the earth itself that is humanity . . .
> He is the inhuman son and she,
> She is the fateful mother, whom he does not know.
>
> She is the day, the walk of the moon
> Among the breathless spices and, sometimes,
> He, too, is human and difference disappears
>
> And the poverty of dirt, the thing upon his breast,
> The hating woman, the meaningless place,
> Become a single being, sure and true.   (454)

The unity that Stevens describes in these lines is indeed curious. But he is certainly not saying that his deprivations, his losses and loneliness, suddenly make sense, or that reality is shown to be "all one." It is the awful things—the dirt of the grave, the loss of the mother, the failure of love, the emptiness of the present—that "Become a single being, sure and true." This odd reconciliation comes about when he feels that "He, too, is human and difference disappears." He takes comfort in the sense of fatefulness, a sense of himself and his losses as folded into a destined and seamless experience. He does not have to feel as the most darkly disappointed feel—marked out and persecuted, living on though exiled from life. Nor is his experience fragmentary and disassociated, but it goes together, as the nature of our "human" earth. Thus, he flirts with a grim harmonization of the elements of experience, so that he may be soothed by the "naturalness" of his losses. It will easily be perceived how dubious a consolation this is, with its recapitulation, in bleaker tones, of Wordsworth's brave assertion: "Nature never did betray / The heart that loved her" ("Tintern Abbey," 122–23).

From the limpid sadness of poems in *Transport to Summer* and *The Auroras of Autumn,* Stevens moves on to still more original, more delicate evocations of disappointment in *The Rock.* His tone becomes somewhat less urgent, and his acute nostalgia for the family romance recedes; he turns to an assessment of the mind's quest, or, to adopt the metaphor in "The World as Meditation," its vigil. All his ranges of affect—despair, indignation, grief, geniality, fortitude, detachment, and so on—are gathered and arranged in subtler patterns than ever before. But this quieter and more nuanced verse incorporates rather than surmounts the fundamental inconsolability of "The Auroras." The extinction of ontological confidence, as described in the earlier volume, is taken for granted in *The Rock*; its lyrics pursue the varieties of regret and accommodation in a musing aftermath. The mind, after all, must go on cogitating; it moves while it lives, even though its movement is ultimately aimless. As Stevens observes in "The River of Rivers in Connecticut," the mind is our "great river this side of Stygia," but it is a river "that flows nowhere, like a sea" (533).

The Soul Is Not a Soul

WHEN STEVENS REGRETS not that there is nothing but that "There is so little that is close and warm," he anticipates the characteristic pathos of qualification in John Ashbery, his poetic heir. Ashbery is always modest enough to discover a tender mercy or two, in "night," for example, which "gives more than it takes" (*SP* 2); yet when he tempers the expression of disappointment in this way he makes it seem the more sincere. "As One Put Drunk into the Packet-Boat" opens with such a precise, penetrating lament: "I tried each thing, only some were immortal and free" (*SP* 1). The freedom Ashbery craves is the touch of the transcendent, that which makes the self feel autonomous and bold. Of course, he never possesses this freedom in the present, but he is always recalling it with an ambivalent nostalgia. Like Stevens he envies and disparages his younger self, with its ambition after existential freedom. At least he was ambitious then, instead of being, as Yeats would say, "but a broken man" ("The Circus Animals' Desertion"). However, again like Stevens, he finds to his mortification that the cancellations are never final. His ontological dreams are thickly layered and ever-renewing; veil after veil falls from the form and countenance of all as he pursues his work of discrimination through ever subtler reaches of disappointment. He finds himself saying, at last, "Farewell to an idea," or as he puts it, farewell to "the dream that sustains all dreams," though he knows that, since the mind is porous, he will not be able to maintain the clarity of this negation. The author is not the master of his own mind, as Ashbery recalls in the concluding lines of "Self-Portrait in a Convex Mirror":

> The hand holds no chalk
> And each part of the whole falls off
> And cannot know it knew.   (SP 83)

Though his poems, those "cold pockets of remembrance," may record his meanings, their maker himself is ever departing from his acquaintance with them.

With all his avant-garde effects—among them his deliberate obliquity, his promiscuous figurative language, and his pointedly indecorous diction —Ashbery would seem to be a distinctly postmodern or postromantic poet. But, though contemporary in his poetics, Ashbery is in his themes a romantic. Any number of critics, including Harold Bloom and John Shoptaw, have demonstrated the continuity between Ashbery's concerns and those of his romantic predecessors. Some have suggested that Ashbery takes up where Wordsworth, Shelley, Tennyson, Browning, and Yeats left off, whereas others have described him as recapitulating the conclusions of romanticism in order to deny or subvert them. All these critics try to assess Ashbery's stance toward romanticism, but the more fundamental question is what he takes romanticism to be, and which themes it is exactly that he reprises. According to Bloom, Ashbery attacks the "High Romantic insistence that the power of the poet's mind could triumph over the universe of death," whereas Shoptaw has more circumspectly deduced that "Ashbery tends to identify romanticism not only with skeptical, idealist questioning but with subjective, erotic response."[1] This chapter will show that Ashbery does not address either of these—or any similar—creative or hopeful versions of romanticism. He is preoccupied with the psychological theme of Wordsworth's crisis lyrics, namely, the failure of "genial spirits," or the experience of ontological disappointment. In this bleak version of romanticism, disappointment remains unrepaired by a therapeutic resolution; there is no restored contact with the transcendent, nor any true accommodation to its loss.[2]

Along with Stevens, Ashbery eschews the lyric "I," preferring a more impersonal "you" or "we," and a corresponding generality of expression. This shared strategy might be contrasted with Wordsworth's: whereas Wordsworth ascribes his sense of loss to a particular occasion and leaves it to us to reinterpret the nature of this loss in larger terms, Stevens and Ashbery choose an abstract language and describe a universal deprivation. Yet subtler effects of their poetry suggest how disheartening each poet has found these putatively theoretical losses. Ashbery is even more willing than Stevens to expose the bumbling of the subject demeaned in its conception of its subjectivity.

Ashbery has said that his poems "are about the experience of experience"; this second-order experience is often that of surprise and consternation at the ruin of existential dreams. Like Wordsworth's his dreams are ontological or existential in that they embody linked assumptions about the uniqueness of the self and the promise of time. The self seemed to be marked out for a special destiny, at the very least in its capacity to understand and appreciate its experience, while the apparently teleological structure of time corroborated this sense of privilege by creating an expectation of achievement and growth. These are assumptions Ashbery did not necessarily know he harbored, but whose quiet decay he discovers in mid-adulthood, perceiving the value of his dreams at the point of their dissolution. Like many earlier romantics, he must measure the distance between his invigorating archaic assumptions and their defeat in maturity.

His disappointment precipitates him into the state of psychological impasse explored by Wordsworth, Stevens, and Shelley. He finds himself in an unenviable new situation in which he is burdened both with an ambivalent attitude toward his past self and an empty prospect for the present and future. He will sometimes react to this impasse with a burst of frustration, as in "Crazy Weather." There he angrily repudiates both his present and past selves:

> I shall never want or need
> Any other literature than this poetry of mud
> And ambitious reminiscences of the times when it came easily.
>
> (*HD* 21)

Ashbery can be powerful in such moments of bitterness and disgust, but his apprehension of seemingly irreversible loss tends to issue in his distinctive elegiac strain, muted and stoical. He observes his loss and feels helpless, as at the end of "The Gazing Grain":

> Rooted in parched earth I am
> A stranger myself in the dramatic lighting,
> The result of war. That which is given to see
> At any moment is the residue, shadowed
>
> In gold or emerging into the clear bluish haze
> Of uncertainty. We come back to ourselves
> Through the rubbish of cloud and tree-spattered pavement.
> These days stand like vapor under the trees.   (*HD* 11)

The faint reviving lyricism of the last line is also typical of Ashbery; in his disinclination to self-pity, he swerves from his own laments and tries to make the best of it in an effort at resignation, or surrender to sadness. In framing this subtle hopelessness, he is aided by the fact that, unlike Wordsworth, he does not represent his disappointment as the result of dramatic reversal or sudden discovery; instead, he recognizes that his disappointment has come about through the slow and certain erosion of "dreams."

His disappointment is inevitable, but ordinary and unworthy of any special sympathy. No trauma or loss awakens it: it is folded into the course of life, transpiring gradually and emerging as already familiar. It has no relation to a particular way of living, or to the fate of a particular life, and therefore it is profoundly recalcitrant: it remains a chronic disappointment, incapable of either precipitating a tangible crisis or of being resolved. It is significant, it is stubborn, and it hurts; yet it can only be recognized in order to be forgotten again. That this disappointment is chronic reflects its depth; that it is cerebral produces its subtlety; it forms like a cloud rolling over a landscape, dissolving, condensing, and dissolving again. To experience this kind of existential disappointment is in a sense a luxury; but on the other hand, it can be said to embrace and subsume the other manifestations of disappointment. In elucidating his unhappiness over the condition of being a subject, Ashbery propels the representation of disappointment toward what would appear to be its destiny: thought of the greatest inwardness, delicacy, impersonality, and irresolution.

His elegiac mode is various and understated; it incorporates highs and lows, turnings, recoveries, and humor. These modulations and qualifications actually contribute to the evocation of disappointment; for what has been lost in disappointment are the wellsprings of grandeur—the rhetorical authority that follows upon the flaring up of the determined self. Pathos is interrupted, like everything else. Bravery is interspersed with cowardice, anguish with boredom, intensity with distraction and silliness. Some thoughts are evaded, others entertained as truths that straggle along without the force of a commanding negation. Ashbery eschews the drama of conclusiveness, along with the clarity of form and strict economy. When he does make "statements," they can seem banal, and that effect is deliberate: Ashbery has a keen sense of bathos and likes to expose the clumsiness of the declarative mode and the want of glamour in the sources of his disappointments. His poetry pursues the track of thought, with the result that it seems spontaneous, flowing, elliptical, redundant, and whimsical; but with the aim, always, of carrying the fragile sense of mourning and unease that stirs the meditation. His sorrow may then console itself with dubious charities that substitute the obscure charms of experience for the lost treasure of the autonomous self. Shelley's speaker in "Lerici" reaches for anodyne comforts and fails to attain them; Ashbery's finds are real, but to embrace them signals the incorporation of diminishment. There is in Ashbery's voice a modulation out of poverty that would not be permitted in the uncompromising mode of Shelley's late lyrics; yet this digression arises out of the same decline in the pride and power of the subject.

"Soonest Mended" strikes the defeated but equivocal note characteristic of Ashbery. The poem plainly concerns a Stevensian theme: the decay, in maturity, of the self's hopes for itself, and specifically, its expectation that it is to be the light of its own experience.

> These then were some hazards of the course,
> Yet though we knew the course *was* hazards and nothing else
> It was still a shock when, almost a quarter of a century later,

> The clarity of the rules dawned on you for the first time.
> *They* were the players, and we who had struggled at the game
> Were merely spectators, though subject to its vicissitudes.
>
> (*DDS* 18)

"Soonest Mended" was written in spring 1969, "almost a quarter century" after Ashbery's adolescence, at a time when he had come to know
not just the nature of the rules but their "clarity." To know the "clarity"
of the rules means to have beheld them coalesce with one's experience,
which is in turn to recognize that they have the force of necessity and
will not be abrogated on one's behalf. The rule in this case is the rule of
the self's being curiously incidental to its own experience: it is "subject"
to the "vicissitudes" of life, but without feeling itself to have cognitive
mastery over them, nor even to be entirely the site of their occurrence.

   Earlier in the poem, Ashbery had described the dawning recognition
of this disappointment, its subtle repudiation, and its working its way
into life at last.

> And then there always came a time when
> Happy Hooligan in his rusted green automobile
> Came plowing down the course, just to make sure everything was
>   O.K.,
> Only by that time we were in another chapter and confused
> About how to receive this latest piece of information.
> *Was* it information? Weren't we rather acting this out
> For someone else's benefit, thoughts in a mind
> With room enough and to spare for our little problems (so they
>   began to seem),
> Our daily quandary about food and the rent and bills to be paid?
> To reduce all this to a small variant,
> To step free at last, minuscule on the gigantic plateau—
> This was our ambition: to be small and clear and free. (*DDS* 17)

In this ambition there is already a curtailment of grander desires. Here
the self no longer hopes for the assurance of a transcendent origin, but is
willing to accept its "smallness" in exchange for the feeling of being, at
least, "free." "Free" might mean capable of determining its fate, but is

more likely to mean capable of governing experience cognitively, so as to float apart from and beyond it, to be "minuscule on the gigantic plateau." This self would have a circumscribed, intellectual measure of transcendence, insofar as it could see everything, even itself, *sub specie aeternitatis*.

Even this reduced ambition fails, yet it does not lose its stature or its romance for all that. The subject from whom it departs feels guilty, as if diminished by his own demystification, and uncertainly nostalgic for his high-minded dreams:

> Alas, the summer's energy wanes quickly,
> A moment and it is gone. And no longer
> May we make the necessary arrangements, simple as they are.
> Our star was brighter perhaps when it had water in it. (*DDS* 17)

Ashbery does not congratulate himself on growing wiser or throwing off an illusion. On the contrary, he pays homage to his earlier self, which, in spite of being deluded, was bolder and in some way more admirable than his present self. The star that was once brighter descends from the Intimations Ode ("The Soul that rises with us, our life's star" [59]). In language that is a little absurd and yet charged with pathos, it is commemorated for having "had water in it." The water is perhaps the water of tears, or at any rate of a lost intensity and earnestness of self-dramatization. The transcendental ambitions of adolescence are replaced by a humiliating struggle to maintain equilibrium:

> Our star was brighter perhaps when it had water in it.
> Now there is no question even of that, but only
> Of holding on to the hard earth so as not to get thrown off,
> With an occasional dream, a vision: a robin flies across
> The upper corner of the window, you brush your hair away,
> And cannot quite see, or a wound will flash
> Against the sweet faces of others, something like:
> This is what you wanted to hear, so why
> Did you think of listening to something else? We are all talkers
> It is true, but underneath the talk lies
> The moving and not wanting to be moved, the loose
> Meaning, untidy and simple like a threshing floor. (*DDS* 17–18)

Now one steadfastly attends to reality, only to be reminded of higher ambitions by "an occasional dream, a vision," something out of the ordinary that arouses an old intensity or longing for intensity, and "wounds" one with what is at once a reproach and a recollection of futility. A Wordsworthian adult feels respect, suspicion, and mourning for the mirage of power and meaning in experience. We are all talkers, tempted to pass the time in idle chatter, desiring and yet dreading to break the frame, "moving and not wanting to be moved."

When the "clarity of the rules" dawns on Ashbery, he recognizes first that disappointment is the rule, second that he is not to be exempted from encountering it, and third that what it means to undergo this disappointment is precisely not to be able to embrace it as a cognitive achievement. For then the disappointment would have its compensation and would no longer be a disappointment. Though he might wish to claim skepticism as the accomplishment of his chastened maturity ("the fantasy makes it ours, a kind of fence-sitting / Raised to the level of an esthetic ideal" [*DDS* 18]), the loss is instead an inveterate and grueling one, which keeps recurring without dissipating its force. It is the exact opposite of the kind of loss by which the self might feel deepened or ennobled. It cannot be interpreted as an intellectual advance, with the result that it is doubly disheartening:

> Night after night this message returns, repeated
> In the flickering bulbs of the sky, raised past us, taken away
>   from us,
> Yet ours over and over until the end that is past truth,
> The being of our sentences, in the climate that fostered them,
> Not ours to own, like a book, but to be with, and sometimes
> To be without, alone and desperate.   (*DDS* 18)

Ontological disappointment threatens to empty the events of everyday life, yet according to the logic of this disappointment, such a loss can serve no purpose. Therefore, it is preferable to resist the evacuation of significance, to cling to the old ways, and defy the claims of a spurious "maturity," especially because the association of maturity with the progress of understanding has been scuttled:

> Better, you said, to stay cowering
> Like this in the early lessons, since the promise of learning
> Is a delusion, and I agreed, adding that
> Tomorrow would alter the sense of what had already been learned,
> That the learning process is extended in this way, so that from
>   this standpoint
> None of us ever graduates from college,
> For time is an emulsion, and probably thinking not to grow up
> Is the brightest kind of maturity for us, right now at any rate.
>   (*DDS* 18–19)

Here is the last but not the least of the ontological disappointments to be weighed by the poem. Time, it turns out, does not act on understanding in such a way as to allow for the accumulation and incorporation of knowledge; time does not allow our understanding to be progressive. On the contrary, we are always losing insight, forgetting, displacing, and rearranging our knowledge, so that we never arrive at conclusions that we can hoard and treasure as permanent possessions. Ashbery confirms the justice of these observations—that "the promise of learning is a delusion" and that "probably not thinking to grow up / Is the brightest kind of maturity"—but now it is with a sudden, profound gloom, for to accept the sacrifice of cognitive achievement means that the pain of experience —including the pain of ontological disappointment—has no creative end: "And you see, both of us were right, though nothing / Has somehow come to nothing." Ashbery goes on to affirm the substance of everyday life stripped of ontological value, but not wholeheartedly. It is clear from his aversive language that he regards the new life as a sorry compromise:

>   the avatars
> Of our conforming to the rules and living
> Around the home have made—well, in a sense, "good citizens"
>   of us,
> Brushing the teeth and all that, and learning to accept
> The charity of the hard moments as they are doled out. (*DDS* 19)

His humility and his resignation to bourgeois mundanity are sources of oppression in themselves, but like Wordsworth he must, because he has

no recourse, embrace the "strength" in "what remains behind," and take
for what it is worth our meandering, oblivious, unproductive life:

> For this is action, this not being sure, this careless
> Preparing, sowing the seeds crooked in the furrow,
> Making ready to forget, and always coming back
> To the mooring of starting out, that day so long ago.   (*DDS* 19)

A subject that must always be "making ready to forget" must relinquish its hopes of having cognitive command over its experience.
Such command, the faculty of seeing sub specie aeternitatis, is what
Kierkegaard identified as the futile though desperate desire of "the existing subject," who longs to abstract himself from the abyss of temporality.[3] Kierkegaard reflects on this longing and its defeat in *Concluding
Unscientific Postscript*, a polemical attack on historical and "speculative"
(that is, Hegelian) approaches to Christianity. He argues that the impersonal and definitive solutions offered by historical inquiry or speculative
philosophy are useless to the individual, for whom the question of existence is solely (and urgently) personal and particular. The goal of thinking sub specie aeternitatis is a false goal for beings who are not eternal
but subject to time, who must change with time, and whose thoughts
must consequently alter with time: "Every subject is an existing subject,
and therefore this must be essentially expressed in his knowing and must
be expressed by keeping his knowing from an illusory termination in
sensate certainty, in historical knowledge, in illusory results."[4] To exist is
to have to keep asking the question of existence; "sensate certainty,"
"historical knowledge," and "illusory results" all offer to settle the question factitiously, for any settling of the question is delusive. And yet one
does not want to become trapped in the obscure labor of maintaining
uncertainty. We want to grow richer in knowledge—not out of simple
narcissistic impulses, but out of a more subtle, perhaps more elemental,
derivative of narcissism: we want our relation to time to be productive.
It should not present a succession of scattered moments, but should be
genuinely progressive, amassing a result that can be regarded as having
tangibility, or permanence, or some sort of extratemporal substantiality—
something to transcend the manner of its creation. The movement of
time should be teleological. By contrast, the prospect of having to remain

in perpetual suspense, or of living without creative issue, is humiliating. Behind Kierkegaard's particular argument lies the intuition that the desire for teleology is inevitable but doomed because teleology is at odds both with the actual nature of time and with that of subjectivity bound to time.[5]

"Self-Portrait in a Convex Mirror" is Ashbery's most sustained and moving examination of the frustrations of the self enmired in time. The discovery of being an "existing subject" unable to transcend the moment in which it exists strikes a harsh blow to the self's natural penchant for self-aggrandizement. With the death of the soul's dreams for itself, the abyss of temporality is reopened: one must face the question of how to occupy the diminished self in a world in which time has lost its teleology, and even "the promise of learning is a delusion." "Self-Portrait" thus reprises the themes of shorter poems like "Soonest Mended," but does so at great length, which is part of the point.

Many of Ashbery's volumes—*Rivers and Mountains*, *The Double Dream of Spring*, *Houseboat Days*, and *Self-Portrait in a Convex Mirror* among them—comprise a series of short poems on related themes and then a long poem in which those themes are explored iteratively and in detail. "Self-Portrait" concerns the trouble of being steeped in time, and the poem itself is steeped in its own prolonged, irresolute meditations. It takes up certain questions and anxieties again and again, without arriving at decisions or solutions; it illustrates the crisis of an ephemeral subjectivity in the form of its own ellipses. In its meandering, the poem enacts the habit of dwelling in the paradigm of disappointment, which Ashbery's shorter poems only narrate: "Self-Portrait" shows what it is to think in accordance with an intermittent but irresolvable grief. Ontological disappointment of the order Ashbery suffers is not susceptible of conclusion, for it is chronic; it poses the very question of what to do with time. It is important for this reason to trace the poem's progress—or rather, the want of it—patiently, for the failure of dramatic structure in the poem reflects the plight of the speaker who has determined that time itself lacks the structure of promise. He sees his very thought as nonteleological: that is, as an adventure that transpires without the expectation of an issue or end. The poem spools out in the manner of the temporality that it describes.

There are two major schools of thought about "Self-Portrait in a Convex Mirror." One, a more classical tradition, sees the poem as focused on problems of aesthetics or poesis, and the other, the deconstructive approach, reads the poem as an exposé of false hopes for representation in general and language in particular.[6] This chapter departs from both of these views in interpreting the poem as a stark lament over the condition of being a subject. It will be shown that, despite appearances, Ashbery's poem is not primarily about art and its lapses but about the self's disappointment with its own being. Critics of the first school have taken it that the "self" or "soul" whose erosion the poem regrets is either the poetic self or the self as represented in art.[7] Such readings necessarily tend to obscure the considerable pathos of the poem. When Ashbery weeps to see the message in Parmigianino's painting "that the soul is not a soul," he weeps over the fate of the soul in general, not because his poetic powers are fading, nor because the soul is distorted and "imprisoned" by art. He grieves because there is no soul as the self is bound to dream of it.

To read the poem this way means reorienting the usual notion of Ashbery's romantic and Stevensian heritage. Most accounts of Ashbery's poetic relations in "Self-Portrait" build upon the idea that the poem is an aesthetic meditation and therefore follows after works such as Keats's "Ode on a Grecian Urn"[8] or Stevens's "The Poems of Our Climate" and *The Man with the Blue Guitar*.[9] One of the most perspicuous essays on this subject, Lynn Keller's "Thinkers without Final Thoughts," maintains that Ashbery draws upon Stevens's poetics and also such of his metapoiec themes as "the artist's frustrated desire to capture 'things as they are' . . . ; the problem of solipsism—is all art self-portraiture?—and the recurrent question from 'The Idea of Order at Key West' whether the sea or the self shapes art's order."[10] But they share a deeper mode of ontological and epistemological elegy. Keller asserts "Both men are content to be 'Thinkers without final thoughts.'" However, it can be argued that though they are indeed without final thoughts, they are not content to be; both express what they know to be an intractable atavistic desire for the clarity which would have sprung from an ultimately masterful self.

Deconstructive readings of the poem come closer to this interpretation, in addition to being more attentive to the poem's pathos, because they enlarge the scope of Ashbery's themes: he is not concerned just with the failures of art or poetry, they say, but with the disappointments of representation, which means with the self's ability to represent itself to itself.[11] Questions of being thereby come into play; Ashbery is shown to recognize the failure of self-coincidence, which follows from the fault in being, or the absence of presence. Jody Norton lucidly remarks, "'Self-Portrait' is in part an elegy for the soul—for a time when the soul existed by virtue of its own Wittgensteinian self-certainty, its own assumption of itself."[12] Or as Anita Sokolsky puts it, more astringently, "the equation of 'I=I' [is] converted into an endlessly insufficient and approximate asymptote."[13] These readings agree, then, that the "soul" at risk is the soul in its metaphysical conception.[14]

Yet it is just at this point that such readings take an odd turn and develop a convoluted relation to Ashbery's pathos; for if the questioning of transcendental hopes is defined as desirable, indeed as proof of Ashbery's intellectual superiority, then what are we to make of his unabashed dismay at having to part with them? Deconstructive critics define his sorrow as "nostalgic desire" and treat it suspiciously. Sokolsky, for example, reads the poem as a doomed struggle for intellectual authority, which first achieves "disillusionment with narcissism" and relegates the "substantive self" to mere linguistic play, only to relapse in its closing lines, which reinstitute "the mystique of language."[15] Lee Edelman makes the more elaborate claim that the poem, which longs for "a lost plenitude or essence," at the same time exposes the pathos of its competing attitude, "its skepticism," and "the poignancy of the desire that always informs its irony."[16] The speaker knows he is trapped in an irresolvable dialectic, which he then thematizes; in this way he recuperates his authority through "the pose of self-exposure."[17] Ashbery's archaic yearning for presence is "simultaneously hidden and exposed."[18] Both Sokolsky and Edelman deal uneasily with the pathos of Ashbery's poem because they conceive his skeptical insight to be at odds with his "nostalgic desire." But for Ashbery the two points of view are not at odds; he is not embarrassed to feel transcendental longing in the face of its frustration, nor does he imagine that this tenacious longing can be surmounted by force of revelation or of will. His sense of loss is not the clinging residuum of his demystifying insight but the central and naked subject of the poem.

Ashbery begins with a description of Parmigianino's painting, a self-portrait taken from a reflection in a mirror which enlarges what is in the foreground—namely, the painter's hand—and "sequesters" what is in the middleground—the painter's face. The image of "sequestration" comes to have a certain poignancy. For, protected by the giant hand, the face, though "Lively and intact in a recurring wave of arrival," is suspended in its approach. The rounded surface of the convex mirror acts as a sort of visible restraint, a reminder, to Ashbery, of more general ontological restrictions. For, in a compelling twist on a very old cliché, Ashbery interprets the face as an image of the soul—though not of the soul behind that particular face, but the soul of all souls. What the painting reveals, or speaks for, is Ashbery's disappointment with the status of what he thus designates "the soul." (He might have chosen a more noncommittal word, like my word "self," but he means to own his attachment to an archaic fantasy.) The soul is eager to exert its autonomy, to experience its power, or, in the words of "Soonest Mended," "to step free at last, minuscule on the gigantic plateau . . . to be small and clear and free," but because it is not really powerful or free, it "has to stay where it is," wary of the scrutiny that would expose it as illusion:

> The soul has to stay where it is,
> Even though restless, hearing raindrops at the pane,
> The sighing of autumn leaves thrashed by the wind,
> Longing to be free, outside, but it must stay
> Posing in this place. It must move
> As little as possible. This is what the portrait says. (SP 69)

The convex shape of the reflection figures the confinement of the soul, barred by its constitutive limitations from experiencing itself as "free," that is, as metaphysically sovereign and autonomous, divine and real. We are attached to this abstract concept of soul because we are (necessarily) attached to the idea of having a unique and permanent self. But the eager, fragile, "sequestered" face in the mirror, as a figure for the soul, shows how wishful is its metaphysical aggrandizement. The soul does not share in the nature of transcendence; it is instead a precipitate of its occasion, "a ping-pong ball / Secure on its jet of water," without permanence or substance and therefore without a higher destiny.

What is left over under the name of "soul" has none of the qualities we had wanted to attribute to it; it cannot accommodate our longing to have a special self that in its nature surmounts the nature of the time it moves in. Ashbery projects his unhappiness over this recognition unto the gaze of the painter. In a moment of unusually frank grief, he suggests that the demystification of the soul brings with it a sense not of intellectual achievement but of enervating loss:

> there is in that gaze a combination
> Of tenderness, amusement and regret, so powerful
> In its restraint one cannot look for long.
> The secret is too plain. The pity of it smarts,
> Makes hot tears spurt: that the soul is not a soul,
> Has no secret, is small, and it fits
> Its hollow perfectly: its room, our moment of attention. (*SP* 69)

Hamlet may have dared Rosencrantz and Guildenstern to "pluck out the heart of my mystery," but here the occult core of personality is denied. The soul "Has no secret"; it is not an essence from which consciousness flows, but only the gathering of consciousness in this moment, which is the "hollow" it necessarily "fits." Its "room" is the room in the background of the self-portrait, and "our moment of attention," the moment in which we concentrate on this painting; but the room is also the limited provenance of the soul, which only comes into being when we turn our attention to it.

In this view from the outside, the self—which is felt to be focal and real—loses its depth, becoming illusory and slight. Figures of superficiality dominate the closing part of the stanza, where the painting's depiction of the mirror's curved surface is taken to show that in fact "everything is surface"—that the moment is determinant, and nothing in self or experience can be found to maintain an existence outside the moment that produces it.

> But your eyes proclaim
> That everything is surface. The surface is what's there
> And nothing can exist except what's there.
> There are no recesses in the room, only alcoves,
> And the window doesn't matter much, or that
> Sliver of window or mirror on the right. (*SP* 70)

The distortion of the mirror rounds everything in its reflection toward the center, so that the faithful painting of it must repudiate the standard pictorial illusion of realistic perspective. The painting, as interpreted in the poem, declines to suggest that there are spaces exterior to its view, either distant spaces just out of reach or embedded interior ones, still closed, still keeping their secrets. Nothing has autonomy or depth with respect to this representation; there are no withdrawn and private spaces, only the shallow fold of alcoves. As a sly train of association hints, this undulation of the inescapable surface recalls the movement of time and our place within it:

> And the window doesn't matter much, or that
> Sliver of window or mirror on the right, even
> As a gauge of the weather, which in French is
> *Le temps*, the word for time, and which
> Follows a course wherein changes are merely
> Features of the whole.   (*SP* 70)

Time is a fluid "course" of gentle mutation that never mounts to a climax or dramatic rupture, a "break with the past," which might lead to its transcendence; instead, the ribbon flows peaceably on, regathering all variation under its forward momentum. The course blends change into "the whole," as the curvature of the mirror makes "a coral ring" of the background, or as Ashbery says later, "one neutral band . . . boil[ed] down to one uniform substance . . . a magma of interiors" (*SP* 76). The self shares in the nature of time, which creates it, and nothing rests under or supports its tumbling motion:

> The whole is stable within
> Instability, a globe like ours, resting
> On its pedestal of vacuum, a ping-pong ball
> Secure on its jet of water.
> And just as there are no words for the surface, that is,
> No words to say what it really is, that it is not
> Superficial but a visible core, then there is
> No way out of the problem of pathos vs. experience.
> You will stay on, restive, serene in
> Your gesture which is neither embrace nor warning

> But which holds something of both in pure
> Affirmation that doesn't affirm anything. (*SP* 70)

This ephemeral self is not a nothing, but because it is unclear how to describe or to value the small "soul that is not a soul," we cannot reconcile
our experience of self with what we know it, once demystified, to be:
there is "No way out of the problem of pathos vs. experience." The look
of "tenderness, amusement and regret" in Parmigianino's eyes exemplifies this problem: it shows the complex reaction of the self that has
suffered disappointment in its conception of self, but at the same time,
paradoxically, suffered this disappointment as an experience of the new,
"small," pathetic self. This is an impasse, as reflected in the painting's
"suspension" of the face, poised in the center like a balloon, at once
"restive" and "serene," unable to conclude, left to extend its hand dramatically in a gesture of "pure / Affirmation that doesn't affirm anything."

Ashbery sees Parmigianino's self-portrait as exposing the will of individual consciousness to mystify itself—to organize experience around the
assumption of its own integrity, continuity, and uniqueness, when it is in
fact a frail precipitate of the movement of time. We might have expected
this requiem for the soul to serve as the climax in a story of disappointment, but here it is the starting point. The rest of "Self-Portrait" deals
with the way in which time defeats the dream of the soul, and the difficulties Ashbery faces in confronting the failure of the dream, as well as the
various unsuccessful efforts he makes to accommodate or resign himself
to this failure. As in Wordsworth's "Tintern Abbey," time defeats the
soul's self-enchantment when the soul discovers that it is permeable by
the effects of time; it has no independent essence. In the constitution of
the self there is a kind of drift and an incursion of the alien:

> This otherness, this
> 'Not-being-us' is all there is to look at
> In the mirror, though no one can say
> How it came to be this way. (*SP* 81)

The self fails to coincide with itself. It is amorphous and fragmented,
composed of elements that are unfixed, that dissolve and reform, disap-
pear and are replaced by other elements ignorant of what came before
them.

The poem treats this theme implicitly and explicitly: it enacts its apprehension that subjectivity is volatile by means of its own false starts and forgettings. The second stanza begins with a record of distraction: "The balloon pops, the attention / Turns dully away," and the poem contains any number of such records, scatterings of thought as the speaker loses the thread of his meditation, forgets what he saw in the painting and what has moved him. His brain becomes as sand, to borrow Shelley's grim figure from "The Triumph of Life." Ashbery's speaker no longer sees the aspect of the painting he had seen before, as "Clouds / In the puddle stir up into sawtoothed fragments." His idle memories begin to invade his thoughts—

> I think of the friends
> Who came to see me, of what yesterday
> Was like.   (SP 71)

These memories "[intrude] on the dreaming model in the silence of the studio as he considers / Lifting the pencil to the self-portrait"; they are interruptions in the consciousness of the poet as he composes this poem, and yet they are not merely interruptions—nagging distractions of the outer world—but the very material of the self. As he puts it later, "Our landscape / Is alive with filiations, shuttlings." Odd contributions constitute the self, and so reveal the poverty of its claims to autonomy and integrity:

> How many people came and stayed a certain time,
> Uttered light or dark speech that became part of you
> Like light behind windblown fog and sand,
> Filtered and influenced by it, until no part
> Remains that is surely you.   (SP 71)

This recognition of the self's striated character raises the question of its destiny. Is there any constructive order in the assortment of fluid experiences, associations, and memories that go to make up the self? Is it collected according to some principle or in accordance with some teleological aim?

> Whose curved hand controls,
> Francesco, the turning seasons and the thoughts

> That peel off and fly away at breathless speeds
> Like the last stubborn leaves ripped
> From wet branches?   (*SP* 71)

No, there is a blank where the organizing principle of the self should be:

> I see in this only the chaos
> Of your round mirror which organizes everything
> Around the polestar of your eyes which are empty,
> Know nothing, dream but reveal nothing.   (*SP* 71)

Finally, all the material that has made up his experience loses the contours of priority and value. It becomes just so much aleatory intrusion blended into one "magma" of insignificance:

> I feel the carousel starting slowly
> And going faster and faster: desk, papers, books,
> Photographs of friends, the window and the trees
> Merging in one neutral band that surrounds
> Me on all sides, everywhere I look.
> And I cannot explain the action of leveling,
> Why it should all boil down to one
> Uniform substance, a magma of interiors.   (*SP* 71)

The stoical gaze of the painter, who understands the disappointment of the self in the impotence of understanding and can do nothing with his knowledge but to represent it, must serve as a model:

> My guide in these matters is your self,
> Firm, oblique, accepting everything with the same
> Wraith of a smile.   (*SP* 71)

Acknowledging the volatile composition of the self puts an end to the fundamental hope of having a productive relation to time. The soul wants to build up its wealth over time, to understand more, know more, and in short, gain from age and experience. But in fact it keeps the same limited dimensions—"small" and fitting "its hollow perfectly"—because it only mutates, shedding its past experience and its former constitution. A recognition like this discombobulates one's relation to time. It used to be that the events brought forward by time could be interpreted as part of a scheme—the development of the self and its purposes—but now they have been stripped of teleology and exposed as mere "accidents."

> Long ago,
> The strewn evidence meant something,
> The small accidents and pleasures
> Of the day as it moved gracelessly on,
> A housewife doing chores. Impossible now
> To restore those properties in the silver blur that is
> The record of what you accomplished by sitting down
> "With great art to copy all that you saw in the glass"
> So as to perfect and rule out the extraneous
> Forever. In the circle of your intentions certain spars
> Remain that perpetuate the enchantment of self with self:
> Eyebeams, muslin, coral. It doesn't matter
> Because these are things as they are today
> Before one's shadow ever grew
> Out of the field into thoughts of tomorrow.   (SP 71–72)

No longer can the "strewn" or scattered experiences of the self be gathered up into some larger story, treated as "evidence" that gradually reveals the hidden narrative; now these experiences are reduced to a "silver blur," like the blurred background in the curved silver mirror, which captured everything in the one idle moment of the painting's present, so as—this is ironical—"to perfect and rule out the extraneous / Forever." The painting embraces the lustrous materials of the sensual world— muslin, coral, the flashing eyes of the painter—those sensual realities that contribute to the stirring and the comfort of narcissism, but belong strictly to the present, and thus do not solve the problem of the shadowy future, a world of images and thoughts. Now the future has become an object of uneasy dread, having lost the suspense of the purposive without losing its devastating potential.

In the opening lines of the next stanza, Ashbery corrects his emphasis. He realizes that the slackening of teleology leaves us at a loss not so much with respect to our future, but to the present. For it is the present that suffers by the emptying out of the future, when the direction provided by teleology ceases to be credible. Teleology serves to organize our view of time, sending out lines to converge ahead, and justifying the present by means of the future. The present is the terrain actually in need of organization:

> Tomorrow is easy, but today is uncharted,
> Desolate, reluctant as any landscape
> To yield what are laws of perspective
> After all only to the painter's deep
> Mistrust, a weak instrument though
> Necessary. (SP 72)

The loss of teleology damages what we call our "dreams," the aim for the future toward which we orient the present. In this slackening of time, what is one to do with those faulty dreams and hopes, which all depend on the promise of teleology? Ashbery is at his harshest on this subject: dreams are necessary illusions, doomed to be exposed as illusion, and then reformulated in order to sustain the incorrigible master-illusion of teleology, "the source of dreams." For time, which extinguishes dreams, also keeps inventing them, and thus the larger dream of purpose is maintained; and if it should ever be demystified, it would leave stark desolation in its wake:

> What should be the vacuum of dream
> Becomes continually replete as the source of dreams
> Is being tapped so that this one dream
> May wax, flourish like a cabbage rose,
> Defying sumptuary laws, leaving us
> To awake and try to begin living in what
> Has now become a slum. (SP 73)

Dreams serve to sustain the illusion that our present is substantial, ripe with the promises of our future; individual dreams protect the larger myth; and the end of dreams spells the end of direction. When a dream lapses, not only is its particular emptiness exposed, but the emptiness of our time, which is not in the business of bringing us forward. Then we perceive the value of dreams retrospectively, when we have ceased to believe in them.

> "The forms retain
> A strong measure of ideal beauty," because
> Fed by our dreams, so inconsequential until one day

We notice the hole they left. Now their importance
If not their meaning is plain. They were to nourish
A dream which includes them all, as they are
Finally reversed in the accumulating mirror.
They seemed strange because we couldn't actually see them.
And we realize this only at a point where they lapse
Like a wave breaking on a rock, giving up
Its shape in a gesture which expresses that shape.
The forms retain a strong measure of ideal beauty
As they forage in secret on our idea of distortion.
Why be unhappy with this arrangement, since
Dreams prolong us as they are absorbed?
Something like living occurs, a movement
Out of the dream into its codification.   (SP 73)

We return here to one of the problems adumbrated in the first stanza:
the problem of a disappointed or demystified perspective that regards itself as both unproductive and intractable. Ashbery strikes a caustic note,
wondering implicitly what could be the point of perceiving that the
dream of teleology is fallacious. Such knowledge is not useful, and even
more vexing, it is not permanent. We awake to the emptiness of dreams
in order to know that we will forget our knowledge. Despair at the fact
that we have no choice prompts him to ask, unhappily, "Why be unhappy with this arrangement?" The "arrangement" provides the illusions that sustain us between episodes of short-lived insight. "Dreams
prolong us as they are absorbed"; they enable us to persevere by filling
the present and future with distraction and in this way, as he grimly puts
it, "Something like living occurs."

    The sense of deadlock remains through the next stanza, in which
Ashbery insists darkly on the corrosion of the self through time. He begins
to drift again and to "forget" the face of the mirror portrait, but then it
returns in alienated majesty, "Riding at anchor, issued from hazards,"
looking eerie, bold, and vulnerable, "'rather angel than man'" (SP 73).
With a swift stroke of his melancholy, Ashbery transforms this face—
lonely, floating, displaced—into an image of the lost self:

        Perhaps an angel looks like everything
        We have forgotten, I mean forgotten

> Things that don't seem familiar when
> We meet them again, lost beyond telling,
> Which were ours once.   (*SP* 74)

Proust would have endorsed this reflection on the obsolescence of "*l'ancien moi.*" One changes so much as to lose any feeling of continuity with the old self; we cannot remember to remember aspects of ourselves that have disappeared in time, and if we "meet them again," if we find evidence of their having been, they seem puzzling and remote; nothing in us now recalls or speaks for what we were.

In the remaining stanzas of the poem, Ashbery tries out a variety of solutions to the predicament of the self paralyzed by disenchantment with the possibilities of self and stranded in a forlorn vacuum of time. He tries them out and rejects them all one by one. His first pass at a resolution is particularly fleeting. He finds a way to repudiate the anguishing "conclusions" of the painting, but it is one that he himself hardly finds credible:

> Your argument, Francesco,
> Had begun to grow stale as no answer
> Or answers were forthcoming. If it dissolves now
> Into dust, that only means its time had come
> Some time ago, but look now, and listen:
> It may be that another life is stocked there
> In recesses no one knew of; that it,
> Not we, are the change; that we are in fact it
> If we could get back to it, relive some of the way
> It looked, turn our faces to the globe as it sets
> And still be coming out all right:
> Nerves normal, breath normal.   (*SP* 76)

The painting "argues" that time is hostile to us; our relation to it is tragic. Ashbery wants to represent this idea to himself as "stale"—jejune, melodramatic—and to substitute for it a benign version of our relation to time, one in which we are not at odds with it, but move with it, faithfully, as it moves. To accept this view would mean to own our mutations: to think of them as natural or impelled from within. We might simply take a different attitude, or as Ashbery says, adopt a new "metaphor" through which we would regard the subduction of the present under the past with tranquillity: we could "turn our faces to the globe as it sets / And still be coming out all right: Nerves normal, breath normal." And actually we do this routinely; the metaphor is "Made to include us, we are a part of it and / Can live in it as in fact we have done" (*SP* 76).

But this "pleasant intuition" is not to last long. Now its quick vanishing exposes it as a wish-fulfillment, a reaction to the darker thought of the painting, which Ashbery had never really dismissed. The pleasant "dream" leaves its "white precipitate" (reminiscent of some powdery poison) to reassert the tragic perspective, which, after all, harmonizes with "the climate of sighs flung across our world."

> A breeze like the turning of a page
> Brings back your face: the moment
> Takes such a big bite out of the haze
> Of pleasant intuition it comes after.
> The locking into place is "death itself,"
> As Berg said of a phrase in Mahler's Ninth;
> Or, to quote Imogen in *Cymbeline*, "There cannot
> Be a pinch in death more sharp than this," for,
> Though only exercise or tactic, it carries
> The momentum of a conviction that had been building.
> Mere forgetfulness cannot remove it
> Nor wishing bring it back, as long as it remains
> The white precipitate of its dream
> In the climate of sighs flung across our world,
> A cloth over a birdcage.   (*SP* 76–77)

The tragic perspective must be granted. In fact, Ashbery concedes, it is the pressure of time and mortality which in the end give "beauty." Yet self-effacement is the price of affirming this beauty, for the sheen of hope and vulnerability belongs to all lives, and one can affirm this dignifying pathos only at the cost of surrendering one's uniqueness. Hence Ashbery's next sentiment is one of sharp self-contempt:

> I go on consulting
> This mirror that is no longer mine
> For as much brisk vacancy as is to be
> My portion this time.   (*SP* 77)

This "self-portrait" is hardly a self-portrait at all, there being not much to portray but the vague generality of experience. Nor does the author have any special powers of insight; he is just offering up his modicum of banal introspection, or "brisk vacancy."

Ashbery has shown how the self's desire for permanence, continuity and growth cannot be fulfilled. Now he experiments with another mode of absorbing that disappointment: he resigns a portion of narcissism and determines to embrace the strandedness of the present—its status as the only reality though doomed to supersession. This experiment eventually falters, with Ashbery's recollection that in fact the present has no self-sufficient grandeur. We do not forget the other aspects of time or cease to feel the confusion of our abandonment in time. However pressed by conviction and necessity, we cannot come to rest in the present, as in our element. We will continue to experience the sort of division and unease that Kierkegaard described: the unease of an "existing subject," a creature of the moment caught in time but harassed by the call of a transcendent vocation. Stevens was pursuing this intuition in his dictum:

> From this the poem springs: that we live in a place
> That is not our own, and, much more, not ourselves
> And hard it is in spite of blazoned days.
> ("Notes toward a Supreme Fiction," 383)

Ashbery expresses his unease more quietly, in admitting the persistent question:

> But what is this universe the porch of
> As it veers in and out, back and forth,
> Refusing to surround us and still the only
> Thing we can see?   (*SP* 77)

The pressure of transcendent vocation disturbs and devalues our temporal existence, making it seem inadequate. Such an existence does not saturate our capacities or desires; and from this failure the notion arises that existence is no more than a place of trial, the limen or gateway to another world. Ashbery's "porch" is (a characteristically deflated) heir of Stevens's "fragrant portals"; and further back, of the "portal" Shelley wanted to cross in his "Ode to Heaven."

Ashbery nostalgically recalls the experiences that used to appear to fulfill our "higher destiny." At one time love seemed to satisfy the impulse toward transcendence, yet that comfort has somehow faded: "Love once / Tipped the scales but now is shadowed, invisible." It has not been abandoned, but its promise has been reduced, for now it evokes wistful rather than active longings. It remains

> mysteriously present, around somewhere.
> But we know it cannot be sandwiched
> Between two adjacent moments, that its windings
> Lead nowhere except to further tributaries
> And that these empty themselves in a vague
> Sense of something that can never be known
> Even though it seems likely that each of us
> Knows what it is and is capable of
> Communicating it to the other. But the look
> Some wear as a sign makes one want to
> Push forward ignoring the apparent
> Naivete of the attempt, not caring
> That no one is listening, since the light
> Has been lit once and for all in their eyes
> And is present, unimpaired, a permanent anomaly,
> Awake and silent. (SP 77–78)

Love still teases us with its possibilities—and it is not valueless. We still follow the "light" in another's eyes; but by this light we are led back to the amorphous, improvisatory present, where love's intimation of transcendence disappears. A romance with time is left in tatters, as the course of love unfolds

> to the end
> Of our dreaming, as we had never imagined
> It would end, in worn daylight with the painted
> Promise showing through as a gage, a bond.
> This nondescript, never-to-be-defined daytime is
> The secret of where it takes place (SP 78)

It turns out that even love is a thing of today, re-formed in the indifferent present and deprived of a certain future.

It is the issue of this dim, disorienting present, and our unhappy relation to it, that Ashbery takes up next. The present is banal and yet amorphous, beginning all over again from scratch, without much help from
the past. As a consequence, the present in which we are enmired has for
us a baffling, yet anticlimactic mystery. We come into our present feeling
unprepared and a bit bewildered, as if thrust into the project prematurely: "All we know / Is that we are a little early." Yet we are conscious
that the present is the only time accessible to experience and the moment
in which events may happen. The more Ashbery loses faith in the substantiality of the self and its history, the more vivid he finds the reality
and singularity of the present:

> Today has that special, lapidary
> Todayness that the sunlight reproduces
> Faithfully in casting twig-shadows on blithe
> Sidewalks. No previous day would have been like this.
> I used to think they were all alike,
> That the present always looked the same to everybody
> But this confusion drains away as one
> Is always cresting into one's present.   *(SP* 78)

He used to be cavalier about the present; it seemed to consist of a trivial
instantaneity. But the pressure of maturity and years of "cresting into
one's present" have revealed its weighty, somewhat chilling specificity—
the historical character and distinctness of each day—so that his sense
of immediacy has become acute, almost vertiginous: "No previous day
would have been like this."

> Yet one cannot come to rest
> In the present we are always escaping from
> And falling back into, as the waterwheel of days
> Pursues its uneventful, even serene course.   *(SP* 78–79)

The "serene course" of the waterwheel proceeds evenly, in spite of our
restlessness; and our striving to transcend the present can only "fall back
into" or coincide with its "cresting." Yet eagerly and inevitably, we push
out of the tedious present, as the painting shows:

I think it is trying to say it is today
And we must get out of it even as the public
Is pushing through the museum so as to
Be out by closing time. You can't live there.
The gray glaze of the past attacks all know-how:
Secrets of wash and finish that took a lifetime
To learn and are reduced to the status of
Black and white illustrations in a book where colorplates
Are rare. That is, all time
Reduces to no special time. (*SP* 79)

The present itself cannot be isolated and privileged; it is too slight, "You can't live there," and meantime the "gray glaze of the past"—the past however dimmed and faded—nags the present with its anteriority. "All time / Reduces to no special time." For the prospect of death makes any settling in the present impossible. The craving for greatness in the painting itself reminds us of this.

Our time gets to be veiled, compromised
By the portrait's will to endure. It hints
At our own, which we were hoping to keep hidden. (*SP* 79)

Ashbery had anticipated this theme earlier in the poem, in describing the quiet monotony of time, which has lost its character of "promise" and become "unvarying," "Except perhaps to brighten bleakly and almost / Invisibly, in a focus sharpening toward death." But this death is a crude force vitiating all his subtlety:

We don't need paintings or
Doggerel written by mature poets when
The explosion is so precise, so fine.
Is there any point in even acknowledging
The existence of all that? Does it
Exist? Certainly the leisure to
Indulge stately pastimes doesn't,
Any more. (*SP* 79)

Lamenting the apprehension and sorrow of mortality, writing "doggerel" about it, is perhaps no more than a "stately pastime," for which we no longer have the "leisure," that is, the desire. For

> Today has no margins, the event arrives
> Flush with its edges, is of the same substance,
> Indistinguishable.   (SP 79)

The joys of reflection and articulation have lost their mystique, that hint of transcendence that was in them. We are in no position to savor the events of our life; the "margin" of contemplation has disappeared, that sense of being at once the hero, spectator, and judge of one's life. With severity, Ashbery concludes that

> There is no other way, and those assholes
> Who would confuse everything with their mirror games
> Which seem to multiply stakes and possibilities, or
> At least confuse issues by means of an investing
> Aura that would corrode the architecture
> Of the whole in a haze of suppressed mockery,
> Are beside the point. They are out of the game,
> Which doesn't exist until they are out of it.   (SP 79–80)

These "assholes" are none other than Ashbery himself in an earlier phase, when those dreams he has now undone, the dream of the "promise" of time and the dramatic fate of the soul "multi[plied] stakes and possibilities," suffusing his life with a factitious "aura." The aura was sheer mystification—so ridiculous it dwelt in "a haze of suppressed mockery" —and serious thinking about life, he says brusquely, can begin only when that foolish idealization of the self perishes. But this is a desperate claim, for Ashbery does not represent demystification as a way out either. With his angry dismissal, all he has done is to direct his bitterness against himself, for lack of a better object. No wonder he thinks next, sadly: "It seems like a very hostile universe" (SP 80). "The principle of each individual thing is / Hostile to, exists at the expense of all the others": the present, past, and future compete with one another. There is continual war of the spirit, complicated by a disheartening awareness of division between truth and desire.

But the present at least is whole in itself; it is "*This* thing," "mute" and "undivided"—the real, the undistinguished thing. Perhaps it is the writer's task to trace its contours, to recover and speak for this "mute" thing. Yet in another turn, another disappointment, Ashbery finds that

that is not possible: the writer cannot remain "undivided" in this present and be true to it. The artist's hope of immortalizing his insight and skill in art is compromised by the porousness of the self and the present moment in which it dwells:

> *This* thing, the mute, undivided present,
> Has the justification of logic, which
> In this instance isn't a bad thing
> Or wouldn't be, if the way of telling
> Didn't somehow intrude, twisting the end result
> Into a caricature of itself. This always
> Happens, as in the game where
> A whispered phrase passed around the room
> Ends up as something completely different.
> It is the principle that makes works of art so unlike
> What the artist intended. Often he finds
> He has omitted the thing he started out to say
> In the first place. Seduced by flowers,
> Explicit pleasures, he blames himself (though
> Secretly satisfied with the result), imagining
> He had a say in the matter and exercised
> An option of which he was hardly conscious,
> Unaware that necessity circumvents such resolutions.
> So as to create something new
> For itself, that there is no other way,
> That the history of creation proceeds according to
> Stringent laws, and that things
> Do get done in this way, but never the things
> We set out to accomplish and wanted so desperately
> To see come into being.   (*SP* 80)

Here we have again that rather unexpected note of severity and despair —"there is no other way"—which had appeared earlier in the stanza. The medium of utterance distorts what one meant to have said, introducing into the present another kind of fissure—between what one thought or intended and its expression. The artist is not the master of his own work, for the influence of something alien and uncontrolled—a slippage between himself and his "self-portrait"—enters in. But Ashbery refuses to exaggerate the problem, adding that "things / Do get done in this way."

The fate of authorship, though baffling to both the plans and the self-conception of the artist, does not lead to simple failure; the artist ends up with something that, though it may not be what he had in mind, still "secretly satisfies" him. His predicament is not dire. Thus Ashbery resists melodrama, yet his disappointment vividly reemerges at the end of the passage when he confesses that the things which do get done are not those we "wanted so desperately / To see come into being."

Once more, the drift of consciousness enters into the composition of the poem, as Ashbery begins to lose track of his purposes and to stray from his intensities, so that he is left with the detritus of the insight he set out to pursue. He is now stuck with "spoiled" inspiration, as he records with rising disgust:

> A ship
> Flying unknown colors has entered the harbor.
> You are allowing extraneous matters
> To break up your day, cloud the focus
> Of the crystal ball. Its scene drifts away
> Like vapor scattered on the wind. The fertile
> Thought-associations that until now came
> So easily, appear no more, or rarely. Their
> Colorings are less intense, washed out
> By autumn rains and winds, spoiled, muddied,
> Given back to you because they are worthless. (SP 81)

But the original inspiration will not simply vanish and leave him in peace: "their implications are still around *en permanence*, confusing / Issues" (SP 81). He could abandon his vocation, live for the present, "be serious only about sex," yet the past and its messages will not fall completely silent. Even now, Parmigianino's painting continues to exercise its spell —making claims on our attention, seeming to offer answers to pressing existential questions, but ones which we cannot quite decipher. And at the same time its immediacy is dissolving: we "linger in" the painter's face,

> receiving
> Dreams and inspirations on an unassigned
> Frequency, but the hues have turned metallic,
> The curves and edges are not so rich. (SP 81)

We peer into the painting in search of the solution for which we are always casting about; and the painting is tantalizingly urgent, evidently profound, but its point seems somehow to evaporate before it reaches us. As usual, we have to resort to other people's "theories" in order to "decode our own man-size quotient," yet these theories always turn out to be faulty and useless:

> Each person
> Has one big theory to explain the universe
> But it doesn't tell the whole story
> And in the end it is what is outside him
> That matters, to him and especially to us
> Who have been given no help whatever
> In decoding our own man-size quotient and must rely
> On second-hand knowledge.
>
> (SP 81–82)

We easily perceive the parochial and inadequate character of other people's existential "theories," but we are not thereby freed from needing or searching for one of our own. The search is the outcome of endless pressure, which no demystification or recognition of futility can relieve. Ashbery would seem to share Kierkegaard's intuition that solution and satisfaction are available only in the abstract, while the "existing individual" is a "poor, wretched" thing "who stumbles again and again and progresses very slowly from year to year."[19] The whole of "Self-Portrait" exemplifies Kierkegaard's idea that it is the vocation of the subject to experience his subjectivity as disappointing. The very nature of vocation is not to provide its own reward but to be uncertain and unfulfilling.

Turning away from this dead end, Ashbery recurs to the thought of steeping oneself in the pleasures of immediacy—in sensuality and a kind of fond materialism—but he now invokes the prospect in a merely nostalgic mode. It is already too late.

> Once it seemed so perfect—gloss on the fine
> Freckled skin, lips moistened as though about to part
> Releasing speech, and the familiar look
> Of clothes and furniture that one forgets.
> This could have been our paradise: exotic
> Refuge within an exhausted world, but that wasn't

> In the cards, because it couldn't have been
> The point.   (*SP* 82)

The terms in which this "paradise" is characterized already show why it
"wasn't / In the cards." For it would only have been, in Ashbery's beautiful phrase, an "exotic / Refuge within an exhausted world." His "exotic
refuge" was as contrived and intent, as Shelley's pursuit of a benign imagination in "Lerici." It was to represent a self-conscious retreat chosen
and embraced in the shadow of despair. But its dark source would have
compromised it, and "exoticism" here has all the connotations of deca-
dence. A pastoral inner life cannot be willed into being; and more to the
point, a self-conscious fantasy cannot sustain itself.

In the next breath, Ashbery renounces any Zenlike pose of welcom-
ing immediacy. Those who try to "[ape] naturalness," end up with mere
artificiality, not with something spontaneous but with

> a frozen gesture of welcome etched
> On the air materializing behind it,
> A convention.   (*SP* 82)

Ashbery repudiates such "conventions," and with them, the hope of a
cognitive therapy for our unease. The potential consolations (sensualism,
philosophy) have lost their credibility for him, and he suddenly brushes
aside all such thoughts. In one of those bursts of brutality that are so arresting in him, he rejects the aspiration toward acceptance on the grounds
that we are already committed to bewilderment and inauthenticity:

> we have really
> No time for these [conventions], except to use them
> For kindling. The sooner they are burnt up,
> The better for the roles we have to play.   (*SP* 82)

This is a stern remark: it registers Ashbery's determination to regard the
existential problem as intractable. We really are to have no help in "de-
coding our own man-size quotient." For it is not on behalf of a more authentic life that we are to "burn up" or discard poses, but only in order
to adopt the other "roles" already assigned to us. And those "roles" are
the roles we have to play in our attitudes toward our existence: as de-

jected by the littleness of the self, as restless about our place in time, as hopeful, afraid, oblivious, ashamed, arrogant, and deluded. In any case, we will remain Kierkegaardian subjects, incapable of transcending the possibilities time accords us.

It is with this last alternative and its dismissal, near the end of the poem, that Ashbery surrenders the effort to think his way around the "life-obstructing" message of the painting. The painting was right in the end: our relation to time is a tragic one. Ashbery will not put up any more of a fight against its melancholy perspective. He accepts the justice of its representation and asks only to be relieved of its by now unnecessary urgency. It is out of defeat, not rejection, that he pleads: "Therefore I beseech you, withdraw that hand" (SP 82). The painting's insistence is painful because it suggests that we can come to some crisis in our relation to time, cross some Rubicon or make a bold, liberating existential decision; it is this that Ashbery has discovered not to be so. What the painting "says" is accurate and yet anachronistic; for the Rubicon is not to be found, and once more, this time definitively, the momentum of consciousness is forcing the painting's own drama into the background:

> Therefore I beseech you, withdraw that hand,
> Offer it no longer as a shield or a greeting,
> The shield of a greeting, Francesco:
> There is room for one bullet in the chamber:
> Our looking through the wrong end
> Of the telescope as you fall back at a speed
> Faster than that of light to flatten ultimately
> Among the features of the room, an invitation
> Never mailed, the "it was all a dream"
> Syndrome, though the "all" tells tersely
> Enough how it wasn't.
>
> (SP 82)

The poem ends on this note of frustration, as the "waking dream" of Ashbery's encounter with the painting fades out, and his attention is reabsorbed by "the cold, syrupy flow" of the actual. The force of his thoughts evades him; he forgets them, as well as forgetting that he knew them, and though the poem may recall them, it is in a form somehow frozen and inaccessible, in "cold pockets of remembrance, whispers out of time." He is forced to conclude inconclusively, with this ambivalent characterization of writing and a correspondingly ambivalent valediction to his poem. He remains steeped in time, in a present already departing from the time in which the poem was composed. He concedes, like Wordsworth, in his perplexity and chagrin, "I cannot paint / What then I was" ("Tintern Abbey," 75–76). For the hand that paints, the mind that represents, loses its knowledge, "And cannot know it knew" (*SP* 83). Like Wordsworth, Shelley, and Stevens, Ashbery is endlessly, painfully surprised to find a definitive blank where the soul's last resource, its own authority over itself, should be. "Self-Portrait in a Convex Mirror" demonstrates that this is a truth never to be fully grasped, assimilated or overcome.

"Self-Portrait in a Convex Mirror" tracks shifting responses to disappointment in a single episode of thought, an episode that may be imagined as occurring over the space of an afternoon, or a day, or maybe only twenty minutes. The poem expands as it follows the curve of thought from recognition to repudiation through struggle and return. But still it is only fifteen pages. The reader might wonder about the role of disappointment in longer narratives. Although this book has shown that the romantic and postromantic lyric particularly cultivated the delineation of disappointment, it has naturally been a subject of interest to many modern authors. Formal reasons, perhaps, have made it the special province of poetry. This afterword considers the difficulties of representing disappointment in story or novel form, and the signal successes some authors have had.

If poetry provides the appropriate venue for the description of disappointment, it does so in part because of its temporal frame: the meditative or lyric poem can portray a delimited psychological moment. This is essential for the representation of disappointment, which perceives itself, paradoxically, both as chronic and as encased in a frozen present. A poem arrests the psyche in crisis; any succeeding psychic movement is necessarily abbreviated. But what about novels and stories, narratives in which time unfolds? Is it possible to portray a *course* of disappointment, or how exactly can a narrative that covers months or years depict an iteration of panic?

In fact, it is difficult for narratives to work within the constraints of the temporal moment, and for this reason prose treatments of disappointment are rare. Narratives of disillusionment, however, are common, especially novels that portray a series of disillusionments. This is the usual trajectory of the nineteenth-century bildungsroman, the novel in which a main character ages by experiencing the loss of ideals. For example, Flaubert's *Sentimental Education* recounts the story of the fool Frederic, who comes to Paris in pursuit of the high life and after dispiriting adventures sees through the "artificial world in which he had suffered so much" (409). Flaubert delights in describing the gradual erosion of his obtuse hero's enthusiasm, but just at the point of its consummation —when Frederic has attained to the balked life of disappointment— Flaubert drastically foreshortens his tale. He moves into generalization because his hero has begun to lead a monotonous interior life, in which all experience is repetitive:

> He travelled.
> He came to know the melancholy of the steamboat, the cold awakening in the tent, the tedium of landscapes and ruins, the bitterness of interrupted friendships.
> He returned.
> He went into society, and he had other loves. But the ever-present memory of the first made them insipid; and besides, the violence of desire, the very flower of feeling, had gone. His intellectual ambitions had also dwindled. Years went by; and he endured the idleness of his mind and the inertia of his heart. (411)

This aimless life is represented as deadening, rather than anxious, which helps to justify the brevity of its description. Frederic's dreary middle age is the wan conclusion of the life he has wasted; it can be summarized efficiently because it lacks the variety and suspense that make for narrative.

Flaubert treats disappointment elliptically, as being in some sense beneath representation because it is an enfeebled, antidramatic condition. In an approach to the problem that may be typical in its own way, Mary McCarthy takes the opposite tack: in her novel *Birds of America*, disappointment is so terrible a state she will not lessen it by representation but has to leave it to be imagined. Her protagonist's serial disillusionment builds to a devastating qualitative change, but the novel stops short at the point of this catastrophe.

An idealistic, leftist college student spends his junior year abroad in

Paris, where his high standards, his generous views, and his precise ethics come to grief. Wherever he takes refuge—in art, nature, a Kantian personal morality—his refuge is soon invaded and destroyed. Yet he is open-minded and largely brave, flexible and resilient until the last chapter, when everything goes wrong and his morale collapses. He finds a clocharde huddled on the landing in his apartment building, and having been disturbed about the clochardes for a long time, because he is disgusted by them and yet also feels responsible for them, he takes her in. After making her a bed, he lies awake all night, filled with repugnance, anxiety, and guilt. His scheme to be good has fallen apart, and with it his belief in the Kantian rationale for goodness:

> If this *clocharde* seemed more alien to him than any brute creature, it was just *because* she shared with him, supposedly, a moral faculty that animals did not have, and this moral faculty in man was a regulatory instinct that kept him in balance with the natural things of the world, which were good without putting out any effort. But it was hard to believe that there was any such universal moral faculty when you had a proof to the contrary a few feet away from you. If it was not the *clocharde's* choice that she had got into this grisly state, then there was no freedom of the will, and if it *was* her choice, of which tonight he felt convinced, then the will's objects were not the same for everybody. Either way, everything he cared about fell to pieces. As for the great "Know yourself," after tonight, he would rather not. It was no use pretending that there was common humanity in *him* when all he could think of in the midst of his philosophizing was how many minutes still had to pass before dawn came to his rescue. (333)

The deepest content of his disillusionment is self-disgust. By means of losing an abstract ideal, he loses his self-interest or self-respect, and so is put on the path to ennui. The next morning he discovers from newspaper headlines that the United States has started bombing North Vietnam. He goes to the park with a shallow friend, and because he is an amateur ornithologist, he insists on visiting the water birds; at the pond, his friend teases the wild swans, and one of them bites Peter viciously. He gets a severe infection and is admitted to the hospital in a state of delirium. His mother comes to visit, seeming to him weak and wavering ("She had no authority for him any more"). He has a horrible delirious vision of Kant. It is with this that the novel ends:

"I was thinking of you yesterday," Peter went on . . . "I guess it was yesterday. In the Jardin des Plantes. Something our professor said you said about the beautiful things in the world proving that man is made for and fits into the world and that his perception of things agrees with the laws of his perception. It sounded better when he read it in German." "'*Die schönen Dinge zeigen an* . . .' *Ach, ja!*" Kant bowed his head and sighed.

"Excuse me, sir, you have something to tell me, don't you?" The tiny man moved forward on the counterpane and looked Peter keenly in the eyes, as though anxious as to how he would receive the message he had to deliver. He spoke in a low thin voice. "God is dead," Peter understood him to say. Peter sat up. "I *know* that," he protested. "And you didn't say that anyway. Nietzsche did." He felt put upon, as though by an impostor. Kant smiled. "Yes, Nietzsche said that. And even when Nietzsche said it, the news was not new, and maybe not so tragic after all. Mankind can live without God." "I agree," said Peter. "I've always lived without Him." "No, what *I* say to you is something important. You did not hear me correctly. Listen now carefully and remember." Again he looked Peter steadily and searchingly in the eyes. "Perhaps you have guessed it. Nature is dead, *mein kind*." (343–44)

Peter's unconscious informs him of his conviction that "Nature is dead." What does this dictum mean? First, it refers to his sentimental love for wild birds, which has been deflated by his encounter with the malignant swans. "Nature" is now dead for him, having become alien and unkind. It is no longer available as a refuge from what he finds unsatisfactory in the human world. Nature's "beauty" has turned out to be factitious. Thus, "Kant" sighs when Peter eagerly and longingly recalls his professor's paraphrase, "the beautiful things in the world [prove] that man is made for and fits into the world." A whole set of teleological propositions and benevolent attitudes dies with that axiom, and Peter's episode of disenchantment shows its affinity with similar moments in the history of romantic and postromantic poetry.

McCarthy represents this last disillusionment as discontinuous with the series Peter has previously experienced; it is not one among others, but the sum of them all, the death of "the dream that sustains all dreams." This meta-loss is definitive; when we last see him, Peter seems to be on the verge of a complete collapse, not prepared to pick up and move on, as he had been in the face of previous reverses, but wary and exhausted at last. McCarthy halts the novel at this threshold of disappointment, leaving the reader to speculate about what will become of Peter after his emotional apocalypse. What can be the content of his inner life now? In truth, it cannot have a possible content: McCarthy has chosen to represent the end state of Peter's disillusionment (which is clearly disappointment) as a punctum rather than a permanent condition. In this way, she does not address the problem of representing its constitutively chronic nature, the (often deceptive) feeling that one must dwell in it forever.

In contrast with both McCarthy and Flaubert, F. Scott Fitzgerald pursued the prolonged afterlife of disappointment into its wasted reaches. Out of an autobiographical interest, Fitzgerald battened on stretches of degeneration when his characters become not climactically, but slowly and incrementally more disoriented and more spent. His aging expatriates, stunned by the collapse of the Jazz Age, and his straggling alcoholics hardly know what to do with themselves in lives that have survived their essential moment, or in which a psychic wound has proved permanent and debilitating. As Fitzgerald chillingly put it,

> One writes of scars healed, a loose parallel to the pathology of the skin, but there is no such thing in the life of an individual. There are open wounds, shrunk sometimes to the size of a pin-prick but wounds still. The marks of suffering are more comparable to the loss of a finger, or of the sight of an eye. We may not miss them, either, for one minute in a year, but if we should there is nothing to be done about it. (*Tender Is the Night* 168–69)

The failures and losses from which his protagonists suffer are irreversible. Fitzgerald was fascinated by the corrosive effects of demoralization, and he sought to represent its slow, obscure, erratic history in his novels *The Beautiful and Damned* and *Tender Is the Night*, condemned by some critics as wandering and lugubrious.

Chekhov wrote the perfect short narrative of disappointment. In the typical course of his stories, a protagonist who is sad at the outset finds reason to become more so; a pregnant woman discontented with her husband suffers a miscarriage; poor people at a rural station see a beautiful woman pass by in a train and feel despair; a professor loses interest in his work and family after being diagnosed with a terminal illness—he turns to a beloved daughter surrogate for comfort, but she is distracted by her own miseries, and they are unable to help one another. Such are some of Chekhov's many vignettes of pure and deepening sorrow.

Though the example of Chekhov suggests that the short story is preferable for the exploration of disappointment, the great counter example is Proust, chronicler of the decline of magic of every kind. He gives a meticulous record of the gradual erosion of his narrator's ideals and of his capacity for idealization, as summarized by his reencounter with the withered husks of the figures he once held in awe. This reencounter occurs in the last party scene, the matinee at the Guermantes's, in *Le Temps Retrouvé*, when he recalls the glamour with which he once invested his hero Swann, the artist Bergotte, and the elegant Duchesse de Guermantes. It has been years since these people seemed marvelous to him, but the memory of that time comes back and of the "origines presque fabuleuses, charmante mythologie des relations devenues si banales ensuite" (III, 974). There would appear to be nothing left of the narrator's fascinations, and yet in his perspicacity Proust does not allow disenchantment to have the last word. He shows that the narrator's desiccation is a fictitious accomplishment, for he has never really resigned the naive idealizations from which he imagines he has freed himself. He has survived but not transcended his longings. The memory of pleasures experienced under the spell of the dream still moves him. After all, these pleasures are irreplaceable; though their power may be lost, their charm cannot be. Their memory rises up in him again like wavelets in the stream; they refuse to be dismissed. And so he sees that he is not the master of his feelings and history, but a creature of disappointment, helpless and amazed:

> bien que je ne crusse pas à l'amitié, ni en avoir jamais véritablement éprouvé pour Robert, en repensant à ces histoires du lift et du restaurant où j'avais déjeuné avec Saint-Loup et Rachel j'étais obligé de faire un effort pour ne pas pleurer. (III, 688).

Introduction

1. Fitzgerald, "Crack-Up," 81.
2. Lyotard, *Peregrinations*, 3.
3. Kierkegaard, *Concluding Unscientific Postscript*, 256.
4. Ibid., 217.
5. Ibid., 130.
6. Proust himself portrays the self pared down in its own esteem when he breaks the retrospective frame of his novel, briefly, to sketch out an image of the narrator's present condition: "moi l'étrange humain qui, en attendant que la mort le délivre, vit les volets clos, ne sait rien du monde, reste immobile comme un hibou et, comme celui-ci, ne voit un peu clair que dans les ténèbres" (2:982). The narrator regards himself not as an author triumphantly reaping the reward of his vocation (shut up in his cork-lined room writing *A la recherche du temps perdu*) but as a ghostly invalid surviving into an anonymous, marginal existence. This moment of self-reduction should serve to correct the basic misreading of Proust in which he is thought to celebrate art's redemptive powers.
7. Kristeva, *Black Sun*, 4.
8. Ibid., 3.
9. Freud, "Mourning," 170.
10. Freud, "Family Romances," 41.
11. Ibid., 44–45.
12. Ibid., 45.
13. Klein, "Mourning," 353.
14. Ibid., 345.
15. Ibid., 349. In her recent biography, Phyllis Grosskurth has shown that "Mrs. A" is Klein herself.
16. Ibid., 360.
17. Klein, "Sense of Loneliness," 305.
18. No doubt his relief at discovering (or deciding) that he has not been inwardly emptied motivates his claim that with Dorothy's help, he "Maintained . . . a saving intercourse / With my true self (for, though impaired, and changed / Much, as it seemed, I was no further changed / Than as a clouded, not a waning moon" (10.908 ff.).
19. Klein, "Mourning," 355.
20. Rycroft, "On Idealization," 36.

21. "The shaken belief in the good objects disturbs most painfully the process of idealization, which is an essential intermediate step in mental development" (Klein, "Mourning," 357). Note that she says "intermediate"; she will say a page later that at the end of mourning the mourner can acknowledge the imperfections of the dead loved object. But also note that the idealization of the *inner* good object must (logically) go on, for the inner good object is constitutively idealized.

Chapter 1. Wordsworth

1. Through Petrarch and Augustine—the poetry of erotic anxiety and the discourse of spiritual anxiety—Wyatt and Herbert had discovered the theme of disappointment, and the potential it offered for subtlety in psychological representation. But their discovery remained incidental—it hung in the abyss because there was no sufficiently stimulating secular discourse of psychological analysis for it to join, whereas the poetry of sensibility and romanticism was cross-fertilized by the dense and intricate philosophical psychology of eighteenth-century empiricism and its successor, transcendental idealism. Wordsworth and Coleridge owed as much to Locke, Hartley, Hume, and Kant for elaborating the description of complex psychology as for providing a particular vocabulary of subject and object, imagination, and their relations. Without such a discourse, the potential for the lyric description of psychological impasse introduced by Wyatt and Herbert remained largely dormant until the later eighteenth century.

As it happens, Cowper was fascinated by Herbert, particularly during an episode of severe depression at the age of twenty-one, when by his own testimony he found relief only in reading Herbert, though whether it was Herbert's "piety" or his melancholy that drew him remains unclear: "I was struck not long after my settlement in the Temple with such a dejection of spirits as none but they who have felt the same can have the least conception of. Day and night I was upon the rack, lying down in horrors and rising in despair. I presently lost all relish to those studies I had been before closely attached to; the classics had no longer any charm for me; I had need of something more salutary than mere amusement, but had none to direct me where to find it. At length with Herbert's poems, gothic and uncouth as they were, I yet found in them a piety which I could not but admire. This was the only author I had any delight in reading. I pored upon him all day long and though I found not there what I might have found, a cure for my malady, yet it never seemed so much alleviated as while I was reading him. At length I was advised by a very near and dear relation to lay him aside, for he though such an author was more likely to nourish my melancholy than to remove it" (*Letters*, 1:8–9).

2. Jacobus, *Tradition*, 107.

3. Wordsworth, *Lyrical Ballads*, 68.

4. Manning, "Wordworth and Gray's Sonnet," 56.

5. Both Lamb and Byron quoted in Jacobus, *Tradition*, 85.

6. In a late preface to his collection of sonnets, Bowles describes himself as having first undertaken to write his poems when "in youth a wanderer among distant scenes, I sought forgetfulness of the first disappointment in early affections."

7. See Hunt, "Wordsworth and Charlotte Smith," 101.

8. The quotations in Smith's sonnet on forgetfulness are from Boothby and Warton. Her habit of quotation shows that Smith is aware of working within eighteenth-century codifications of poetic sentiment. They may even suggest that she is eager to align her elegiac intensities with preestablished tradition. Throughout her sonnets we find a disconcerting swerve into impersonality—a reticence and appeal to generality—which contrasts oddly with their concentration on her personal anguish. In her prefaces Smith again and again justifies the relentless grimness of her poetry by arguing that it came out of her life; her poems may be "gloomy," but at least she is "exempt from the suspicion of *feigning* sorrow for an opportunity of shewing the pathos with which it can be described—a suspicion that has given rise to much ridicule, and many invidious remarks, among certain critics, and others, who carry into their closets [an] aversion to any thing tragic" (11). There is something a little strange about Smith's having to insist that her sad poems express a sadness she really felt. Perhaps her critics were responding to a certain species of ambiguity in her poems which arises from their insistence on bringing acute personal pain under the cover of universal feeling and conventional description. From our much later perspective, we might be tempted to call this a failure of nerve on Smith's part. It is a familiar enough observation that the romantics managed to develop a persuasive autobiographical discourse out of the rather vague "I" of eighteenth-century meditative poetry. But one must assume that Akenside, Cowper, Thompson, and the like did not themselves feel their poetry to be deficient in this respect; only the innovations of romanticism made it seem so, in retrospect. With Smith the matter seems somewhat more complicated, because she defends an aesthetic of autobiographical accuracy in her prefaces. But she fails to persuade herself, for she remains quite anxious about the charge that her poems exhibit egotism and self-pity. Compare Adela Pinch, "Sentimentality and Experience in Charlotte Smith's Sonnets," chapter 2 in *Strange Fits of Passion*, 51–72.

9. As Wallace Jackson has argued, one distinction between the eighteenth-century and the romantic description of emotion lies in the earlier period's emphasis on identification and separation; by contrast, the romantics were more engaged in exploring undercurrents, contradictions and subtle modulations of feeling ("Wordsworth and His Predecessors: Private Sensations and Public Tones").

10. This phrase is taken from Smith's sonnet "The Laplander," which contrasts the experience of the Laplander, waiting in the dark months for the sun's return, with that of a "sufferer" who has no hope, "who, o'er the waste / Of joyless life is destin'd to deplore / Fond love forgotten, tender friendship past, / Which, once extinguished, can revive no more! / O'er the blank void he looks with hopeless pain; / For him those beams of heaven shall never shine again" (9–14).

11. George Dekker's *Coleridge and the Literature of Sensibility* explores the early romantics' identification with the sensibility poets, their inheritance from those poets of certain images of creativity, and certain ideas about it, including the idea that the exercise of imagination is allied with excessive sensibility, madness, and suicide. In a suggestive aside, he adds that "the literature of Sensibility was haunted quite as much by recollections of lost powers and ecstasies as by premonitions of suicide and madness." (133).

12. Their reaction is described in Holmes, *Coleridge: Early Visions*, 321, and also in Thomas McFarland, "The Symbiosis of Wordsworth and Coleridge," 56–103 of *Romanticism and the Forms of Ruin*, 77.

13. "The Mad Monk" is skipped here because, though it is certainly a poem of disappointment, it is not presented as autobiographical and its authorship is disputed.

14. Paul Magnuson, *Coleridge and Wordsworth: A Lyrical Dialogue*, 175. Magnuson also rather acutely describes "Frost at Midnight" as a poem of intense loneliness, or "seclusion," and argues that "Tintern Abbey" "identifies its generating text" in "Frost at Midnight" (170) by treating the theme of seclusion. Magnuson goes on to assert that "Tintern Abbey" overcomes the impasse delineated in "Frost at Midnight" by restoring the self's fluid relation to its past and future selves: "Wordsworth portrays his maturing as a continuous growth, a process in which the activities of childhood are transformed into the adult's power of insight and sympathy" (175). This book disagrees with Magnuson's conclusion, as will be seen from the discussion of "Tintern Abbey" that follows.

15. For different versions of the relationship between Coleridge and Wordsworth, and their mutual influence and indebtedness, see McFarland and Magnuson, as well as Heath, *Wordsworth and Coleridge*, and Ruoff, *Wordsworth and Coleridge*.

16. Coleridge wrote "Sonnet: To the River Otter," his imitation of Bowles's "To the River Itchin," in 1793. (The year before he had written a poem "To Disappointment," but unfortunately, this poem, despite its title, is a conventional ode celebrating the virtues of a heavily allegorized Hope, with its "Laughing Hours, and Social Pleasures.")

17. Averill, *Wordsworth and the Poetry*, 43.

18. Ibid., 45.

19. Roe, *Wordsworth and Coleridge*, 273.

20. Abrams, "English Romanticism," 325.

21. Ibid., 329.

22. Ibid., 329.

23. The first of Wordsworth's figures to be paralyzed by the defeat of youthful idealism is the murderer-protagonist of *The Borderers*. In his explanatory essay on the play, Wordsworth associates Rivers's moral collapse with the enthusiasm and subsequent frustration of his public spirit: "He has deeply imbibed a spirit of enterprize in a tumultuous age. He goes into the world and is betrayed into a great crime— That influence on which all his happiness is built immediately deserts him. His tal-

ents are robbed of their weight—his exertions are unavailing, and he quits the world in disgust, with strong misanthropic feelings" (30). Wordsworth's striking phrase "His talents are robbed of their weight" evokes that vexing deadlock in which one's powers have been rendered unusable, though they are still operative. Jacobus rightly draws a connection between the character of Rivers, in *The Borderers*, and the solitary of "Yew-Tree." In moving from play to poem, Wordsworth "discard[ed] the gothic paraphernalia of crime and guilt," and retained what really interested him in both characters—namely, "the theme of morbid disappointment" (31).

24. Roe, *Wordsworth and Coleridge*, 321.

25. It appears that Coleridge may have written these lines. Their equivocation and dubiety would certainly seem characteristic of him.

26. Jacobus, *Tradition*, 32.

27. Frost took up Wordsworth's narrative or third-person description of disappointment. See "The Death of a Hired Man."

28. The "close third person" of novels—which represents subjective experience in a quasi-impersonal voice—is another exception. Novels are discussed in my afterword.

29. Coleridge himself pursued the representation of disappointment in a number of touching late poems, including "The Visionary Hope," "Youth and Age," "Work without Hope," and "The Pang More Sharp than All."

30. Jacobus, *Tradition*, 98.

31. Marcel, "Sketch," 60.

32. Ibid., 52.

33. Johnson, *The Idler*, 182.

34. It makes little difference whether Wordsworth's speakers occupy poems with technically optimistic or pessimistic conclusions; their fate is the same. "Composed upon an Evening of Extraordinary Splendour and Beauty," for example, is a redaction of the Intimations Ode, written roughly fifteen years earlier. This poem moves through an emotional order that is the reverse of the Intimations Ode (not climbing out but falling back); yet the dialectical relation of hope and disappointment in the two poems is the same. In both it becomes clear how Wordsworth's characteristic "gratitude" and "hope" emerge out of disappointment and remain tinged by it, constituting not its transcendence but its epiphenomena. In "An Evening of Extraordinary Splendour," the speaker is at first teased with a recurrence of a "glimpse of glory," and then devastated by its precipitate withdrawal. "Dread Power! whom peace and calmness serve / No less than Nature's threatening voice, / If aught unworthy be my choice, / From THEE if I would swerve; / Oh, let Thy grace remind me of the light / Full early lost, and fruitlessly deplored; / Which, at this moment, on my waking sight / Appears to shine, by miracle restored; / My soul, though yet confined to earth, / Rejoices in a second birth! / —'Tis past, the visionary splendour fades; / And night approaches with her shades."

His very prayer *expresses* his disappointment. The recurrence of feeling has pro-

voked his desperation: it has made him aware of his usual stagnation. At first anguished by this recurrence and frustrated by its futility, he abjures himself to be grateful, but his gratitude is only a masquerade of piety acting as a conduit of despair.

35. Wordsworth, *The Poems*, 978.

36. In 1802, at the same time that he wrote the first four stanzas of the Intimations Ode, Wordsworth also addressed themes of disappointment in such diverse
first-person poems as the blithe-seeming "I Wandered Lonely As a Cloud" and the
sly, complex, self-aware "Resolution and Independence." The fading glamour of
the self inflects "I Wandered Lonely as a Cloud," insofar as the poem celebrates a
merely temporary antidote for a constant of inner tedium. This "vacant or pensive
mood" is a state of apathy in which the self feels itself to be an empty, stagnant place.
Then Wordsworth's memories come to fill his solitude and with their "flashing"
spontaneity, to make the mind seem rich with its hidden and unconscious store. The
invisible treasure of visual memory brings into being that "inward eye" that makes
the mind fascinating to itself; it gives the mind its own body, or to put it another
way, divides the mind into separate capacities which can interact, befriend, and surprise one another. And so the poem ends with a burst of gratitude and relief. But
this influx of happiness emerges out of a very fragile consolation. Against the background of chronic loneliness and boredom, the frolic of mental images is an insubstantial comfort.

"Resolution and Independence," too, is a poem about disappointment, and also a
parody of one. The speaker is seized by the fear that a fate of disappointment awaits
him. But disappointment cannot really be anticipated; by definition, it replaces a
"naive" state that was incapable of expecting or foretelling it. Hence the strange situation of the speaker and the odd humor of the poem. It is hard to take the speaker's
anxiety seriously because it involves an illegitimate rehearsal for disappointment.
But the note of self-consciousness already tinges Wordsworth's poem, most obviously in the tension between its subject matter and its peppy Spenserian stanzas.
The poem constitutes Wordsworth's parody of his own fascination with disappointment, and like all parodies, it does homage to its source. For that which the speaker
dreads emerges as a dark, powerful, and legitimate object of dread, even if neither
the speaker nor the poem is fully able to grasp in advance what it will be.

Hazlitt once described Wordsworth as "the spoiled child of disappointment"
("Mr. Wordsworth," 143), by which he meant that stupid opposition had exasperated Wordsworth into a certain dogmatism and laziness. But Hazlitt's phrase is
suggestive because it points to a dialectic in Wordsworth. Wordsworth saw the two
terms as paired; disappointment overcomes a self that seems in retrospect to have
been a "spoiled child" ("a happy child of earth" [31]), living a life of narcissistic contentment and ease. The writer in the discovery of his vocation and in the first flush
of his creativity is such a "spoiled child," persuaded that the power in him spells
uniqueness and that it guarantees special treatment, satisfaction, and safety. That is

the argument of the famous stanza: "I thought of Chatterton, the marvellous Boy / The sleepless Soul that perished in his pride; / Of Him who walked in glory and in joy / Following his plough, along the mountain-side: / By our own spirits are we deified: / We Poets in our youth begin in gladness; / But thereof come in the end despondency and madness" (ll:43–49).

This "despondency" particular to writers does not stem primarily from disappointment of the hope for recognition and success. Rather, it is the hope being sustained in "self-deification"—of continuing to feel pleasure in being *this* self—that fails. The Poets seize on precisely that sense of self-sufficiency and full-fatedness— that ontological contentment—that Wordsworth's speakers always crave. But the narcissistic pleasure of vocation tends to collapse of its own accord. The "Poets" come to find that writing betrays its promises to the writer. And so "pride," "glory," "joy," and "gladness"—and what is a large part of them, the confidence of their persistence—go under in time.

At this point, the Leech-Gatherer fortuitously comes upon the scene as an example of the fate of disappointment the speaker is dreading. Like so many of the impoverished, unfortunate figures with which Wordsworth is fascinated, he has apparently exhausted the possibility of his life, yet he perseveres in a superogatory survival. He has lost his place, fallen by the way of the fluid course of life, and become, even literally, a wanderer, without house or home. He is something of an embarrassment, a "cumber-world," as Chaucer's Troilus would say. For he is not a tragic hero like Chatterton; he is an utterly humble figure, who never followed a great arc or even had a destiny, and who has now been reduced to eke out his life doing something disgusting (leech gathering!). His lot does not have the passionate grandeur of "despondency and madness"; but it is for this reason precisely that we recognize him as a true figure of disappointment—or what the speaker calls "Solitude, pain of heart, distress and poverty."

Even when the speaker begins to try to regard the Leech-Gatherer as an incarnation of his future self, from whose example he might draw some courage, he is unable to see the Leech-Gatherer as he really is. Instead the speaker shies away, taking refuge in a solipsistic "dream": "The old Man still stood talking by my side; / But now his voice to me was like a stream / Scarce heard; nor word from word could I divide; / And the whole body of the Man did seem / Like one whom I had met with in a dream" (ll:106–10).

The speaker's vision of "mighty Poets in their misery dead" returns, and he presses the Leech-Gatherer for instruction to apply in the future: "How is it that you live, and what is it you do?" The Leech-Gatherer answers, but the speaker listens only enough to construct out of the Leech-Gatherer's tale a fleeting, tragic allegory: "In my mind's eye I seemed to see him pace / About the weary moors continually, / Wandering about alone and silently" (135–37). It is only in the last verse that the speaker's understanding yields to the truth: that to suffer disappointment is to become, not a figure of pale agony, but an ordinary man like this one. So there is no more mystery, no urgent question of how to live and what to do. The problem takes care of itself. The poem ends with a (figurative) burst of laughter, though it is not exactly pleasant or relieved: "I could have laughed myself to scorn to find / In that decrepit Man so firm a mind" (137–38). And, with this, the speaker accepts the continuity of his lot with that of the degraded Leech-Gatherer: "'God,'" said I, 'be my help and stay secure; / I'll think of the Leech-Gatherer on the lonely moor!'" (139–40).

To accept fellowship with the Leech-Gatherer is to begin to enter into the psychology of disappointment, to accept the necessity of one's own degradation. It is in this way that the poem, in spite of its parodic tonality, becomes grave and represents the gravity of disappointment. The poem touches on a delicate form of disappointment, and that is the very dread of it —which already participates in its dynamic, since dread reflects an implicit incorporation of the thought that one will not be spared. In the ambivalent resonance of its last line—triumphant, grim and ironic—the speaker, along with the poem itself, both mocks and honors his apprehensions.

37. The word "disappointment" is flagged in the argument of book 3, "Despondency": "Conversation exhibiting the Solitary's past and present opinions and feelings, till he enters upon his own History at length—His domestic felicity.—Afflictions.—Dejection.—Roused by the French Revolution.—Disappointment and disgust.—Voyage to America.—Disappointment and disgust pursue him.—His return.—His languor and depression of mind, from want of faith in the great truths of Religion, and want of confidence in the virtue of Mankind." Wordsworth, *The Poems*, 93.

38. He proceeds to enthusiastic support of the French Revolution, only to be "disgusted" by its failure; he seeks renewal in "the Western World," only to find that people are selfish and petty there—and that the savage is not noble at all; he returns to England in "disgust," having found so little to admire or to hope for in human life and suffering from a species of philosophical discouragement or existential angst.

39. Contrast the crushed figures in the narratives of "The Ruined Cottage" or "Michael," or in Wordsworth's major autobiographical poems, who are not tempted to articulate their anguish in general philosophical terms; they feel their disappointment as acutely personal, and so as susceptible only to a subjective cure ("subjective" in Kierkegaard's sense; what is *my* fate, what am *I* to do?). Even if Wordsworth comes around to a general solution in the Intimations Ode, it is clear that he invents it just to help *him*. But the Solitary is not uneasy within himself, or struggling within himself; the disappointed figure now has an interlocutor, so that the complex representation of psychology is voided and replaced by a trite spiritual debate. In fact, disappointment in our terms is already subdued and resigned, and it is capable of considerable piety; but its piety exacerbates the condition rather than providing relief.

40. In the following selection of quotations, "hope" is complexly characterized:

"That man was only weak through his mistrust / And want to hope, where evidence divine / Proclaimed to him that hope should be most sure" (10:143–45).

"O friend, / It was a lamentable time for man, / Whether a hope had e'er been his or not / A woeful time for them whose hopes did still / Outlast the shock; most woeful for those few— / They had the deepest feeling of the grief— / Who still were flattered, and had trust in man" (10:354–60).

"Not without one memorial hope, not even / A hope to be deferred—for that would serve / To chear the heart in such entire decay" (10:963–65).

"for there I found / Hope to my hope, and to my pleasure peace" (12:177–80).

41. Compare Hartman's reading of "The Solitary Reaper," *Wordsworth's Poetry*, 3–18.

42. Thomas Weiskel's ambivalent interpretation of Wordsworth, for example, attributes it to his highly mystified and naive confidence in Imagination that he escaped the paralyzing fate of "desublimation," that is, the conflict of analytical intelligence and poetic aspiration that befell his more self-conscious contemporaries (particularly Coleridge and Shelley). See *The Romantic Sublime*.

43. Abrams, "English Romanticism," 327.

44. Ibid., 324.

45. McGann, *The Romantic Ideology*, 88.

46. Levinson, *Wordsworth's Great Period Poems*, 25, 45, 58.

47. Liu, *Wordsworth*, 216.

48. Ibid., 217.

49. Levinson, *Wordsworth's Great Period Poems*, 48.

50. Coleridge, for example, described "The Recluse" as "a poem in blank verse addressed to those who, in consequence of the complete failure of the French Revolution, have thrown up all hopes of the amelioration of mankind, and are sinking into an almost epicurean selfishness, disguising the same under the soft titles of domestic attachment and contempt for visionary *philosophes*" (September 1799; quoted in Nicholas Roe, *Wordsworth and Coleridge*, 268.)

Chapter 2. Shelley

1. Bloom, introduction to *Percy Bysshe Shelley: Modern Critical Views,* 18.

2. Ibid., 3.

3. Shelley, *Shelley's Poetry,* ed. Reiman, 69.

4. Ibid., 70.

5. Sartre, *Being and Nothingness,* 800.

6. The present chapter draws on, and in some cases departs from, earlier work that I did on Shelley. The history of critical debate about Shelley's skepticism and pessimism is discussed in the third and fourth chapters of *Literary Power and the Criteria of Truth.* For the argument behind my assertion about Shelley's rejection of

fatalism, see the chapter called "Daimonic Splendor," especially pp. 98–109. I discuss "Lines Written in the Bay of Lerici" at greater length in *Literary Power,* pp. 127–40.

7. But compare the treatment of two first-person lyrics from Shelley's middle phase: "Ode to the West Wind," discussed previously, and "Stanzas Written in Dejection," which follows.

8. Sperry, *Shelley's Major Verse,* 193.

9. See the discussion of Byron's poem in the introduction.

10. Compare Keach's last chapter, on the sense of dismay and personal failure in Shelley's final lyrics.

11. Figures of anachronism, so common in Shelley's late lyrics, appear as well in *Epipsychidion,* which laments that its addressee is "O too late beloved! O too soon adored, by me!" and recalls that an earlier sexual encounter had scorched the "leaves" of Shelley's "green heart," "until as hair grown grey / O'er a young brow, they hid its unblown prime / With ruins of unseasonable time." This language will recall the somewhat more subtle figure of anachronism in *Adonais:* "He is secure, and now can never mourn / A heart grown cold, a head grown grey in vain" (ll:337–38).

12. Shelley, *Poetical Works,* 667. "The Magnetic Lady to Her Patient" is not in the standard *Shelley's Poetry and Prose,* ed. Reiman.

13. Ibid., 667.

14. Richard Garnett, editor of *Relics of Shelley* (London: Edward Moxon, 1862).

15. See also *Prometheus Unbound,* 454 ff.

16. This is the line as Richard Holmes reads it in *Shelley: The Pursuit,* 724. But in his facsimile edition of the poem, Donald Reiman does not make a reading of the last word; see "Peter Bell the Third", 269.

Chapter 3. Stevens

1. Bloom, *Wallace Stevens,* 360.

2. Vendler, *Wallace Stevens,* 6.

3. Ibid., 11.

4. Ibid., 11.

5. Ibid., 4.

6. Stevens, *Letters,* 832.

7. Bloom, *Wallace Stevens,* 359.

8. Ramazani, *Poetry of Mourning,* 127.

9. Bloom, *Wallace Stevens,* 364.

10. Vendler, *Wallace Stevens,* 28.

11. Contrast Vendler: "Old age, seemingly prehistoric in its survival, is in fact inhabiting a pre-history, as the soul, not yet born, waits to be reincarnated. One morning in March it will wake to find not ideas about the things, that intellectuality of old age, but the youthful thing itself" (*Extended Wings,* 311–12).

12. Ramazani, *Poetry of Mourning,* 123.

13. He maintains this tone of shadowed neutrality in "The Plain Sense of Things," another poem with a turn at the end, but one in which the language is subdued enough to scotch affirmative readings. The poem begins in an evocation of disappointment with the very terms of existence. Stevens turns upon his earlier hopes for himself, upon his unspoken desire to be chosen and to transcend ordinary fate. Now he regards his effort to escape as "fantastic"; he is as incredulous as he will be when he calls his marriage "a queer assertion of humanity" (in "The Rock," 525). It is as if there is nothing more for the mind to do, now that its work has been exposed as fantasy, and it can be seen to have no effect on the imperturbable course of "things." "It is as if / We had come to an end of the imagination / Inanimate in an inert savoir" (502). The only thing the imagination seems good for is to accomplish its obsolescence.

But with the fourth stanza, Stevens seems to revive himself, and to reassert the claims of the imagination: "Yet the absence of the imagination had / Itself to be imagined" (503). The poem now argues that the very starkness of the "plain sense of things" represents a vivid and intense work of imagination. There would seem to be a triumph for the imagination in these claims. And yet the measured tone in which they are advanced dampens any feeling of pleasure we might expect. A cloud of fatality continues to hover about the passage, for instead of discovering a new form of freedom, the imagination regards itself as bound by "necessity"; even its skepticism, its self-demystification, is "required" like another verse in the round. No higher perspective has been achieved, and Stevens's tone remains somber, as he demonstrates the unexalted origin of the mind's latest self-negation.

14. Shelley, *Poetical Works,* 633–34.

15. Bornstein, *Transformations,* 173.

16. Stevens, *Necessary Angel,* 82.

17. Vendler, *Extended Wings,* 231.

18. Ibid., 231.

19. Stevens, *Letters,* 678.

20. Thus, this mother is not merely a symbol, but the actual mother as well; she derives her symbolic power from having been actual. The tenderness and security she offers here is to be contrasted with various expressions of alienation from the purely symbolic mother, Mother Nature, in other Stevens poems:

> Since by our nature we grow old, earth grows
> The same. We parallel the mother's death.
> She walks an autumn ampler than the wind
> Cries up for us and colder than the frost
> Pricks in our spirits at the summer's end,
> And over the bare spaces of our skies
> She sees a barer sky that does not bend.
>
> ("Anatomy of Monotony," 108)

> He is the inhuman son and she,
> She is the fateful mother, whom he does not know.
>
> ("World without Peculiarity," 454)

> His grief is that his mother should feed on him, himself
> and what he saw.

("Madame La Fleurie," 507)

Stevens's tenderness for the mother in "The Auroras" is tenderness for his human mother and for the capacity to trust what she represents. The pastoral scene in canto 2 of "The Auroras" is therefore not one in which alienation from experience is reversed, but one in which it is tempered by the company and kindness of the actual mother. The dyad of mother and child is secure in a powerful if contracted happiness; but outside the threat—the wind and the boreal night—go on.

21. For more on Stevens's anxious masculinity and its transumption in his late work, see Frank Lentricchia's *Ariel and the Police*.

22. Stevens, *Letters*, 174.

23. Stevens, *Opus Posthumous*, 185.

24. Bloom, *Wallace Stevens*, 261.

25. Riddell, *The Clairvoyant Eye*, 272.

Chapter 4. Ashbery

1. Bloom, introduction to *John Ashbery*, 3. Shoptaw, *Outside Looking Out*, 87.

2. Ashbery acknowledges his romantic origins most explicitly in "Variations, Calypso and Fugue on a Theme of Ella Wheeler Wilcox," an edgy poem, half mocking and half lyrical, that reprises the themes of "Tintern Abbey" and the Intimations Ode. The poem addresses the question of how to manage the discouragements of maturity. Ashbery makes it clear that he considers his loss not as an advance but as sheer disheartenment. With tart irony, he declares that the defeat of his capacity to idealize has the merit of "preparing" him for a future of repeated disappointments: "Well, it is a good experience, to divest oneself of some tested ideals, some old standbys, / And even finding nothing to put in their place is a good experience, / Preparing one, as it does, for the consternation that is to come."

Like the Wordsworth of "Tintern Abbey," he has learned "Later in the vast gloom of cities" that the inevitable trend of experience is to expose the factitiousness of all idealization, and therefore to "strip" him bare, or humiliate him in his own eyes: "the ideas were good only because they had to die, / Leaving you alone and skinless, a drawing by Vesalius." This brutal image of dismemberment reflects the extent of Ashbery's horror at a demystification that seems to leave behind no productive effects and no consolations.

In the rollicking couplets of the "calypso" variation that follows, Ashbery takes what appears to be the opposite stance, professing his resignation and contentment. What he offers is in fact a parodic version of Wordsworthian resignation, a resignation that is porous and ineffective, though only as much as it ever is in Wordsworth himself. Ashbery claims that as a result of abandoning his aesthetic (and more deeply, narcissistic) investments, he came to discover the "joys of home"; but it is clear that this discovery actually represents a retreat or self-circumscription brought about by the disappearance of older powers and pleasures. He resigns himself to limitation—supposedly—though the repulsive image of "the hole of truth" where he is "snug as a bug" testifies to his continued dissatisfaction.

Ashbery at first seems to enjoin self-reliance, but ultimately he does so with irony and self-consciousness, identifying at once the empty grandeur, the anachronism, and the besieged value of this "dream." His sense of deprivation—of how much is lost with the loss of this dream—comes out in the next lines, with their brief evocation of romantic lyricism, and then its bathetic undoing: "It is the wind that comes from afar / It is the truth of the farthest star." Ashbery has concocted a pastiche of a Wordsworthian and Shelleyan rhyme, but his pastiche reflects nostalgia and homage. The far wind and the farthest star are romantic images of transcendence—specifically the tingeing of mundane experience with the autonomous meaning and power of imaginative or aesthetic discovery. These images are highly compromised in Wordsworth and Shelley, and they meet with no better fate here. From the promise and the dream of aesthetic transcendence, Ashbery descends into the bathos of conventional or rote learning: "In all likelihood you will not need these / So take it easy and learn your ABCs." He does not need these images of transcendence, for the "you" addressed here (Ashbery himself) has been forced to acknowledge what Wordsworth and Shelley had already identified as the mediocrity of life. As usual, perceiving both the falsehood and the charm of his old fantasies, Ashbery requires of himself that he should want less, dream less, and accept less than he used to do. He teases himself with the injunction to resume his "trust in [a] dream" he knows is barren. And now his bitterness—or bite—reemerges. For he reprises both the psychological impasse and the nostalgic language ("dream," "gleam") of the Intimations Ode in a futile command to regress: "And trust in the dream that will never come true / 'Cause that is the scheme that is best for you / And the gleam that is the most suitable too."

This is ironical self-consciousness rather than the tortured humility of Wordsworth's speakers. In the conclusion of "Variations," we are closer to the deadlock of Shelley's late lyrics, in which neither resuscitation of ideals nor adaptation to their absence can be imagined.

3. Kierkegaard, *Concluding Unscientific Postscript*, 81.

4. Ibid., 81.

5. Compare the discussion of Kierkegaard in this book's introduction.

6. There is also some dispute about how deeply skeptical or how elegiac the poem is. Alfred Corn advances a fairly optimistic reading: the poem's "principal theme" is that "art is like a distorting mirror wherein we discover a more engaging, mysterious and enduring image of ourselves than unmediated experience affords" ("Magma of Interiors," 89). A more tempered version of this epistemological optimism appears in Altieri, who measures the poem's "impulse to lucidity" against its "impulse to lyricism" (656), and finds that, however rigorous, the poem retains a constructive

ambition, "clarifying for us where we stand and what powers the imagination pre-serves out of time" ("Motives in Metaphor," 687). More recent critics have treated the poem as predominantly subversive.

7. For examples, see McCorkle, *Still Performance*, Leckie, "Art, Mimesis," and Bloom, "Breaking of Form."

8. Kalstone, *Five Temperaments*, 184.

9. Edelman, "Pose of Imposture," 99. See also Gardner, "Bishop and Ashbery," and Leckie, "Art, Mimesis." Stein's "Stevens and Ashbery" is a critique of Ashbery based on the misconceived notion that he is "an incorrigible wiseacre."

10. Keller, "Thinkers," 241.

11. In addition to Norton and Sokolsky, see Looper, "Ashbery's 'Self-Portrait,'" and Stamelman, "Critical Reflections."

12. Norton, "Whispers," 291. The "time" referred to is apparently a historical time, rather than a time in Ashbery's own distant past, as one might take it to be. Compare Edelman: "The more profound absence takes shape as a questioning of the spiritualized, the transcendental claims made on behalf of the self" ("Pose of Imposture," 100).

13. Sokolsky, "Commission," 239.

14. Contrast Shoptaw: "every self is imprisoned within its self-image, guarded by the intercepting expectations of others or itself" (*On the Outside*, 181).

15. Sokolsky, "Commission," 242, 248, 249.

16. Edelman, "Pose of Imposture," 110, 113.

17. Ibid., 113.

18. Ibid., 107.

19. Kierkegaard, *Concluding Unscientific Postscript,* 256.

Abraham, Karl. "A Short Study of the Development of the Libido." In *Selected Papers on Psychoanalysis*. London: Hogarth, 1927.

Abrams, M. H. "English Romanticism: The Spirit of the Age." In *Romanticism: Points of View*, 2d ed., edited by Robert Gleckner and Gerald E. Enscoe, 314–29. Detroit, Mich.: Wayne State Univ. Press, 1970.

Altieri, Charles. "Motives in Metaphor: John Ashbery and the Modernist Long Poem." *Genre* 11 (1978): 653–87.

Ashbery, John. *The Double Dream of Spring*. New York: Echo Press, 1966.

———. *Houseboat Days*. New York: Penguin, 1977.

———. *Self-Portrait in a Convex Mirror*. New York: Penguin, 1975.

Averill, James H. *Wordsworth and the Poetry of Human Suffering*. Ithaca, N.Y.: Cornell Univ. Press, 1980.

Berger, Charles. *Forms of Farewell: The Late Poetry of Wallace Stevens*. Madison: Univ. of Wisconsin Press, 1985.

Blake, William. *The Songs of Innocence and of Experience*. Oxford: Oxford Univ. Press, 1967.

Bloom, Harold. "The Breaking of Form." In *John Ashbery*, edited by Harold Bloom, 115–26.

———. *Wallace Stevens: The Poems of Our Climate*. Ithaca, N.Y.: Cornell Univ. Press, 1976.

———, ed. *John Ashbery: Modern Critical Views*. New York: Chelsea House, 1985.

———, ed. *Percy Bysshe Shelley: Modern Critical Views*. New York: Chelsea House, 1985.

Bornstein, George. *Transformations of Romanticism in Yeats, Eliot and Stevens*. Chicago: Univ. of Chicago Press, 1976.

Bowles, William Lisle. *"Sonnets and Other Poems," and "The Spirit of Discovery."* Edited by Donald H. Reiman. New York: Garland, 1978.

Brown, Marshall. *Preromanticism*. Stanford, Calif.: Stanford Univ. Press, 1991.

Byron, George Gordon, Lord. *The Complete Poetical Works*. 7 vols. Edited by Jerome McGann. London: Oxford Univ. Press, 1980–93.

Coleridge, Samuel Taylor. *Poetical Works*. Ed. Ernest Hartley Coleridge. Oxford: Oxford Univ. Press, 1969.

Corn, Alfred. "A Magma of Interiors." In *John Ashbery*, edited by Harold Bloom, 81–90.

Cowper, William. *The Letters and Prose Writings of William Cowper*. 5 vols. Ed. James King and Charles Ryskamp. Oxford: Clarendon Press, 1979–86.

————. *Poetical Works*. London: Oxford Univ. Press, 1967.

Dekker, George. *Coleridge and the Literature of Sensibility*. New York: Harper & Row, 1978.

Edelman, Lee. "The Pose of Imposture: Ashbery's 'Self-Portrait in a Convex Mirror.'" *Twentieth Century Literature* 32 (1986): 95–114.

Gardner, Thomas. "Bishop and Ashbery: Two Ways Out of Stevens." *Wallace Stevens Journal* 19 (1995): 201–18.

Gray, Thomas. *Gray and Collins: Poetical Works*. Edited by Roger Lonsdale. Oxford: Oxford Univ. Press, 1977.

Fitzgerald, F. Scott. "The Crack-Up." In *The Crack-Up*. New York: New Directions, 1945.

————. *Tender Is the Night*. New York: Scribners, 1933.

Flaubert, Gustave. *Sentimental Education*. Translated by Robert Baldrick. New York: Penguin, 1964.

Freud, Sigmund. "Family Romances." In *The Sexual Enlightenment of Children*. Edited by Phillip Rieff. New York: Macmillan, 1963.

————. "Mourning and Melancholia." In *General Psychological Theory*. Edited by Phillip Rieff. New York: Macmillan, 1963.

Frye, Northrop. "Towards Defining an Age of Sensibility," *ELH* 23 (1956): 144–52. Reprinted in *Fables of Identity*, 130–37. New York: Harcourt, 1963.

Glen, Heather. *Vision and Disenchantment: Blake's 'Songs' and Wordsworth's 'Lyrical Ballads.'* Cambridge: Cambridge Univ. Press, 1983.

Grosskurth, Phyllis. *Melanie Klein: Her World and Her Work*. New York: Knopf, 1986.

Hartman, Geoffrey H. *Wordsworth's Poetry, 1787–1814*. New Haven, Conn.: Yale Univ. Press, 1964.

Hazlitt, William. "Mr. Wordsworth." In *The Spirit of the Age*. London: Oxford Univ. Press, 1904.

Heath, William. *Wordsworth and Coleridge: A Study of Their Literary Relations in 1801–2*. Oxford: Clarendon, 1970.

Holmes, Richard. *Coleridge: Early Visions*. London: Penguin, 1989.

————. *Shelley: The Pursuit*. London: Thames and Hudson, 1974.

Hunt, Bishop C. "Wordsworth and Charlotte Smith." *The Wordsworth Circle*, 1, no. 3 (1970): 85–103.

Jackson, Wallace. "Wordsworth and His Predecessors: Private Sensations and Public Tones." *Criticism* 17 (1975): 41–58.

Jacobus, Mary. *Tradition and Experiment in Wordsworth's Lyrical Ballads (1798)*. London: Oxford Univ. Press, 1976.

Johnson, Samuel. *The Idler and Adventurer*. Edited by W. J. Bate. New Haven, Conn.: Yale Univ. Press, 1963.

Kalstone, David. *Five Temperaments*. New York: Oxford Univ. Press, 1977.

Keach, William. *Shelley's Style*. New York: Methuen, 1984.

Keller, Lynn. "'Thinkers without Final Thoughts': John Ashbery's Evolving Debt to Wallace Stevens." *ELH* 49 (1982): 235–61.

Kierkegaard, Soren. *Concluding Unscientific Postscript to "Philosophical Fragments."* Edited and translated by Howard V. Honig and Edna H. Honig. Princeton, N.J.: Princeton Univ. Press, 1992.

Klein, Melanie. "Mourning and Its Relation to Manic-Depressive States." In *Love, Guilt and Reparation & Other Works 1921-1945*. New York: Delta-Dell, 1975.

———. "On the Sense of Loneliness." In *Envy and Gratitude and Other Works: 1946–63*. London: Hogarth, 1975.

Kristeva, Julia. *Black Sun: Depression and Melancholia*. Translated by Leon S. Roudiez. New York: Columbia Univ. Press, 1989.

Leckie, Ross. "Art, Mimesis and John Ashbery's 'Self-Portrait in a Convex Mirror.'" *Essays in Literature* 19 (1992): 114–31.

Lentricchia, Frank. *Ariel and the Police: Michel Foucault, William James, Wallace Stevens*. Madison: Univ. of Wisconsin Press, 1988.

Levinson, Marjorie. *Wordsworth's Great Period Poems: Four Essays*. Cambridge: Cambridge Univ. Press, 1986.

Liu, Alan. *Wordsworth: The Sense of History*. Stanford, Calif.: Stanford Univ. Press, 1989.

Looper, Travis. "Ashbery's 'Self-Portrait.'" *Papers on Language and Literature* 28 (1992): 451–56.

Lyotard, Jean-François. *Peregrinations: Law, Form, Event*. New York: Columbia Univ. Press, 1988.

Magnuson, Paul. *Coleridge and Wordsworth: A Lyrical Dialogue*. Princeton, N.J.: Princeton Univ. Press, 1988.

Manning, Peter J. "Wordsworth and Gray's Sonnet on the Death of West." In *Reading Romantics: Texts and Contexts*. New York: Oxford Univ. Press, 1990.

Marcel, Gabriel. "Sketch of a Phenomenology and a Metaphysics of Hope." In *Homo Viator*. Translated by Emma Crawford. New York: Harper, 1962.

McCarthy, Mary. *Birds of America*. New York: Harcourt Brace Jovanovich, 1971.

McCorkle, James. *The Still Performance: Writing, Self and Interconnection in Five Postmodern American Poets*. Charlottesville: Univ. Press of Virginia, 1992.

McFarland, Thomas. "The Symbiosis of Wordsworth and Coleridge." In *Romanticism and the Forms of Ruin*. Princeton, N.J.: Princeton Univ. Press, 1981.

McGann, Jerome. *The Romantic Ideology: A Critical Investigation*. Chicago: Univ. of Chicago Press, 1983.

Merrill, James. "The Book of Ephraim." In *The Changing Light at Sandover*. New York: Atheneum, 1982.

Norton, Jody. "'Whispers out of Time': The Syntax of Being in the Poetry of John Ashbery." *Twentieth Century Literature* 41 (1995): 281–305.

Pinch, Adela. *Strange Fits of Passion: Epistemologies of Emotion, Hume to Austen.* Stanford, Calif.: Stanford Univ. Press, 1996.

Proust, Marcel. *A la recherche du temps perdu.* 3 vols. Paris: Gallimard, 1954.

Quinney, Laura. *Literary Power and the Criteria of Truth.* Gainesville: Univ. Press of Florida, 1995.

Ramazani, Jahan. *Poetry of Mourning: The Modern Elegy from Hardy to Heaney.* Chicago: Univ. of Chicago Press, 1994.

Riddel, Joseph N. *The Clairvoyant Eye: The Poetry and Poetics of Wallace Stevens.* Baton Rouge: Louisiana State Univ. Press, 1965.

Roe, Nicholas. *Wordsworth and Coleridge: The Radical Years.* Oxford: Oxford Univ. Press, 1988.

Ruoff, Gene W. *Wordsworth and Coleridge: The Making of the Major Lyrics, 1802–4.* New Brunswick, N.J.: Rutgers Univ. Press, 1989.

Rycroft, Charles. "On Idealization, Illusion and Catastrophic Disillusion." In *Imagination and Reality.* New York: International Universities Press, 1968.

Sartre, Jean-Paul. *Being and Nothingness.* Translated by Hazel Barnes. New York: Simon & Schuster, 1966.

Shelley, Percy. *Letters.* 2 vols. Edited by F. L. Jones. London: Oxford Univ. Press, 1964.

————. *"Peter Bell the Third" and "The Triumph of Life."* Edited by Donald H. Reiman. The Bodleian Shelley Manuscripts, vol. 1. New York: Garland, 1986.

————. *Poetical Works.* Edited by Thomas Hutchinson. London: Oxford Univ. Press, 1970.

————. *Shelley's Poetry and Prose.* Edited by Donald H. Reiman and Sharon B. Powers. New York: Norton, 1977.

Shoptaw, John. *On the Outside Looking Out: John Ashbery's Poetry.* Cambridge, Mass.: Harvard Univ. Press, 1994.

Sickels, Eleanor. *The Gloomy Egotist: Moods and Themes of Melancholy from Gray to Keats.* New York: Columbia Univ. Press, 1932.

Smith, Charlotte. *The Poems of Charlotte Smith.* Edited by Stuart Curran. New York: Oxford Univ. Press, 1993.

Sokolsky, Anita. "'A Commission That Never Materialized': Narcissism and Lucidity in Ashbery's 'Self-Portrait in a Convex Mirror.'" In *John Ashbery*, edited by Harold Bloom, 233–50.

Sperry, Stuart. *Shelley's Major Verse: The Narrative and Dramatic Poetry.* Cambridge, Mass.: Harvard Univ. Press, 1988.

Stamelman, Richard. "Critical Reflections: Poetry and Art Criticism in Ashbery's 'Self-Portrait in a Convex Mirror.'" *New Literary History* 15 (1984): 607–30.

Stein, William Bysshe. "Stevens and Ashbery: The Wrinkles in the Canvas of Language." *Wallace Stevens Journal* 3, nos. 3–4 (1979): 56–69.

Stevens, Wallace. *The Collected Poems of Wallace Stevens.* New York: Knopf, 1975.

————. *Letters of Wallace Stevens*. Edited by Holly Stevens. New York: Knopf, 1966.

————. *The Necessary Angel: Essays on Reality and the Imagination*. New York: Vintage, 1951.

————. *Opus Posthumous*. Edited by Milton J. Bates. New York: Knopf, 1989.

Vendler, Helen. *On Extended Wings: Wallace Stevens' Longer Poems*. Cambridge, Mass.: Harvard Univ. Press, 1969.

————. *Wallace Stevens: Words Chosen out of Desire*. Knoxville: Univ. of Tennessee Press, 1984.

Weiskel, Thomas. *The Romantic Sublime: Studies in the Structure and Psychology of Transcendence*. Baltimore, Md.: Johns Hopkins Univ. Press, 1976.

Wordsworth, William. *The Poems*. 2 vols. Edited by John O. Hayden. New Haven, Conn.: Yale Univ. Press, 1981.

————. *Poetical Works*. Edited by Thomas Hutchinson and E. D. Selincourt. Oxford: Oxford Univ. Press, 1936.

————. *The Prelude: 1799, 1805, 1850*. Edited by Johnathan Wordsworth, M. H. Abrams, and Stephen Gill. New York: Norton, 1979.

Wordsworth, William, and Samuel Taylor Coleridge. *Lyrical Ballads*. Edited by Michael Mason. London: Longman, 1982.

Yeats, William Butler. *Selected Poems and Two Plays of William Butler Yeats*. Edited by M. L. Rosenthal. New York: Collier, 1966.

Stevens, Wallace (*continued*)
The Man with the Blue Guitar, 116,
147; "Le Monocle de Mon Oncle,"
107, 116; "Montrachet-le-Jardin," 99;
The Necessary Angel, 117; "No Pos-
sum, No Sop, No Tatters," 116;
"Notes Toward a Supreme Fiction,"
108; "O, Florida, Venereal Soil," 109;
"An Ordinary Evening in New
Haven," 99, 117; *Parts of a World,* 116;
"The Place of Solitaries," 110; "The
Plain Sense of Things," 105, 187 n. 13;
"The Planet on the Table," 101; "The
Poems of Our Climate," 147; "The
River of Rivers in Connecticut," 135;
"The Rock," 104, 122; *The Rock,* 95,
105, 119, 135; "Song of Fixed Ac-
cord," 102; "Stars at Tallapoosa," 110;
"Sunday Morning," 107–8, 130;
"Things of August," 123; *Transport to
Summer,* 116, 118, 135; "Two Illustra-
tions That the World Is What You
Make of It," 131; "Waving Adieu,
Adieu, Adieu," 130; "The Well-
Dressed Man with a Beard," 104;
"Wild Ducks, People and Distances,"
106, 127–28; "The World as Medita-
tion," 101, 135; "World without Pecu-
liarity," 131–35, 187 n. 20

Tennyson, Alfred, Lord, xii; *In Memoriam,* xiii, 137

Vendler, Helen, 96–98, 103, 116, 119;
*Wallace Stevens: Words Chosen Out of
Desire,* 96–98; *On Extended Wings:
Wallace Stevens' Longer Poems,*
186 n. 11

Weiskel, Thomas, *The Romantic Sublime:
Studies in the Structure and Psychology
of Transcendence,* 185 n. 42
Whitman, Walt, 96
Williams, Jane, 68, 86

Winnicott, D. W., 19
Wordsworth, William, 12, 18, 20–66, 78,
86, 96, 106–9, 113, 119–20, 132, 135,
137–39, 143–44, 152, 170; and crisis
lyrics, xi, 36–37, 64–65; and elegiac
poetry, 31, 53; and French Revolution,
32–33, 59, 184 n. 38, 185 n. 50; and
hope, 36–37, 41–42, 46–47, 59–61, 64;
and mourning, 53–57; and political
disillusionment, 32–33, 35, 58; and
self-loss, 53, 55, 65; and time, 43–49.
Works: "A Ballad," 31–32; *The Borderers,* 180–81 n. 23; "The Brothers,"
35; "Composed upon an Evening of
Extraordinary Splendour and
Beauty," 181 n. 34; "Elegiac Stanzas
Suggested by a Picture of Peele Castle," 48, 53–57, 64, 106; *The Excursion,*
35, 58; "Intimations Ode," xi, 24, 27,
30, 39, 46, 48, 50–54, 57, 60, 64, 66, 69,
73, 78, 87, 109, 113, 133, 142, 181 n. 34,
184 n. 39, 188 n. 2; "I Wandered
Lonely as a Cloud," 182–83 n. 36;
"Lines left upon a Seat in a Yew-
Tree," 34–35, 58–59; "Lines written in
Early Spring," 37; *Lyrical Ballads,* 33;
"Michael," 35, 58, 184 n. 39; "My
Heart Leaps Up," 39; "The Old
Cumberland Beggar," 47; "Preface to
the Second Edition of *Lyrical Ballads,*"
23; *The Prelude,* 35, 37, 41, 43–45,
58–62, 181 n. 29; "Resolution and
Independence," 113–14, 182–83 n. 36;
"The Ruined Cottage," 35, 58,
184 n. 39; "Simon Lee," 35; "The
Solitary Reaper," 62; "Tintern Abbey,"
xi, 21, 24, 27, 35, 37–43, 46, 48–50,
53–55, 57, 59–61, 63–64, 66, 69, 113,
119–20, 133, 135, 152, 170, 188 n. 2
Wyatt, Thomas, 20, 178 n. 1

Yeats, William Butler, xii, 137; "The Circus Animals' Desertion," xiii, 136